CONCANIM-INGLEZ DICIONAR

KONKANI-ENGLISH DICTIONARY

CONCANIM-INGLEZ DICIONAR

KONKANI-ENGLISH DICTIONARY

GYAN

Published by

Gyan Publishing House
5, Ansari Road
Daryaganj, New Delhi-110002
Phone: 011-47034999, 9811692060
E-mail: books@gyanbooks.com

Distribution Network
gyanbooks.com
India, USA, Canada, UK, Australia, France

ISBN : 978-81-212-4475-6 (PB)
First Published, 1930

2nd Impression 2020

Printed at: Gyan Press, Delhi.

Konkani-English Dictionary

BHARI ZANNAUNNI.

Hea dicionaracho puro faido mellonc goroz assa tache mand-davollichi sozmonni geuncheac, tea pasun hea dicionaracho upeog cortelean socla boroilam tem chotraen vachchem.

Dicionarachim utram manddleant chalte ritin: utor suru zatanam zoddim consoantam asat tancho upeog corunc nam caddun matr *th*, tea vorvim vachpeac kuincheim utor sodun caddunc sompem zauncheac. *'G'* sodanch fort, *e* anim *i* adim ailear verian: exempl: *gutti, geunc, girann.* Him utram vach-chim boroilelea porim: — *gueunc, guirann.* 'S'-cho suar so-danch s; don suaram modem s aslear tica z-cho suar nam: exempl: *maso, couso.* Concanim naunvam uprant *m f* vo *n* dilea tanchi sozmonni tem tem naum *masculin, femenin* vo *neutr.*

Concanim sobdachi puri sozmonni inglezicho poilo uchar vo sobd dita anim; galun utram kherit keleant tim omkeanch soeganim upeartat vachanache vo sentensache sozmonne por-monnem.

Ho dicionar upegacho zauncheac amim tancta tea por-monnem gas mosagotgetlea, vodic corun concanim sobdanchi niz sozmonni diuncheac. inglezin anim hem sompeponni am-cheam vachpeanim sozmoncheac zaite codden exemplanim tancho upeog dacoila. Tosich minot getlea inglez utranchem soletrasaum sarkem corun diuncheac. Oxem astanam thoddeo bhou chuki urleat asteleo teo tike vachpean sozmon geuncheo. He torichem pustoc poilem amche modem anim tem nittier galunc kitleo sonkesttaeo asteleo teo cannacui sompeponnim gomteleo.

Editores.

DICIONAR
CONCANIM-INGLEZ.

A The first letter of the Roman Alphabet.

Ab *f* brim, flap.

Aba ! ah ! (exclamation).

Abade *m* abbot, friar.

Abeci *f* aphabet.

Abediata *n* indivisibility.

Abgat *m* treason, perfidy, unfaithfulness.

Abgat corunc to betray, to attack, to fall upon.

Abgatan traitorously, disloyally.

Abgati *m* traitor, disloyal, unfaithful.

Abisttai *f* indigestion, (fig) want of ardour in a discourse etc.

Abkea *f* filth, uncleanliness, (fig) impurity.

Abort *n* abortion, premature birth or event.

Abras *m* embrace.

Abril *m* the month of April.

Abru *f* honour, esteem.

Abru diunc to honour, to esteem ;

Abrucho,-i,-em vo
Abrudic vo
Abruvont } honourable, respectable, decent, laudable.

Absuart *m* avarice.

Absuarti avaricious, covetous.

Absugun *f* error, fault.

Ac *n* shout, call.

Ac bossonc to feel the effects of an imprecation, to be moved by a curse.

Ac marunc to shout, to call.

Acanddo, Aconddo *m* thumb.

Acant *m* affliction, trouble.

Acantaunc to afflict, to frighten.

Acantonc to be frightened, to be afraid of.

Acar *m* means, possibility, aspect.

Acar *m* appraisement, valuation; "He zomnicho *acar* kelo", this plot of ground was appraised or valued.

Acar corunc to value, to esteem.

Acas *m* heaven, sky.

Achar *f* pickle, preserved fruit in vinegar and Indian condiments.

Achar *m* superstition.

Achar dorunc vo Acharunc to be superstitious.

Achari superstitious.

Achircaen, Ochircaen carefully, prudently.

Achircai, Ochircai attention, carefulness.

Achucponn *n* infallibility.

Acoi *f* aunt, father's sister.
Acolt *m* acolyte, assistant priest at Mass.
Acondd solid, firm, perfect.
Aconddo thumb
Acrec lastly, in conclusion.
Acttem *n* furnace, burning fire
Acudd narrow, short.
Acuddai *f* narrowness.
Acuddunc to be frightened, to shiver with cold.
Acxer *n* letter.
Acxi *f* linseed.
Adãochem patoc original sin.
Adar *m* help, assistance.
Adar diunc to help, to assist, to protect.
Adari *m* protector, helper.
Adarunc to commit, to perform, "Patoc adarunc", to commit a sin."
Adau *m* profit, advantage, gain.
Adaunc to touch, to feel the touch ; to meet physical obstacle.
Adavacho, -i, -em profitable, useful.
Adavan with effect.
Add against, opposite.
Add very far ; "Mojeam dolleam add tum voch", go far away from my sight.
Add *f* bone.
Add bossoinar *m* bone-setter.
Add eunc lay down. "To bajer add poddlo, he has laid down on bed".
Add eunc vo vochonc to oppose, to contradict.
Add galunc to overcome, to defeat, to oppose, to contradict.
Add-naum surname, nick name.
Add poddonc to lie down, to rest.
Add vellar jeunc to dine at irregular hours.
Add vogot *n* unusual time.
Addambo *m* door or window bar.
Addambo galunc to put the door or window bar.
Addangi restless, uneasy, turbulent, noisy.
Addangpon *n* trick, wile, prank.
Addantrim indifferently.
Addao *m* grater, an instrument for grating.
Addaunc to commence, to start work.
Addaunc to stop, to obstruct, to prevent from doing something ; to occupy, to fill up. "Hea goran sogli suat addailea", this house has occupied the whole place, to begin, to commence. "Antonin gor bandunc *addailam*", Anthony has commenced to build a house.
Addaunni *f* obstacle, impediment. "Connem anga addaunni galea", who has put obstacle here.
Addaunni, Mudol beginning, a start. "Pedrun gor bandunc addaunni kelea", peter has made a b ginning to build a house.

ADDCHON *f* cause of involuntary delay.

ADDCHONE to meet obstacles.

ADDCHOUNE to oppose, to create difficulties in the way of another man or his doings.

ADDCOL *n* difficulty, obstacle.

ADDCULO, -I, -EM round, circular.

ADDCUTT *n* skeleton.

ADDECHI GUIRESTAI *n* recent wealth.

ADDECHO, -I, -EM occasional, accidental, contrary to the ordinary course, recent.

ADDECHO SAUCAR *m* new merchant, an upstart.

ADDGAM-NODDGAM *n* tricks.

ADDGOT *n* unexpected, advantageous, cheap.

ADDGOT MELLONC to secure advantageous terms accidentally.

ADDGOT ZOLM *m* premature birth.

ADD-MASS *f* marrow.

ADDMUTT mischievous.

ADDNADDI senseless, thoughtless.

ADDNADDPON senselessness.

ADDNATTI a small grain measure.

ADDNEM *m* act of bringing.

ADDNOM *m* wooden bar for fastening a door or window.

ADDO *m* fence.

ADDO (PACRUM) marroco.

ADDONEM, ADOUNEM, *n* touch, push.

ADDOS *f* protection against sun, rain and wind.

ADDOVO *m* a bundle of corn containing 5 or 6 sheaves.

ADDPONC to overcome himself, to contain himself.

ADDPUNC to overcome, to subdue.

ADDSOR *f* an unripe cocoanut.

ADDUNC to bring, to fetch.

ADDVALLI skeleton.

ADDVARLOLO,-I,-EM prohibited, forbidden. "Tuvem addvarlelem foll khaum naie" you must not eat forbidden fruit.

ADDVARNEM *n* prohibition, interdict.

ADDVARUNC to prohibit, to forbid.

ADDVEM-TIDDVEM disorderly state.

ADDVO, -I, -EM, acros, prostrate.

ADDVO PODDONC to fall prostrate ; to lie down.

ADDVOL *n* a piece of female garment.

ADDVON slope, declivity.

ADES *m* half the day. "Sacallcho ades", morning, "Sanjecho ades", evening.

ADEUS *n* good-bye, farewell.

ADIC, ODIC more, better. "Aichea poros cal odic maslli poddleli", there was more fish yesterday than to-day. "Adic boro Judas zolmo naslo zalear", it would have been better if Judas were not born." "Amvem sogleanc vicharleat munn sang adic corun mojea isttac", give my compliments to all,specially to my friend.

ADIC ADIC more and more.

ADICAR *m* leading man, a person in charge.

ADIM before, previously, before hand. "Hea adim", before this.

ADIM BUD DIUNC to caution, to advise before hand.

ADIM CORUNC to anticipate.

ADIM PAVONC VO VOCHONC to precede, to go before.

ADIM POLLOUNC to foresee.

ADIM PORIANT from the beginning.

ADINCH before hand, previously. "To adinch toiar zala", he was ready before hand.

ADINCH ADDUN DOURUNC to provide, supply.

ADIPOTI *m* chairman, chief, person responsible for an undertaking.

ADISTON *n* fatherhand, one's own native place.

ADIT, SURIO, DIS *m* sun.

ADIXEA Ill luck, mischance.

ADLI TARIK GALUNC to antedate.

ADLO, -I, -EM previous, old. "Adlem lissaum add", bring the previous lesson.

ADLO CALL antiquity, ancient times.

ADLONC to touch.

ADLOS *n* part of building above its foundation.

ADMAS *n* surmise, probability.

ADMINISTRADOR *m* administrator, manager.

ADNEAUM *m* fault, mistake, offence.

ADNEAUNCAR, INE offender, criminal.

ADON water for cooking rice.

ADON DOURUNC to keep water boiling to cook rice.

ADUFAM *n* lattices.

ADVENT *n* advent.

ADVOGAD *m* advocate, lawer, pleader.

AEL *f* oil of fresh cocoanuts.

AEM *n* the laying open of trees.

AEN *n* cury-stuff.

AEUNC to cool down and thicken (a liquid).

AFIN *n* opium.

AFINI *m* opium-eater.

AFODDNEM *n* touch, sense of feeling.

AFODDONC to touch.

AFODDUNC to touch.

AFOINAR, APOINAR one who calls.

AFOT indisposition of health.

AFOUNC, APOUNC to call.

AFOUNEM, APOUNEM *n* call, the act of calling.

AFOUNNOM *m* call-boy.

AFRAMENT perpetual lease of land.

AFURKIM secretly, unknowingly, stealtily.

AG, UZO *m* fire.

AG PADDCHO FATOR *m* flint.

AGA, AGE, AGO respectful greeting usually addressed to

elders, except the last one "ago" which is addresssed to young female.

AGBOT *f* steamer, ship.

AG-GADDI *f* railway.

AGICHI CADDI match stick.

AGICHI PETT, AG-PETTI matchbox.

AGIO SOROP *m* carpet snake.

AGLLO, -I, -EM, VO OGLLO,-I,-EM more, superior. "He petent ogllem zata", in this box contains more. "To amchea gaunvant ogllo", he is superior in our village.

AGLLUNC, AGOLL DIUNC to dye, to stain.

AGODD, AGOTT difficult, hard.

AGODDAI, AGOTTAI difficulty, hardness.

AGOLL *n* liquid decoction.

AGON *f* motions.

AGON LAGONC to suffer from diarrhoea.

AGONC, UDCADDE ZAUNC, BAIR ZAUNC to ease nature. } to have motions,

AGOR *m* salt-pan.

AGORVONNEM *n* reprehension, censure.

AGOST *n* the month of August.

AGOURI the start of rising tide.

AGOURI EUNC to begin the flow of rising tide.

AGRI *m* salter, dealer in salt.

AGRUM *n* disease of foul tongue, inflammation.

AGTTEM *f* conflagration, glowing sight.

AGTTEM furnace.

AGTTEM LOHARACHEM forge.

AGUADOR *m* watering pot.

AGUARDENT strong liquor.

AGVALO *m* stoker, fireman.

AHAD *n* bone.

AHO NOLLEANCHO owen for baking tiles.

AI ! AH ! exclamation of pain.

AIA *f* dry nurse, female servant.

AIAU *f* a married woman whose husband is living.

AIAUPON *n* married state.

AIB *n* omen, indecency.

AIBEUNE to feel supertitiously, to consider an incident as a bad omen.

AIC! exclamation: hark ! Hear, hear !

AICHEAN from to-day.

AICON GEUNC to pay attention.

AICONC, AICUNC to hear, to obey. "Tuca, borem aicota", do you hear well. "Tuca, caido assa avoichem aiconc", it is your duty to obey your mother.

AICONNEM hearing, obeying.

AICOTOLO, -I, -EM, hearer.

AIDON vessel, vase. "tambeachem aidon", a copper vessel.

AIDONN MATIECHEM earthen pot.

AIDONN MOSCO CORCHEM churn.

AIDONN PITTULCHEM brass vessel.

AIDONN RANDUNCHEM cooking pot.

Ailean near by, this side.
Ailo, -i, -em, first, who is near.
Aimbem *n* mushroom.
Aind waist.
Ainim, oinim without salt, insipid, tasteless.
Ainn *n* nursery of plants for transplantation.
Aino *m* fan.
Airat *f* abyss.
Aitar *m* sunday.
Aitepon *n* promptitude, disposition.
Aiti *f* form.
Aito, -i, -em, ready.
Aitomon *n* readiness, disposition, preparation.
Aixi, Auxi lazy, idle.
Aiz to-day.
Aiz legun, Aiz passun, Aiz porian, Aiz than, Aiz ver, Aiz verian } from to-day. "Aiz legun tem falea legun", from to-day till tomorrow.
Ajam, Naim *m* barber.
Ajam zaunc to digest.
Ajap *n* p. ojab.
Ajapi, Ojapi admirer.
Ajent agent, broker, reprensentative.
Aji *f* grand-mother.
Ajir present, ready.
Ajir asnem presence.
Ajir assonc to attend, to be present.
Ajir corunc to get ready.
Ajirassunc vo, Ajir zaunc } to be present.
Ajir nassunc to be absent onc's self-from, be absent.
Ajir zauncho uronc to be absent.
Ajiri *n* muster, call for duty.
Ajiri diunc to be present at muster.
Ajiri gueunc to call out names from the muster-roll.
Ajirn indigestion.
Ajust *m* bargain.
Ajut *n* clyster.
Akem, -i, -o, absolute, whole, entire.
Aker *f* conclusion, end.
Akercho, -i, -em, last one.
Akeunc to shout, to bawl out.
Akram irregularity.
Alaito,-i,-em, changeable, fickle, not firm.
Alarmarki easy work.
Alaxiro *m* help, protection.
Albot certainly, of course.
Alcachi biscut ginger nuts.
Alcacho soro ginger wine.
Alcatif *m* carpet.
Alco, -ki, -kem inferior, simple. "Hem lugot alkem", this cloth is inferior, "to vaur alco", that work is simple.
Alcott mean, contemptible.
Alcunch *n* surname.
Alegr zaunc to be merry with drink.
Alem *n* ginger.
Alett night watchman's shout "alert".
Alett marunc to shout at appointed times of night-watch.
Alfand *n* custom duty.

Alfandachem gor *n* customhouse.

Alfas lettuce.

Alfiat, Darji *n* tailor.

Alfinet *f* pin.

Algoz barbarian, inhuman person.

Alim lately, not long ago.

Alincho,-i,-em of short time, actual.

Allu light, soft.

Allu lightly, softly.

Allu field-mouse.

Allu light, less in weight.

Alum calladium esculentum.

Almanac calendar.

Almar *f* cup-board.

Almar ropachi *n* wardrope.

Alment *n* holy water.

Almentachem pixol sprinkler.

Almentachi pi *f* font.

Almus *n* breakfast.

Alnem *n* movement, motion.

Alô lull, "Burgueac alô curone", to lull a child.

Alonc, Alunc to move, to shake, to balance.

Alounc to move, agitate.

Alounem agitation, movement, (fig.) flirt.

Alpabuzon *f* temperance.

Alsi linseed.

Alsupão trap-door.

Altar *m* altar.

Altar cuxicho side altar.

Altar modlo high altar.

Altaracho fator altar stone.

Altaracho tualo altar cloth.

Altaracho ussul altarage.

Alto,-i,-em agitated, troubled.

Altoddi this side of the margin of a river.

Alvis social rejoicing, entertainment on a happy occasion, presents.

Am (exclamation) yes, agreed.

Amâ wet nurse.

Amal domestic servant.

Amanat aslo toslo intact.

Amanim quietly, slowly.

Amant lover.

Amas *f* new moon.

Ambaddi, Ambo mango.

Ambaddo hog plum (fruit)

Ambaddo hog plum tree.

Ambeunc to bellow, "Gai am beta" the cow bellows.

Ambil gruel, conjee of nachnim (grain).

Amble pendants, parts of glassware hanging like pendants.

Ambli *f* green mango.

Amblo pendant.

Ambo (zad) *m* mango tree.

Ambog humbug, deceit.

Ambogui deceitful, cheating.

Amboi (massoli) *f* peg fish.

Ambott sour.

Ambott-tic biting tart.

Ambrut *n* sweetness, gentleness.

Ambrut ambrosia, heavenly food.

Ambuli (zad) *f* small mango tree.

Amburco ans[illegible] *m* a smile.

Amburco anssunc to smile.

Amburkeunc, Piconc to get ripe.

Amburpico, -ki, -kem nearly riped, half riped.

Amchean we, "Amchean temcoıum eta", we can do that.

Amcho, -i, -em, our.

Amddunc to drive, to expell.

Amend *n* almond-tree.

Amendam *n* almonds.

Amgelo, -i, -em our.

Am-ham ! cry of warning.

Amim we.

Amir peer, nobleman, rich man.

Amolic, Omolic precious.

Amolicai, Omolicai preciousness.

Amôr *n* mulberry tree.

Amor *n* mulberry.

Amori time of "Ave Maria" prayers, Angelus.

Ampulhet *f* hour glass.

Amttan *f* tamarind.

Amttaunc to make sour.

Amttelelo, -i, -em fermented.

Amttem *n* ferment, leaven.

Amtteunc to get sour, to be fermented.

Anad food stuff, grain.

Anai immorality.

Anayi immoral.

Anbavarthi faithless.

Anc *m* figure.

Ancarunc to set sail, to drive "Tarum ancarlem", the ship set sail. "Gaddi ancarunc", to drive the carriage.

Ancddo *m* hook.

Ancddonc (**xivan vo invan**, to shiver with cold.

Anchi, Topal post.

Ancodde again, once more.

Ancoddonc to be uneasy, to feel reluctant.

Ancor, Ancri, Combri a young shoot of a tree, bud.

Ancor futtonc to sprout.

Ancottem ulounc to speak nonsence, to speak unreasonably.

Ancotto, -i, -em impertinent, unreasonable, nonsencical.

Ancreo futtonc to sprout shoots.

Ancreunc, Paleunc to bud, to sprout shoots.

Ancuar *f* virgin, unmarried, maid.

Ancuar dadlo bachelor.

Ancuarpon *n* virginity, celibacy.

And the place built for storing water, testicle.

Andar *m* calloc, obscurity, darkness,(massolecho) a shoal of fish, (fig) multitude.

Andaro darkness, obscurity.

Anddi, Toplem *n* copper pot.

Anddlepon, Curddepon *n* blindness.

Anddlo, -i, -em blind.

Anddo *m* caldron.

Andoc, Ondoc p. **andar.**

Andôl *m* bier.

Andurli, Dongorpulli a pimple, a little swelling in the eyelids.

Aneaum, Guneaum fault, error, mistake.

Aneauncar culpable, guilty, in fault.

Anenes *n* pine apple.

ANENÊS *f* pine apple tree.
ANG, CUDD body.
ANG BAILEM right side, exterior side of cloth.
ANG-BAILEM superficial, outward. "Bailem ang borem assa", outwardly it is good.
ANGA, ANGOR, INGA here, there, in this place.
ANGACHEAN from here, from this place.
ANGACHO, -I, -EM from here, of this place. "Ti bail angachi", that woman is from here.
ANGACHO of body. "Tachea angachem rogot vaunta," his body bleeds.
ANGAILIM clothes, raiment.
ANGAN bodily.
ANGAR fire.
ANGASSORLEM, ANGACHEM from here.
ANGDDECAR *m* stall keeper, shopkeeper, merchant.
ANGLEM, ANGOSTR *n* dress, clothes, garment.
ANGLOTT *f* corpulency, fleshy.
ANGLOTT state of the body.
ANGODD, POSRO *f* stall, shop, market, fare.
ANGOJIN *f* complexion, constitution.
ANGONN *f* vow, promise.
ANGONN court-yard, farm-yard, yard.
ANGONN CORUNC p. angounc.
ANGOR p. ANGA.
ANGORLEAN p. ANGACHEAN.
ANGOSTR *n* garment, dress. clothes.
AGOTTI, FAI *f* swadding clothes, swaddling band.
ANGOTTONN corpulence, fatness.
ANGOUNC to promise, to make a vow.
ANGOUNNECHO, -I, -EM obtained by vows, fulfilling vows, attracting vows.
ANGUL *n* finger.
ANGULI *f* midle finger.
ANGULL bath.
ANGUR fig tree, also its fruit.
ANGUSTAN, DEDAL *n* thimble.
ANIM and, also.
ANINC more.
ANISCHAI indetermination.
ANJ *m* angel, a spiritual being.
ANJIR *n* figg.
ANN *f* to take another man's oath, adjuration.
ANKIDDEO guts, bowls.
ANNOM *m* anna.
ANNOS *f* a chape, a steel or silver tip at the end of scabbard.
ANNUNC, ONNUNC to press, to shorten.
ANON *n* bull-heart.
ANON *f* bull-heart tree.
ANS *f* duck.
ANS *m* drake.
ANS LAUNC to bait, to entice.
ANSO *m* laughter, smile. "Tuzo anso sobonam", your laughter is not pleasant "Amurco anso", smile.
ANSO MARUNC to laugh loudly.
ANSONC, ANSUNC to laugh.
ANSOUNC to make one laugh.
ANSVEL *f* bear.

Ant, **Anter** custard apple.
Ant (zad) custard apple-tree.
Ant masllechem inside part of fish usually cast away.
Antarjnam intuition.
Antcolleo intestines.
Antlean through this.
Antlo, -i, -em from this, from inside.
Antor large bamboo matting.
Antoscorn, **Ontoscorn** *n* heart.
Antoscorn conscience, interior light.
Antroll, **Ontroll** heaven, firmament.
Antrunc to spread, to put.
Antum, **Intum** in this, here, inside.
Anturn bed, bedding.
Antu'unc p. **Antrunc**.
Antuun *n* bed, couch.
Anupeog inutility.
Anupeogui invalid, unfit.
Anvallo myrobalan, emblico.
Anvem myself, I.
Apaplis *f* apoplexy.
Apaplo, -i, -em one's own "zonn eiclean apapleam corneanchi zortti diunchi poddteli", aach one will have to give an account of one's own actions.
Apapnnem each one.
Apĺea vadeacho capricious, mettlesome, stubborn, obstinate.
Aple budin arbitrarily, of his own free will or pleasure. "Tannem aple budin gor bandlem", he built the house by his own free w i.
Aple sotecho, -i, -em independent.
Aplo, -i, -em p. **Apaplo**.
Apnna bitor ulounc to speak within one's self, to soliloquize.
Apnnagelo, -i, -em p. **Aplo**.
Apnnanc to himself or herself.
Apnnanc diunc to apply one's self-to, to devote one's self-to.
Apnnapunn vo apnnapich by himself, by itself.
Apnnem p. **Apapnnem**.
Apoddonc to touch, to pollute by touch.
Apoddonc to remove untouchability by touching.
Apoinar one that calls.
Apol (frut) apple.
Apost bet, challenge.
Apost marunc to bet, to challenge.
Apostl apostle, upholder of some great cause of humanity,
Apoti *f* rent.
Apounc, **Afounc** to call.
Apounem *n* call, calling, invitation.
Apros *m* cocoanut juice.
Aprub *f* esteem.
Aprub incomparable.
Apsim self-acting, automatically.
Apsuarth *m* avarice, greediness.
Apsuarthi avaricious, greedy.
Aptton knocking about, belabouring.

Apttonc to be knocked about, to belabour one's self.

Apttunc to knock down, to beat with great strength.

Apunn he or she.

Apunnom call-boy, messenger for purpose of invitation.

Apunnuch he or she only, he himself, he alone.

Apunnuim he also, she also.

Apúrai corunc to fondle, to love excessively.

Apurbai, Opurbai *f* affection, esteem, regard, liking.

Apurbaicho, -i, -em darling, favourite.

Apurbaien (adv.) fondly, lovingly.

Apurtai insufficiency.

Apurto, -i, -em insufficient.

Apxim by himself, herself or itself.

Ar *f* a file, a line. "Sipaicanchi ar", a file of soldiers.

Ar *m* necklace, collar. "Tinnem motiancho ar golleant gala", she wore a pearl necklace or she put around her neck a pearl necklace.

Ar (pidda) paralysis.

Ar (sorop) boa, constrictor.

Ar fouzichi army filled up in battle-array.

Aramkhor idler, parasite.

Ararutt arrowroot.

Aratt *m* clamour, out crying.

Arattonc to shout, to clamour, to wail, to scold, to scream.

Arbott indelicate, mannerless.

Arbottponn indelicacy, mis behaviour.

Arc *n* arch.

Arc (rebecacho) *m* fiddle-bow.

Arcanj *m* archangel.

Arcebisp *m* archbishop.

Arcediag *m* archdeacon.

Ardo, -i, -em one-half.

Are form of addressing a boy or a young man.

Are form of addressing a married young woman.

Arecan *f* a woman that suffers from paralysis.

Arecar *m* a paralytic, a man that suffers from paralysis.

Argam, Orgam *f* thanks giving, acknowledgements.

Argam diunc to thank, to show one's gratitude.

Argol handle, hook.

Argolin pendant.

Ari *f* awl. "Mochi arien moche siunta", shoe maker stitches shoes with an awl.

Arji petition, memorial.

Arji-boroinar petition-writer, memorialist.

Arluc religious medal.

Arm, Bonduc *n* gun, carabine.

Armachi nolli barrel.

Armacho cão trigger.

Armon armonium.

Arnunc to fasten, to tighten.

Aro poro soon, very shortly.

Arodd loud noise.

Aroddonc shouting.

Arog *m* health.

Arponc to be very busy.

Arpunc to complete, to finish.

ARSO mirror, looking glass.
ARTH p. ORTH.
ARU a shout, a song.
ARUN, SUNCR dawn of day, dawn.
ARVALLI, ARVOLLI quitch-grass.
AS, AXIA ambition, desire.
ASCAR aspiration.
ASCAR SUSCAR SODDUNC to sigh, to desire earnestly.
ASCARONC, ASCARUNC to aspire, to inhale.
ASCOTTEO eye-brows.
ASDDOP winnowed.
ASDDUNC to winnow.
ASKITTEO (VOILEO) *f* lashes.
ASKITTEO (SOCOILEO) *f* eye brows.
ASMAN sky, heavens, airy region.
ASPAS round about, on all sides.
ASPAU *m* iron tools, a set of tools.
ASPUS search, inquiry, diligence.
ASRAI, AXIRAI p. OXIRAI.
ASRAUNC to defend, to protect from.
ASRAUNC PAUS to save one's self from being wet by rain.
ASRAUNNEM defence, repair.
ASRONC, ASRUNC (PAUS) to cease rain, to stop raining.
ASSIGNAD signature.
ASSO, (BATĂCHO) grain of paddy (with husk).
ASSOL loyal, true, original.
ASSOLPONN loyalty.
ASSONC, ASSUNC to be, to exist, to have. "Deu sorvol suatar assa". God is every where. "Antoninc ec gor assa", Anthony has got a house.
ASSONNEM *n* existence.
ASSOR *n* protection, assistance.
ASSUC, OSSUC small pox.
ASTI skeleton.
ASTIC rich, beautiful.
ASTOGIM, OSTOGIM bodily, "Aple ostogim, personally, by himself.
ASVAD absence, separation.
ASVADIN in absence.
ASVEL *n* bear.
AT *m* hand.
ATA BHAIR PODDONC to lose hopes of recovery.
ATA KHAL DOURUNC to control.
ATA'KHALTO,-I,-EM subordinate.
ATAC *m* aggression.
ATAC CORNAR *m* aggressor.
ATAC CORUNC to attack.
ATAC NERVANCHO fit of hysteria.
ATAM now, at this moment.
ATAM LEGUN / ATAM PASSUN } up to now, up to this moment.
ATAM THAN from to-day, hence forward.
ATAM VERIAN even now.
ATAN GUEUNC to start work.
ATANCHO,-I,-EM of the present time: actual.
ATANCHO CALL contemporary times.
ATANT in hand, power. "Hi chacri mojea atant nam", this job is not in my hands.
ATANTLO,-I,-EM from a hand, beyond one's power. "Ti vost

mojea atantli noi, that business is beyond my power.
ATARVON *f* cheat, deceit.
ATHIRPONN incertitude.
ATIAR *n* an instrument of hand such as sword, spear etc.
AT-LAUNC to pilfer, to filch.
AT-LAUNNOM petty thief.
ATMEACHE GUNN qualities, talents.
ATMEACHI VISSOR self-oblivion.
ATMO, OTMO *m* soul.
ATO (FUL) ata.
ATODDI hammer.
ATON, SOUEM *n* a large mat.
AT-PAEM ALOUNC to move one's body, to work and live.
AT-PAIKI skill in manual tricks.
ATREVID bold.
ATRI *f* a mat.
ATT eight.
ATT PAUTTIM eight times.
ATTAPONC to seclude one's self, to limit one's self.
ATTAPUNC to close, to finish.
ATTAVOLLI benefit, advantage.
ATTESTAD certificate, official confirmation of an event.
ATTIBHOJAN intemperance.
ATTO iron hoop, wooden hoop.
ATTODDO *m* eight days, a week.
ATTONC to condense, to dry.
ATTONNEM *n* condensation.
ATTOU rememberance,memory.
ATTOU CORUNC to remember, to think over.
ATTOU ZAUNC to remember.
ATTOUNC to make dry, to congeal.
ATTOUNC UPCAR to thank, to acknowledge a favour.
ATTOUNEM p. ATTONNEM.
ATTVO eighth, eighth in consecutive order.
ATVO,-I,-EM stranger, new, exquisite.
AU *f* (ponsachi) a small jackfruit tree.
AUC *n* life, duration of life.
AUCHIT suddenly, unexpectedly.
AUCHITUCH suddenly.
AUKAS interval.
AUM I.
AUMCH I only.
AUMDEUNC to desire earnestly, to aspire.
AUMR *n* inundation.
AUMRO *m* bean, kidney-bean.
AUNDUM,OUNDUM current year.
AUSSAI, ALLOSSAI *f* laziness, slothfulness, sluggishness.
AUT, ATIAR *n* an instrument, a tool.
AUTHOR author of literary works.
AUTHOR complainant in criminal case.
AUTRI mat.
AUXEPON *n* laziness, sluggishness.
AUXI lazy, sluggish.
AUZAI VO AUZALLI turbulent, uneasy, unquiet, riotous.
AVALO an tact of transfering.
AVALO DIUNC to promise to pay on a fixed day, to transfer one's debt to another person.
AVALO GEUNC to accept a pro-

mise made on account of debt.
AVANCO *m* conjecture, opinion.
AVANCONC, AVANCUNC to conjucture.
AVATAR godlike man.
AVAZ *m* sound.
AVELI *f* palace, a big house, princely mansion.
AVER, AER the day before yesterday.
AVESSOR *m* chapter.
AVICHAR unmindfulness, desattention.
AVIZ message, notice.
AVOI *f* mother,
AVOI bapui, parents.
AVOIPON *n* maternity.
AXA *n* desires, ambition.
AXAMIM *m* person.
AXAVONT desirous, ambitious.
AXIERI the piles.
AXIL gain, advantage, usefulness.
AXIR narrow, tight.
AXIR CORUNC to shorten, to tighten.
AXIR ZAUNC to shrink.
AXIRVOZONN *n* blessing.
AYUKTI impropriety.
AZ to-day.
AZ-CAL in these days, at present time.
AZAM p. AJAM.
AZAR one thousand.
AZARCAR, INE a man extremely rich, millionaire.
AZCAR protection, help.
AZCARI *m* protector.
AZI, XAMAIM *f* grand-mother.
AZO, XAPAI *m* grand-father.
AZUL blue.
AZUN still.
AZUN PASSUN } up to now, still.
AZUN VERIAN } up to now, still.
AZUNUIM, } up to now, still.

B

B the second letter of the Roman Alphabet.
BAB, BABA *m* a child, an infant, a little boy.
BA-BAU *m* brothers.
BABDDEPONN *n* helplessness, forlorness.
BABDDO,-I,-EM helpless, forlorn.
BABLEM a little female child.
BABOT insufficient, unfit.
BABRO, -I, -EM big, thick "Babre vontt," thick lips.
BABU *m* p. BABA.
BABUL *f* acacia.
BABULO a little male child.
BAC, BACO *f* hiccup, "Baco eunc", to get hiccup.
BACALHAU cod liver oil.
BACBAC barking of dog.
BACBACUUC VO BONCUNC to bark, to bark like a dog.
BACHI *f* niece.
BACHO *m* nephew.
BACOR VO BACRI *f* hand made bread.
BAD *n* discount, deduction.
BAD GALUNC to deduct, to discount, to diminish.
BAD ZAUNC to be deducted, to gain and lose nothing.
BADD immoral gain, profit of illicit services.
BADDEAC DIUNC VO LAUNC to give on hire.

BADDEAC GEUNC to hire.
BADDECAR *m* one who hires something, lessor.
BADDEM *n* rent, hire, freigth.
BADDIO hireling, ordinary person.
BADD-KHAIRO, -I, -EM unprincipled person, one doing any mean work for gain.
BADDKI lark.
BADI *f* fringe.
BADOM *n* almond.
BAF heat, steam, breath of life.
BAFI using steam-power.
BAG *f* inclination, curve.
BAG *m* company, society.
BAG, VANTTO *m* portion, share. "Hea veparant maca bag nam", in this business I have no share.
BAG *f* happiness, felicity. "Sasnanchi bag", eternal happiness.
BAG *f* garden, flower garden.
BAG GUEUNC to bend, to become agreeable, to drop pride.
BAGARUNC BAGAR DIUNC to add seasoning stuff in working.
BAGAUNC to bend, to incline.
BAGEDAR *m* partner.
BAGELI *m* partner.
BAGEVONT *m* blessed, happy.
BAGIAM *f* beatitudes.
BAGLOLO, -I, -EM lean, meagre, weak.
BAGONC to grow lean, to be satisfied. "To dissan dis bagta." he daily grows lean. „Soglem khaun tachi as bagli" — by eating all, he was satisfied.
BAGOTTAI *f* leaness.
BAGOTTIO, -I, -EM lean, thin, weak.
BAGOUNC to make lean, or thin, to pay, to satisfy, "Taca jeunc dinastanam bagollo", he was made lean without giving him food. "Pedrun Antonichem rin bagollem", Peter paid the debt of Anthony.
BAGOUTA TOSLEM flexible.
BAI *n* an infant girl, a baby.
BAI *f* lady, mistress.
BAIBOLEA PORIM effeminately.
BAIBOLO, -I, -EM effeminate.
BAIBOLPONN *n* effeminacy.
BAIL *f* woman.
BAIL ANCUAR maid, spinster.
BAIL CAZARI *f* wife.
BAIL DOVORLOLI concubine.
BAIL MANSUKECHI lady.
BAIL ZAUNNEM puberty.
BAILE BABOT ZAUNC to become effiminate, to undergo influences of emasculation.
BAILEA-BAIR outwardly.
BAILEAN *n* outwardly, superficially.
BAILO, -I, -EM from outside, stranger.
BAILOGO *m* p. BAIBOLO.
BAIM *f* well.
BAIR out, outside.
BAIR *n* operation, motion.
BAIR GALUNC to dismiss, to exclude.
BAIR ZAUNC to have motions.

Bairaunc to separate, to exclude.

Bairaunnim *f* separation, exclusion.

Bairi *f* a purgative, a laxative.

Bairo corunc to dismiss, to send away.

Bairo zaunc to take leave (fg.) to disappear.

Baji *f* green, pot herbs.

Bajn party of singers and music players, serenade.

Baju-toddop a kind of female dress.

Baki *f* balance, difference "baki caddunc", to substract or find the difference of.

Bakicho, -i, -em remaining, excessive.

Balchão pickle.

Baldi, Bali *f* arrow.

Baldi (udcachi) *f* bucket.

Balguem female hyena.

Balgunc to secure, to save.

Ball child, infant.

Ballo *m* (zadd) purping cacia.

Ballu beaver.

Balluc *m* infant.

Balo *m* lance, dart.

Balsamar corunc to embalm.

Bamb *m* eel.

Bamb thick long rope.

Bambolli playing rope.

Bambor *n* mud or mire.

Bambracho, -i, -em muddy.

Bambtto, -i, -em destitute of character, disorderly, shameless.

Banc bank.

Banc *m* bench.

Banc dudduancho bank.

Bancacho donim banker.

Bancal carpet.

Bancrutt insolvency.

Bancrutti insolvent, penniless.

Bancrutti zaunc to lose one's business, or occupation, to be destitute of means.

Band *m* edge, fence, a long foss.

Band (golleacho) *m* comforter.

Band (pencottacho) waist-band.

Bandavoll *f* construction.

Banddar *n* treasure, riches.

Banddem *n* stomach,

Banddvoll *n* treasure, capital.

Bandfas, Bandpas *m* knot.

Bandi paddy-field near a river.

Bandon vo Badop *n* tie, bandage, construction, building.

Bandpi builder, constructor.

Bandunc to tie, to join.

Bandunc, Bonduc *n* carbine,

Bandunc dondd to levy taxes. rifle.

Bandunc gor to construct, to build.

Bandunc udoc to stop the flow of water.

Bandunc tanduanchi muddi to pack up "chorac bandun galunc", to catch a thief.

Bandvott a snare, difficult situation.

Bang parting of hair.

Bang foddunc to part the hair.

Bang-pannim full tide.

Bangar *n* gold, jewels. "Tichea golleantlem bangar", the jewels from her neck or her necklace.

BANGAR MALLUNC to adorn one's head with gold articles.

BANGDDO *m* mackarel.

BANIAN jacket.

BANN *m* rocket.

BANN (AIDON) *n* a large mud vessel.

BANN (DEG) *f* border, margin "Voddeachi bann" border of the boat.

BANNIAN *n* small shirt.

BANXIRO, -I, -EM worthless person

BAONC to fade.

BAONT CORUNC to assist a child birth.

BAONT VO BALLONT parturient.

BAONT ZAUNC to bring forth young, to produce.

Mazor *baont zaunc,* to kitten, *colgem* to whelp, to puppy, *ducon,* to pig, to farrow, *bocddi,* to yean, *goddi,* to foal, *gai,* to calf, *coli,* to cub.

BANSIREM *n* dirty rag.

BAOLOLO,-I,-EM withered, faded (fig) sad, discouraged.

BAP *m* father.

BAPAI SARCO inheriting qualities of ones father, like one's own father.

BAPAIPONN *n* paternity.

BAPUDDO, -I, -EM orphan, helpless.

BAPUI *m* p. BAP.

BAPULBAU *m* he cousin.

BAPULBOIN *f* she cousin.

BAPULO *m* paternal uncle.

BAR *m* weight.

BAR valuátion.

BAR sense of responsibility; weight.

BAR due time, season.

BAR, BAUSACHO *m* rigours of rainy weather.

BAR (FULANCHO) *m* time of abundance.

BARA *m* twelve.

BARABOR VO BOROBOR in company of.

BARADIC heavy.

BARADIC (ULOUP) serious.

BARADIC MUNIS person of weight and influence.

BARAN CHOLONC to walk with seriousness.

BARAR in the season of, in time.

BARAVO, I, EM twelfth.

BARCAI *f* acuteness, delicacy of wit, kind manners, wisdom.

BARCON *f* cold.

BARIC thin.

BARIM big, large.

BARIONC to be proud, to lose simplicity.

BARKELO, -I, -EM fine, small.

BARMEYCHO NIS barley water.

BARONC (PAUS) to gather rain clouds.

BARONC (TANTIM) to form a chicken into an egg.

BARUNC to appraise, to estimate, to value.

BAS *f* language, idiom.

BAS *m* (VAZOUNCHO INSTRUMENT) bass.

BAS CORUNC to stop, to discontinue.

BAS DIUNC to promise.
BASCOLL, BASCOU *m* liar, bad, cheating.
BASCOUPONN *n* a cheat, fraud.
BASSA-BAS *f* dispute, debate, contention.
BASSA-BAS PODDONC VO ZAUNC to dispute, to contend.
BASSAINAR *m* one who promise,
BASSAINAR person having power to issue orders, instructitions, etc.
BASS AUNC to order, to pass laws.
BASSAUNC to promise.
BASSAUNIM VO BAS *f* promise, vow.
BASSO, -I, -EM stale, not fresh.
BASSO idle gossip, useless talk.
BASSUNC to deny, to contradict one's self.
BASSUNC to dispute to insist-on.
BAT *n* rice, paddy.
BATCAR owner of rice.
BATE *f* bellows.
BATE ZOUNNAR organ blower.
BATELOLO, -I, -EM mouldy.
BATEM *n* food, ration,
BATEUNC to grow mouldy.
BATIO liar, deceiver, flatterer.
BATO *m* bellow.
BATO *m* mouldiness.
BATO MANDONC *m* to get moudly.
BATO (UNDRACHO) skin.
BATSAN *m* moudly taste or smell.
BATT *n* property (of cocoanut trees).
BATTCAN *f* famale proprietor, owner.
BATTCAR landlord.
BATTCAR *m* male proprietor, owner.
BATTI *f* (SOREACHI) distillery.
BATTI *f* (UNDE BAZCHI) oven.
BATTONC to be baptised, to become christian.
BATTOUNC to convert, to make christian.
BAU *m* brother.
BAU, MOL *m* value.
BAUBONDPONN brotherhood.
BAUBONKI *f* fraternity, brotherhood.
BAUL *m* hyaena (zool).
BAULEM *n* figure, statue.
BAULI *f* (DOLLEANTLI) pupil.
BAULLE ALLOUNC to move one's arms, (fig) to struggle with or against.
BAULLO *m* arm.
BAUNTTER *m* deliverance, labour, chuld birth.
BAUNTTER CADDUNC to defray the expense of deliverance or labour.
BAUNTTERACHEM VAITT CORUNC to lie in, to be in labour.
BAUTTO *m* flag.
BAUTTO UBOUNC to raise a flag.
BAVARTH m faith.
BAVARTHI *m* faithful.
BAVARTHPONN *n* faithfulness, fidelity.
BAVOZ, BAUZOI *f* sister-in-law, brother's wife.
BAXA *f* language.
BAXI stale, not fresh, unfit for use.
BAZ *f* bed, couch.

Bazar *m* market, bazar, fare.
Bazar boronc to have a fare.
Bazcheo sorieo gridiron.
Bazodd hard, tough.
Bazonc to heat one's self, to be impatient.
Bazop baking or fryigg.
Bazopi *m* master of a cook's shop.
Bazopin *f* mistress of a cook's shop.
Bazri *f* millet.
Bazunc to bake, to fry.
Bazunc ujean to broil.
Beabit dreadful.
Beabit zaunc to be dreadful, to be afraid of.
Beabitai *f* dread, fear, consternation.
Beat, Beatin pious maid, unmarried female addicted to piety.
Bebdeponn intoxication, curse of drink.
Bebdo *m* drunkard.
Bebdo zaunc to be intoxicated, to be drunk.
Bebo, Manduc *m* frog.
Bebuc *n* small frog.
Becar idle, unoccupied.
Becarponn *n* idleness.
Bechotrai thoughtlessness.
Bechotur imprudent, unwise.
Bêd a clue, secret information.
Bed diunc to disclose secrets of one person to another.
Bed gueunc to obtain information indirectly.
Bed *m* combination.
Beddi *f* manacles.
Beddi galunc to put manacles, to handcuff.
Bedi *m* spy.
Bedonc to conspire, to take part in a conspiracy.
Bedonc to combine, to join.
Bedos (zadd) *f* a kind of jamboa tree.
Bedosturai *f* unusualness; extravagance,
Bedraunc to frighten, to cause admiration.
Bedronc to be frightened, surprised.
Bedunc p. **bedonc.**
Befikir careless, untroubled by cares.
Begari carrier, labourer.
Begim quickly, sharply.
Begot *f* leaf-brass.
Begul *f* bugle.
Behocum without authority, arbitrary.
Beiman untrustworthy person.
Beimani faithless.
Bejar loathing, disgust.
Bejar corunc to cause loathing, to tire.
Bejar zaunc to get tired, to get disgusted.
Bêl *m* branch, "Dakecho bêl", a branch of grape-tree.
Bêll vo **Beli** mixture.
Bel mazor *n* brave cat.
Bel vaimgem *n* tomato.
Belabann *f* incorrigibleness.
Belabannponn *n* incorrigibility.
Belco brain-pan (a term of derision).

BELDAR *m* spendrift, waster.
BELEBAUNN incorrigible.
BELI *f* empty small cocoanut.
BELI *f* cane, sugar stick.
BELO *m* empty cocoanut.
BELLOS *f* rustiness, rankness.
BELLXELELO, -I, -EM mouldy.
BELLXEUNC to get mouldy.
BEM *f* fear.
BEMAN irreverence.
BEMAN dishonour, loss of self-respect.
BEMANI disrespectful.
BEMANIM irreverent, disrespectful.
BEMANUNC VO } to disrespect,
BEMAN-CORUNC } to profane.
BEMBRO *m* the mocus voided by the nose.
BEMORIAD *f* immodesty, dishonesty.
BEMORIADI *m* immodest, dishonest.
BENCDDAUNC to frighten, to cause alarm.
BENCDDAUNNI *f* striking with terror, daunting.
BENCREM *n* chamois, a wild goat.
BENDD, PENCOTT *n* waist.
BENDDO (FOLL) *n* lady-finger.
BENDD (MUZGANCHEM) band of musicians.
BENDDO, (ZADD) *m* lady-finger tree.
BENDDUNC to trim, to cut short.
BENDDUNC to cut down, to destroy, clear a forest of useless wood.
BENDOR *f* parasite plant.
BENDURLEM *n* pruning hook.
BENGI censure, criticism.
BENS property, worldly goods.
BENSAUM blessing, benediction.
BEPORVA CORUNC to despise.
BEPORVA VO BEPORVE contempt, disrespect.
BERDDO, -I, -EM deaf person.
BEREAR PODDONC to be neglected, to remain unheeded.
BEREPONN *n* deafness.
BERESTAR, BRESTAR *m* thursday.
BEREUNC to be stunned, to become insensible, to be deaf.
BERO, -I, -EM deaf.
BERO ZAUNC to be deaf, not to hear properly.
BES *m* state (of life)
BESHEC certainly.
BESSARMAI *f* laziness, carelessness.
BESSARMAI CORUNC to neglect, to be careless.
BESSURVANNO ugty, untidy.
BET stick, walking stick.
BETAUM *m* a splinter, chink.
BETAUM VOCHUNC to cleave, to split.
BET-CANTTI sceptre of authority.
BETT *f* present, offering, gift.
BETT *n* a cane, "raj-bett", sceptre.
BETT CORUNC to offer a present.
BETT *n* (MANNICHEM VO CONDEANCHEM) a ground where bamboo grow.
BETTAN MARUNC to stitch the borders of a garment.

BETTO, -I, -EM idle, without any work.

BETTONC to visit, to meet.

BETTOUNC to offer, to give.

BETTOUNNIM *f* offering, gift.

BEUPEOGUI fruitless, useless.

BEUSANN *f* bad taste, oldness.

BEUXEUNC to get mouldy.

BEXTTO, -I, -EM idle, not occupied, unemployed.

BEZONC to imbibe.

BEZUDD *m* timid, fearful, frightful.

BEZUDDAI *f* timidity, fear.

BEZUDDPONN *n* timidity, fear.

BHAIR GANVAN VOCHNEM emigration.

BHAIR PODDONC to die, to lose.

BHALO javelin.

BHORO ZOLLVACHO load of faggots or firewood.

BI perhaps.

BI *f* the seed (of a fruit).

BIALLO VO BIM seeds.

BIAZ interest, profit due.

BIBEL *n* oil of cajunut shells.

BIBIO VAG *m* panther.

BIBO *m* cashew-tree, anacardium.

BIC *f* alms.

BIC GALUNC to give alms.

BIC MAGONC to beg, to ask alms.

BICAN *f* beggar woman.

BICAR-CHORTTO, -I, -EM petty thief.

BICARI *m* beggar, one that asks alms, mendicant.

BICARPON *n* mendicity, the act of mendicity.

BICON *m* bug.

BICOXA p. BIC.

BICRO, -I, -EM beggarly person.

BID *f* lane, small street.

BIDD *n* bronze.

BIDDA *f* condescencion, compliance.

BIDDEM (SUECHEM) *n* an eye of a needle.

BIDDEST *m* condescending, complying, yielding.

BIDDEUNC to condescend, to be ashamed, to blush.

BIEC *n* hole, opening.

BIEM, BIRANT fear, dread.

BIEUNC to fear, to be afraid of.

BIGOTT *f* leaf-brass, tinsel.

BILCUL entirely, altogether.

BILLO *m* medal.

BIM seed, kernel.

BIM OMPONC to sow, to cast seeds.

BINDLO *m* an Indian earthen vessel.

BING dazzling.

BIPTO VAG leopard.

BIRAD DINAR *m* one who lodges gratuitously.

BIRADD *n* lodging, house for travellers.

BIRADD DIUNC to entertain as a guest, to lodge.

BIRADDI *m* guest, stranger.

BIRANCUL fearful, horrible.

BIRANT *f* fear, alarm.

BIRBO *m* gimlet.

BIREM *n* swarm, a large number of small animals or insects.

BIREU *m* pitch, tar.

BIRLO MADD *m* a wild palm tree.

BIRMOT evil consequence of evil done.

BIRMOT FUTTONC to suffer from misfortune attributed to evil deeds.

BITOR inside.

BITOR GALUNC to put inside, to penetrate.

BITOR GENNEM *n* admission.

BITOR GEUNC to admit, to receive.

BITOR SORONC VO SORUNC to .enter, to come inside.

BITORLEA BITOR interiorly, stealthily, quietly.

BITTBITTAUNC to twinkle, to wink.

BIUAN in the opening, in the hole.

BIUCUTTO, -I, -EM timid.

BIXANNEM *n* bed, all that is laid in a bed.

BIXAT an affair of no importance.

BIZ *n* seed, spesm, source, origin.

BIZLECHO DONDO electric business.

BIZLECHO DONDO CORNAR electrician.

BIZLI *f* electricity.

BIZLI CORUNC to electrify.

BIZLOLO, -I, -EM wet, soaked in water.

BIZOT GALUNC to soak in water.

BIZONC to get wet.

BIZOP *n* wetting, wet state.

BIZOUNC to make wet.

BIZOUNC (MUNXEAC) to throw water on (him).

BIZUDD timid, shy.

BOB *f* shriec, shout, cry, wailing.

BOB O show, ostentation.

BOB MARUNC to shriek, to cry loudly.

BOBALL *m* noise.

BOBATT *f* noise, shout, wailing, shriek, cry.

BOBATT CORNAR *m* reprehender, censurer.

BOBATT CORUNC to reprehend, to admonish.

BOBATT MARUNC to strick, to shout.

BOBATTIO,-I,-EM noisy, one that shouts.

BOBOUNNIM *f* sisters.

BOCDDI *f* she goat.

BOCDDO *m* he goat

BOCDECHEM POR kid.

BOCHOC *n* claw, talon, paw.

BOCHOC MARUNC to take by handful.

BOCHOCBOR handful.

BOCHCUL *n* small handful or paw.

BOCRUNC to eat up greedily, to consume ravenously.

BOCŢ *m* saint, holy person.

BOCTI *m* saint, devout person.

BOCTIN *f* devout person, saint.

BOCTIPONN *n* sanctity, holiness.

BOCUL *m* male cat.

BOCXEM *n* a bunddle.

BODD heredity.

BODDAI *f* fashionableness, pride.

BODDAICAR, IN *m f* a fashionable person.

Boddi *f* stick, cane.
Boddicho,-i,-em of ancestry, hereditary "Ti pidda boddichi" that sickness is hereditary, transmission of qualities of parents to offsprings.
Bodli *f* change.
Bodli corunc to transfer, to change, to replace.
Bodli zaunc to be transfered.
Boddboddo, -i, -em loquacious, talkative, noisy.
Boddboddunc to prattle, to talk much.
Boddcaunc, Bendunc to trim, to cut short.
Boddco, -ki, -kem bald headed.
Boddco head.
Boddic the top, head and front of an animal.
Boddio spirit, angel.
Boddki *f* a bald headed woman.
Bodlam corunc to defame.
Bodlec in the place of, instead of.
Bodol *f* change.
Bodol corunc to change, to replace.
Bodvo *m* angel, spiritual being.
Bogavol *f* possession.
Bogavol caddunc to disposses, usurp.
Boglant *n* calumny, slander.
Boglant galunnc to slander, to calumniate.
Boglanttcar *m* p. **Boglantti.**
Boglantti *m* calumniator, slanderer.
Boglec by the side, near.
Boglechean by the side of.
Bogli marunc to jest, to joke.
Bognar *m* possessor, *duc bognar* sufferer.
Bognar vicissitudes of life.
Bogonc to feel, to bear, to endure.
Bogor without.
Bogsonnem *n* forgiveness, pardon.
Bogsunc to forgive, to absolve.
Bogt *m* saint, holy person.
Bogtancho ectar communion of saints.
Bogul *f* jest, joke.
Bogunc to possess.
Bogunc khast to suffer.
Bogunc suc to enjoy.
Boi *f* fear, grain of any corn. "losnninchi boi", a grain of garlick.
Boi *m* carrier of palanquin.
Boi dissonc to fear, to be afraid of.
Boicot good.
Boin *f* sister.
Boiraji *m* vagabond.
Boireponn *n* deafness.
Boiro, -i, -em deaf.
Boistto, Bestto, -i, -em idle, unoccupied, causeless.
Bokem *n* heron (bird).
Bol *n* cask.
Bol (gonnvancho) cake.
Bolaiki *f* good health.
Bolaikecho, -i, -em healthy, strong.
Bolaiki prosperity, satisfactory life.
Boldi *f* change, substitution.

Boldonc to be changed or reformed, to be revolted.
Boldunc to change, to substitute.
Boli (**chali boli**) *f* agreement, coming to an understanding.
Boli public lecture, speech or address.
Boll *n* strength, vigour.
Bolladic strong, robust, energetic.
Bollan cornem effort.
Bollan corunc to do with an effort.
Bollaboll *f* altercation.
Bollabollcar *m* disputer, wrangler.
Bollandunc to pass, to go across, to overcome.
Bollar *f* white heron.
Bol-lar poddonc to become smiled, to show signs of imbecility.
Bollaunc to entice, to persuade.
Bolleponn *n* goodnees, kindness, benevolence.
Bolleponnim kindly, benevolently, graciously.
Bolli *m* a strong man.
Bolliam without cause, in jest, purposely.
Bollo, -i, -em kind, benevolent.
Bollocottai *f* strength, courage, valour, fortitude.
Bolnar *m* speaker.
Bolnem *n* speech, language, conversation.
Bolonc to speak, to talk.
Bolos pocket.
Bolto, -i, -em other than required.
Bolxi small bag of cloth, pocket of small size.
Bom-anddo *m* act of going round.
Bom-anddo marunc to walk around.
Bõm-ar *f* round about, border, margin.
Bomb *m* bomb.
Bomb (**dud diunc burgueac**) a nipple, feeding bottle.
Bombaddo *m* jet, gush of water, spout.
Bombaist bombayite.
Bombil bombay fish, bombay duck.
Bombil, Bomble bombay fish.
Bombli *f* navel.
Bomgi *m* cleaner of latrines etc.
Bõm-odd *f* a walk.
Bonch *f* bill.
Bonch gueunc to mourn deeply and visibly.
Bonchaunc to eat by bits, to peck.
Boncho mouth.
Bonchro, -i, -em toothless.
Bonconn prison, jail.
Boncunc to bark, (fig) to vociferate, to threaten.
Bonddconn jail, prison.
Bonddi (**maddachi**) tender cocoanut.
Bonddio padri one appearing in priestly dress, but without orders of the priesthood.
Bondir *n* port, wharf.
Bonddo tender cocoanut, green-

or in its early condition.
BONDOR *n* old rag, torn cloth.
BONDRAM CORUNC to rend.
BONDREPONN *n* rudeness, clownish.
BONDRO, -I, -EM rustic, rude.
BONDUC *n* rifle, musket.
BONDVODD *f* jail, prison.
BONG *m* destruction, ruin.
BONG frivolous habits, "polle tache bong, look at her frivolous ways".
BONGEUNC to bud, germinate.
BONGIN *f* female cleaner of latrines etc.
BONGONNAR *m* one that destroys or demolishes.
BONGOUNC to waste, to destroy, to demolish.
BONKI *f* barking of a dog.
BONNS local society in a village, local meeting concerning local affairs.
BONT (VOLICHI) *f* wrapping up or muffling.
BONTO *m* a stopper.
BONVADDO *m* circle, a round about way, a compass.
BONVI *f* the brow or eye brow.
BONVODD *f* a walk.
BONVODD (GADDIEN) a drive.
BONVONC to walk, to go about.
BONVOR *f* butterfly or the great horn beetle.
BONVORCANDDI *f* a screw, vice [pin.
BŎ-ŎG *m* delight, pleasure.
BO-ON-BO-ON from time to time, very often.
BOPXEM, BOUXEM *n* a small fish.
BOR *f* rib.
BOR satisfaction, fullness.
BOR ASSUNC to be satisfied.
BOR DIUNC VO GALUNC to fill up with rubbish.
BOR (FOLL) *n* apple.
BOR (PURNIM) *f* rubbish, "Muttbor" handful, "Gollo bor" up to the neck. "To tonddbor uloita" he speaks frankly or openly. "Aum dollebor polletam" I see with pleasure.
BOR (ZADD) apple-tree.
BORBORIT dragging.
BORCOI *f* jack fruit.
BORCOT *n* health, prosperity.
BORCOTI prosperous, auspicious.
BORCUNC to eat greedily.
BORDDUNC to unusk.
BORE BAXEN well, certainly.
BOREAM GUNNACHI RIT ethics.
BOREAPONNAN frankly sincerely.
BOREM good, yes.
BOREM XICLOLO erudite, learned.
BOREM XICOP erudition, education.
BOREPONN *n* goodness, improvement (in health).
BOREPONNIM good naturedly, sincerely.
BORI CHAL etiquette.
BORNI *f* jar.
BORNUS blanket.
BORO, -I, -EM good, well.
BOROBOR in company of, along with.
BOROBOR (SARKEM) exact, similar.

Borodd *m* weevil.
Borof *n* ice.
Boroinar *m* writer, clerk.
Boronc to fill up.
Boronc (thond) to get cold.
Boronc (meu) to get dirty.
Boronnar potracho editor.
Borop *n* load, burden.
Borop cagdar writing.
Borop fonddar epitaph.
Borop tarvachem freight.
Borop utrunc to copy.
Borop zagranchem drama.
Borounar pustocancho author.
Borounc to write.
Bouronc jevon to feed an infant.
Borounchi rit calligraphy.
Borpi *m* writer, clerk.
Borpi motto great writer.
Borsolet bracelet, wrist jewel.
Borti *f* high water.
Borti, Sucti tide.
Borunc to fill up.
Borunc gonth to gargle.
Borunc meu to stain, to pollute.
Borvonno *m* beater.
Borvonso *m* hope.
Bosca *f* seat.
Boslolo, -i, -em seated.
Bosm *m* ashes.
Bosm corunc to destroy, to burn.
Bosmunc to burn, to reduce, to ashes, to destroy.
Bosnar *m* sedentary, one that sits.
Bossonc, Bossunc to sit down.
Bossonc codelir to sit on a chair.
Bossonc goddear to ride on a horse.
Bossonc ucoddiam to squat, to sit upon one's heels.
Bossounc to make one sit down.
Bosti locality, centre of population.
Bosttaunc to profanate, to pollute.
Bostto,-i,-em idle, without any work.
Posttong to be polluted.
Bosttonnem *n* profanation.
Botelo sailing ship.
Botl *f* **Modtel** *n* bottle.
Bott *m* hindu priest.
Bott *n* finger, bott dacounc, to point-out, to point-at.
Bott (docounchem) *n* forefinger.
Bottatto *m* potato.
Bottcorum *n* a female servant.
Botto caju nut of large size.
Botto dunce, a dull, stupid man.
Bottpon priesthood.
Bou, Boll *n* strength, vigour.
Bou much, largely.
Bou, tantiacho *m* white of an egg.
Boullic *f* sickness, illness.
Boullicar *m* a sick person.
Boullicarine *f* a sick female.
Bounddaunc to make one go about.
Bounddaunc to take round, to circulate.

Bounddecar *m* walker, goer.
Bounddi *f* a walk.
Bounri *f* distaff.
Bounro *m* top. [hair.
Bounro, Kensancho *m* tuft of
Bounro (toclecho) crown.
Bounsa bhair poddonc to be ostracized, to be disowned in one's society.
Bountonn(dor munxachi) environment, surrounding influence.
Bountoun *f* border, margin, circumference.
Bountounim around.
Bouxem *n* small fishes.
Boxi *f* plate.
Bozbozo, -i, -em talkative.
Bozbozunc to prattle.
Boznar *m* worshiper, one that adores.
Bozon *f* adoration, worship.
Bozonc to adore, to worship.
Brestar *m* thursday.
Brim *n* (**lugot**) ticking drill.
Brotar *m* husband.
Buc *f* hunger.
Buc lagonc to be hungry.
Bucando *m* the sacred bone, the flesh that covers it.
Buchcol *f* suffocation.
Buchcolaunc to choke, to throttle, to kill by stopping the breadth (fg) to drown.
Buchcolonc to be suffocated, to drown one's self.
Bud *f* advice, counsel.
Bud dinar *m* counsellor.
Bud diunc to advise, to instruct.
Bud geunc to take counsel, to consult.
Bud zolmachi instinct.
Buddbuddo bubble.
Buddcullem *n* a small earthen vessel.
Buddi, Buddnar *m* a diver.
Buddonc to dive, to plunge, to drown one's self.
Buddonc (gaman) to perspire.
Buddonc (rinnan) to be full of debt.
Buddonc (udcant bitor vochunc) to sink.
Buddounc to put under water, to dip in water.
Buddti *f* deluge, flood.
Budicho, -i, -em wise, cunning.
Budiprocas understanding.
Budvar *m* wednesday.
Budvont *m* prudent, wise, well informed.
Budvont superior, master, adviser.
Buião jar.
Buim *f* (**dorn**) ground.
Buim *f* (**zomin**) land.
Buim poddonc to fall down.
Buim-ar *n* cave, ditch.
Buke moronc to starve.
Buke ravonc to fast.
Bukeloli, -i, -em, bukest hungry.
Bukeunc to be hungry.
Buki (**mutt**) *f* buffet, a blow.
Bul *f* enticement, enchantment, cheat, trick,
Bul *n* (**chauchi**) tea-pot.
Bul *n* (**rozarachem**) bull.
Bullbullit lubricous, slippery.

Bullbullitai *f* lubricity.
Bulloun *f* enchantment.
Bulonc to become passionate, to be passionately in love.
Bulonc (munxeac), to feel a violent passion for.
Bulounno, -i, -em seducer, captivating.
Bund coffee.
Bunhad *f* foundation, base.
Bunhad marunc to make a foundation.
Bunvor circle, act of going round.
Bunvor marunc to go round, to go circling about.
Bunvorkhanddi screwing part of an article.
Bur *n* hernia, fleshy rupture.
Burac *m* hole.
Burac corunc to bore.
Buravoll common people.
Burcaunc to scratch with nails.
Burco *m* paw.
Burddunc to scratch, to rub with the nails.
Burgem *n* child.
Burgem (dactem) baby.
Burgem (zanttem) girl.
Burgeponn *n* childness, infancy.
Burgim children.
Burgo *m* boy, "supurlo burgo," infant, "zalolo burgo," new born-child.
Burio *m* hernious.
Burniz tower.
Burso rustic, rude.
Burxeponn rudeness.
Bus *n* food, ration.
Bus marunc to eat, uto take food.
Buscaunc to suffocate in water.
Buscoll *f* submersion.
But (deuchar) *m* devil, evil spirit.
Butaum *m* button.
Butcannem *n* masonry.
Butic *n* shop, store, dispensary, pharmacy.
Buticar *m* apothecary, salesman, compounder.
Butt (chori) rapine, robberry, theft.
Butt diunc to burn with fire to brand.
Butt launc to steal, to rob.
Buz *n* shoulder, blade bone.
Buznem vo buznar scarecrow.
Buzonc, buzvon diunc to console, to comfort.
Buzonc (paddo) to be frightened, to be surprised.
Buzvon *f* consolation, comfort.
Buzvon diunc to console.
Buzvon, geunc to be consoled, to be comforted.
Buzvonddar consoling consoler.

C

C the third letter of the Roman Alphabet.
Cab (militar) corporal.
Cab (policecho) police officer of subordinate grade.
Cabai tunic, cloak.
Cabar end, conclusion.

CABAR CORUNC to finish, to decide.

CABAR ZAUNC to exhaust.

CABIT *f* rack, clothes stand.

CABLER wig, false hair.

CABLO *m* the outward shell of the cocoanut.

CABLLO MADACHO coir.

CACA, ACOI *f* aunt, father's sister.

CACAD *m* laughter.

CACAD MARUNC to laugh loudly.

CACHERI *f* court (judge's).

CACODDAUNC to frighten, to intimidate.

CACODDONC to shiver, to tremble.

CACOI *f* molasses.

CACON *n* bangle.

CACONCAR VO OLLAR *m* a man that sells bangles.

CACUS *m* latrin.

CACUT *f* mercy, compassion.

CACUT CORUNC to commiserate, to have compassion.

CACUTVONT merciful, kind hearted.

CADDAMODD *f* fatigue, toil or hardship.

CADDI *f* (TONNACHI) straw, *agichi caddi*, matches,

CADDO *m* interest.

CADDNEM *n* removal, abolition.

CADDUN UDDOUNC to abolish.

CADDUNC to take, to remove, *Chunom caddunc*, to whitewash; *xen caddunc*, to put cow dung; *durig caddunc*, to erect a fence or to build a small rough wall; *fondd caddunc*, to sink or dig a grave; *soro caddunc*, to distil; *tel caddunc*, to extract oil; *dar caddunc*, to sharpen (a knife); *Santa Khursache caddunc*, to make the sign of the cross; *dar caddunc*, to open a door; *socla vo khala caddunc*, to lower; *voir caddunc*, to elevate or to place above, to lift; *kadd caddunc*, to shave; *chimtto caddunc*, to pinch; *dud caddunc*, to milk (a cow); *kodd caddunc*, to find fault with or criticise; *dis caddunc*, to pass days or to bear; *jiu caddunc*, to kill or assassinate; *zoc caddunc*, to take measurement; *anglem caddunc*, to undress; *ang caddunc*, to be afraid of, to tremble or to shudder; to draw back or to refuse; *cal caddunc*, to skin; *vaitt caddunc*, to look after a sick man; *pacam caddunc*, to unfeather or to remove feathers; *koullam* (nisteachim) *caddunc* to clean a fish; *moche caddunc*, to remove the boots; *rupem vo bangar caddunc*, to give a silver or gold coating; *zuttie velo caddunc*, to dismiss; *apnnanc caddunc*, to save one's self; *sodun caddunc*, to find out; *samonn caddunc*, to file a law-suit.

CAFI *f* coffee.

CAFO *m* (ZADD) coffee-plant.

CAFUR *m* camphor.

CAGOT *n* paper; *tint puschem cagot* blotting paper.
CAI what.
CAI BOREM how nice! how good!
CAICOI *f* jaundice.
CAIDEACHO,-I,-EM,of obligation.
CAIDEAN justly, by right, according to law or custom.
CAIDO *m* duty, obligation.
CAIDO law, custom, rule.
CAIDO PAUNC to fulfil one's obligation or duty.
CAIL *f* frying-pan.
CAILATO *m* poker.
CAIM something, anything.
CAIM NAM zero, nothing.
CAING *n* water-melon, *caingicho mollo* ground where water melons are grown.
CAINGIN *f* plant of water-melon.
CAIZ *n* heart, courage, affection.
CAIZVONT courageous, bold.
CAL yesterday.
CALAFUR *n* clove.
CALCHO, -I, -EM of yesterday.
CALD *m* broth, soup.
CALDERIN kettle.
CALDIN sweet curry.
CALL time, period.
CALLAU *m* late, delay.
CALLEM CORUNC to dye with black colour.
CALLEM GALLUNC to wear mourning, clothes, to mourn.
CALLEM MARUNC to drape in deep black on mournful occasions.
CALLEM MIRIM black pepper.
CALLIM formerly, olden time. *Mornache callim*, at the hour of death.
CALLIZ NANTLOLO ? callous, destitude of moral feelings.
CALLIZ VO CAIZ *n* heart.
CALLO black, callo zaunc, to become black.
CALLO CORUNC to make black or dark.
CALLOC darkness, obscurity.
CALLSAR darksome.
CALLSO, -I, -EM VO CAUSO, -I, -EM somewhat dark.
CALOR heat, hot weather.
CALOUNC to mix, to mingle.
CALOUNNEM mixture, agitation.
CAL-POR in the last few days.
CALS chalice, wine-cup or glass.
CALSADOR shoe-horn.
CALSAUM pair of trousers.
CALUM *n* oyster.
CALZIVONT, CALJIDAR BOLD courageous, manly.
CAM *n* business.
CAMA PURTO ZAUNC to adapt.
CAMAIS preparation, tillage.
CAMAIS CORUNC to prepare, to till.
CAMANC LAUNC to use.
CAMANCHO, -I, -EM useful, profitable, serviceable.
CAMB rod, bar.
CAMB *f* shingle.
CAMBLECAR work-man, labourer.
CAMBLEM *n* blanket.
CAMELI working man.
CAMEREM working woman.
CAMIZOL chemise, under-wear of females.

Camot *f* a plain field sowed and cultivated generally on the banks of a river.

Camoti *m* agriculturer, farmer.

Camotipon *n* agriculture.

Camounc to cultivate.

Camp *f* trembling or shivering.

Campin *f* a small bell.

Camponc to tremble or to shiver.

Campounc to frighten, to intimidate.

Campro,-i,-em shaky, trembling, timid.

Campro fear, timidity, nervousness.

Camr chamber, municipality.

Camrist member of municipal committee.

Camronc to cover.

Can *m* ear, can bossonc, to become deaf.

Can boire corunc to take no notice of something, to pay no attention to something.

Can diunc to listen or to hear.

Can matrem corunc not to pay any attention.

Canachi fodda-fodd ear-ache.

Canacho burac ear-drum.

Canapo wooden bedstead.

Canari, candri belonging to kanara.

Cancaddo torch light.

Cancaddo *m* tender fruit.

Canculai *f* a cap for chidren.

Candeancho mollo *m* a place where onions are grown.

Candli *f* small onion.

Cando vo Piaų *m* onion.

Candop *n* peeling.

Candpi *n* peeler.

Candpin *f* a female peeler of rice.

Candrunc vo Korpunc to scratch.

Candunc to peel.

Canhus parsimonious.

Cani, dori, dor rope.

Cannim fable or a story.

Cannullem *n* ear-cleaner.

Canos *f* file.

Cansaem pair of cymbals.

Cansaem *n* a musical instrument.

Cansar *m* copper-smith.

Cansèr fatigue, bodily exhaustion.

Canserichem cop wines or spirits for refreshment.

Cansiranc to suffer from hunger.

Canso bowl.

Canso *m* porringer.

Cansou *m* tortoise or turtle.

Cansul temple.

Cansulam *n* temples.

Canti *f* kernel of a cocoanut.

Cantounc to turn as turners do, emcompass, to engrave; *undir* cantounc, to nibble; *nal* cantunc, to scrape; *son* cantunc, *n* to spin.

Cantt upper part or mouth of a vessel, border.

Cantt baincho mouth of a well,

Cantt diveacho fringe or border-end of a lamp.

Canttallo vo Canttao nastines, slutishness, (subs) obsenity.

CANTALLONG, OLXIGONG to detest or to be tired of.
CANTTAM black berries.
CANTTECUOR *f* alve-herb.
CANTTI *f* a thorn-tree.
CANTTIAM *n* fire-wood.
CANTTO *m* thorn, *tagrecho cantto,* the needle of a balance; *goddialacho cantto,* a watch hand; *suri cantto,* knife and fork.
CANULO *m* ear-wax.
CANVET penknife.
CANVIS canvas.
CÃO-ARMACHO trigger.
CAOTO *m* a small cocoanut tree.
CAPAL VO COPOL *m* forehead.
CAPAL FUTTCO unhappy, unfortunate, tachea capalan cainch vochonam, he does not understand.
CAPÃOCORUNG to castrate.
CAPEL chapel.
CAPELÃO chaplain.
CAPNINM *f* cutting hairs.
CAPNNI cut, shave, destruction.
CAPNNIM CORUNG to out hair.
CAPO PONNOS jack fruit tree, yielding dry or less juicy fruit.
CAPO PONNOS jack fruit of dry kind.
CAPODD *n* a dress of an Indian woman.
CAPODDI dealer in cloth, also in sarees used by Indian women.
CAPOT cloak, long coat.
CAPUNG to cut.
CAPUS *m* cotton.
CAPUTTLI VO SOULI *f* a thin piece of wood.
CAPXIN *f* cotton-tree.
CAR,. CROD, RAG *m* anger or wrath.
CAR EUNG to share the taste or inclination of passing events.
CARAB, CARABAM ear-rings usually worn by females.
CARAMOT *f* art or skill.
CARÀMOTIN *f* skilfully or artfully.
CARAN *n* cause.
CARANDAI dispute, discord.
CARANI *m* clerk.
CARANIPON *n* agency.
CARAR contract, agreement.
CARAR CORUNG to settle terms of an agreement.
CARBAR *m* work.
CARBAR management, administration.
CARBARI *m* clerk or headman.
CARCEREIR jailer, official in charge of a jail.
CARCUN *n* clerk.
CARCUNAI *f* clerk's office.
CARETEM *n* a bitter vegetable.
CARGOT, SOMOIO *m* time.
CARGOTICHO wasted or worn by infirmities of old age, very old.
CARMA destiny, invisible power
CAS game for hunting.
CAS VAZONNE to announce a new public order with beating of drum.
CASSAB butcher.
CASSAC VOSSONG to go hunting.
CASTTI loin-cloth, used by Indians of male sex.

CASTTO a form of dressing sarees used by fish-woman.

CAT *f* skin.

CATHI wary, prudent, careful.

CATI (NARLACHI) *f* kernel of a cocoanut.

CATI *f*(RENDRACHI) pruning knife.

CATIAEM *n* small foggels.

CATMAU *f* scrofula.

CATO fibrous material of which coir ropes are made.

CATODDEM VO CATROP *n* cutting.

CATOR pair of scissors.

CATRO *m* a cut ; *catro rodacho*, the tuk of a wheel.

CATROP *n* cutting.

CATRUNC to cut, loum catrunc, to shear, tocxco catrunc, to trim.

CATTACONGI *f* indian potato.

CATTANDUR *m* wood-pecker

CATTI, BETT *m* rod or emblem of anything.

CATTMAN scrofula, king's evil.

CAU red ochre.

CAU psychological moment.

CAU EUNC VO PANONC to reach the time ripe for an event.

CAUGO black, somewhat black.

CAUJEUNC to be frightened.

CAULLO *m* crow.

CAULLO RODDONC to croak.

CAUSAN *f* blackness, darkness.

CAUSO, -I, -EM somewhat black.

CAZ (FOLL) *n* caju; *butavanchem caz*, button hole.

CAZ *n* (ZADD) caju-tree.

CAZAC *n* tail-coat.

CAZAR *n* wedding feast, marriage; *cazaracheo chitti*, bans; *cazari dadlo*, married man.

CAZAR ZAUNC to marry.

CAZOLL. CAZOU *n* soot.

CAZUL *n* chasuble.

CAZULO *m* glow-worm, *diveacho cazulo*, the muff of a candle.

CAZULO *m* (soro) weak liquor of caju.

CEI supper.

CHA *f* tea; *chachi bul*, tea-pot.

CHABCANIM MARUNC to whip, to flog.

CHABCAR biting, dangerous.

CHABDDAUNC to chew, to masticate.

CHABIRO,-I,-EM mordicant, mordacious,

CHABON RAVONT CAROP mastication.

CHABONC, CHABUNC to bite; *pottant chabonc*, to ache.

CHABONC to masticate.

CHABUC whip.

CHAC *n* wheel.

CHACHUR (UDOC) blakish water.

CHACNNEM *n* taste.

CHACONC, CHACUNC to taste, to prove; *chacon polleunc*, to prove by tasting.

CHACOR *m* servant.

CHACORN *f* female servant.

CHACRER ASNNEM to be on duty.

CHACRI *f* employment, job, work.

CHACRI CORUNC to work, to be employed.

CHACRI DIUNC to get (one) employed.

CHADDEO, -II, -IEM intriguer, a talebearer.

Chaddi *f* intrigue, calumny.
Chaddi sangunc to intrigue against, to bear tales.
Chai *f* fey.
Chain *f* sieve.
Chainin galunc to sieve.
Chal *f* walk, habit, custom.
Chal building, in which rooms may be let, big house occupied by many tenants.
Chali-boli *f* friendly intercourse.
Çhalicho,-i, -em usual, accustomed.
Chalis forty.
Challounc to scoff-at, to jest, to worry.
Challunc (chaunc) to sieve.
Chaltic system, government, rule.
Chalto,-i, -em ordinary, usual.
Chamaconc to shine, to glisten.
Chaman (kidd) *f* tick.
Chaman female of shoe-maker's caste.
Chamar *m* a shoe-maker, sadler.
Chambddem *n* leather.
Chamcou *m* wart.
Chanchaunc to slash, to cut, to tread, to pound.
Chancholl luxurious.
Chanchollai *f* luxury.
Chand, Chondrim *m* moon ; *chand udeunc*, to appear the moon.
Chandi *f* silver.
Chandnem moon light.
Chandon *n* sandal.
Chanim *f* squirrel.
Chao marunc to turn up the grain laid out for drying.
Chaonc to irritate, to get angry.
Chaonem *n* irritation.
Chaott, Chauonnem irritating individual.
Chaounc to make one angry.
Chapanni idlers' gossip.
Chapaunc to babble, to speak munch.
Charnem *n* moon-light.
Charo *m* pasture, food, nourishment.
Charounc to graze.
Charounc to put into pasture.
Chatto, -i, -em a miser, a stingy person.
Chattunc to eat voraciously.
Chauddi meeting place, public office.
Chaunc (bat) to turn over.
Chaunnem galunc to sift.
Chavi *f* p. chai.
Cheabuc *n* scourge, whip.
Cheabucaunc to flog, to punish.
Cheacu *m* penknife.
Chealis *m* forty.
Cheddi *f* prostitute, whore.
Cheddiepon *n* prostitution.
Cheddo *m* a boy, male child.
Cheddum *n* a girl.
Cheir perfume, smell.
Chenchaunc to smash, to compress, to suffocate, to crush.
Chenchaunem *n* act of treading.
Chenchlolo, -i, -em oppressed, downtrodden, unfortunate.
Chenchnim compression, pressure, overcrowding.

CHENCHONC to be pressed, to be crushed.
CHENCHUDD small quantity of coir pressed for igniting, a poor female.
CHENCHUNC to compress.
CHEP *n* squashing.
CHEP GALUNC to squash, to crush.
CHEPEM *n* hat.
CHEPNNI act of crushing or squashing.
CHEPONC to be compressed, to yield, to submit.
CHEPONNEM *n* compression.
CHERN VO CHERONA verse.
CHEROL movable and open oratory, to be carried in procession.
CHESTAUNC to jest, to joke, to make a mockery of.
CHESTTAECAR (KESTTAECAR) *m* derider mocker, jester.
CHESTTE *m* fun, mocking.
CHESTTE CORUNC to mock.
CHETNY uncooked curry.
CHIBAT riding whip.
CHIBUDD *n* melon.
CHIBUDDIN *f* melon plant.
CHICAN deceit, treachery.
CHICHANDOR *f* mouse.
CHICOL *m* mud.
CHICHONDOR *m* embolus, sucker of a pump.
CHICNALLI *f* syringe.
CHICOLIO, -I, -EM dirty, muddy.
CHICOT whip.
CHICOT DIUNC VO MARUNC to whip.
CHICOT MATI *f* argil, clay.
CHICOTT *n* sticky, glutinous.
CHICOTTAI *f* sticking, clinging, union.
CHICR *n* tea-cup.
CHIDDAUNC to compress, to tread.
CHIDDONC to be crushed.
CHIDDOUNC to excite, to provoke.
CHIL (BURAC) *f* leak.
CHIL *n* gunny bag.
CHILAR cash money, coins.
CHILIMB smoking pipe.
CHIM *n* slate pencil.
CHIMBU *m* brass water-pot.
CHIMTTAUNC to pinch.
CHIMTTI *f* snuff.
CHIMTTO *m* pinch.
CHIMTTO (LOCNACHO) tongs.
CHINCH (FOLL) tamarind.
CHINCH (ZADD) *f* tamarind-tree.
CHINCHARO VO CHINCHRO tamarind seed.
CHINDI rag, piece of cloth.
CHINEL *n* slipper.
CHINEM *n* Indian potato.
CHINGULO (VAGI) *m* lobster.
CHINI chinese, belonging to China.
CHINTEST *f* sad, melancholic.
CHINTNA *f* thought, mind.
CHINTNECHO, -I, -EM thoughtful, considerate, sensible.
CHINTONNEM *n* reflection, consideration, thinking.
CHINTUC to think, to reflect, to consider.
CHINVAR *m* jeweller.
CHIONC to suck, to lick.
CHIP *n* silence.

CHIP (DOULO) large spoon.
CHIPOTT *n* spoon.
CHIRDDONC to be crushed.
CHIRDDUNC to crush, to press.
CHIRECAR *m* quary, man.
CHIRI *f* money-bag or purse.
CHIRIMIRI *f* a recompense, reward.
CHIRO *m* stone, zodd chiro, very heavy.
CHIROCAMI *m* mason.
CHIRODD *f* crowd, a throng.
CHIROP *n* sawing, cutting.
CHIRPUT *f* toss, fillip.
CHIRPUTT (ZADD) poppy.
CHIRU *f* louse, crab.
CHIRUNC to cut, to saw.
CHIRUTT *n* cigar.
CHIT *n* attention.
CHIT (LUGOT) *n* chintz, printed calico.
CHIT DIUNC to pay attention.
CHIT DINAM ZAUNC to pass over, to omit.
CHIT DIUN AICUNC to hear attentively.
CHITAN attentively.
CHITARI *m* painter.
CHITARUNC to paint.
CHITAVITI opinion.
CHITR *n* painting.
CHITT *f* letter.
CHITTCAUNC to glue, to paste on.
CHITTI *f* a spek, a spot.
CHITTI GALUNC to bespinkle, to dash, to corn.
CHITTI PODDONC to be bespinkled.
CHITTI VACHUNC to publish of a forthcoming, marriage.

CHITTIANCHO,-I,-EM of specks.
CHITTOU *n* wild-goat.
CHIUM *f* button of teat.
CHIUMNNEM sucking.
CHIUNC to suck, to lick.
CHIUNLOLO,-I,-EM sucked, dry, sapless.
CHOBCO *m* claw, talon paw,(fig) the hand; *chopcobor*, handful.
CHOC pure, good.
CHOCHAL MANACHO irresolute.
CHOCHOG four by four.
CHOCMOC *n* link, steel.
CHODD much.
CHODD increase "Chodd assa punn bor nam"
CHODDAU *m* increase, excess; *chodd mollo*, very fat; *chodd rodd zaunc*, to be prosperous.
CHODDCHODDE *m* throbbing, beating, palpitating.
CHODDCHODDUNC to throb, to beat, to palpitate.
CHODDFODDE *m* affliction, pain, [trouble.
CHODDFODDUNC VO CHODDFODDE BOGUNC to grieve, to afflict one's self.
CHODDIT ZAUNC to get drunk.
CHODDONC, CHODDUNC to climb up, to creep, to increase, to rise; *maddar choddonc*, to climb up a cocoa-nut tree; *halam-paianim choddonc*, to creep; *dissan dis callantor choddta*, day by day the interest increases; *raticho zor choddtia*, the fever rises at night.
CHODDONNEM *n* ascension, going up, mounting.

CHODDOP p. choddonem.
CHODDOUNC to make one climb, to increase, to exagerate.
CHODOR *n* bed-sheet.
CHODDTI VATT steep path.
CHOKOTT beautiful, nice.
CHOKOTTAI *f* beauty, handsomeness.
CHOLI *f* girl.
CHOLLI *f* bodice.
CHOLNAR walker, a courier on foot.
CHOLO *m* boy.
CHOLONC, CHOLUNC to walk, to flow; *rupia cholonc*, to be current, to be in vogue; *voddilam codde boro corunc cholonc*, to conduct one's self well with one's superiors; *hatam paianim cholonc*, to go on all four; *vepar cholonc*, to continue a business; *somoia pormonnem cholonc*, to accomodate one's self according to time; *khoxe pormonnem cholonc*, to act in conformity, to agree, to be of the same opinion.
CHOLONNEM *n* gait, pacing; *eca dissachem cholonnem*, a day's journey.
CHOLOUNC to make one walk.
CHOLOUNC GADDI to drive a carriage.
CHOLOUNC ISCOL to conduct a school.
CHOLOUNC VEPAR to manage a business.
CHOLTO, -I, -EM going, errant.
CHOMBO a number, crowd.
CHOMCONNC to walk.
CHOMCONNEM VO CHOMCONN p. CHOLONNEM.
CHOMDDI *f* a small bundle, a parcel.
CHOMDDO *m* a cork or stopple, (fig) effeminate.
CHON MARUN RAONC to entrench.
CHONCRO, -I, -EM stammering.
CHONDALL wicked.
CHONDON *n* sandal-wood.
CHONDONC to be closed or obstructed.
CHONDRIM *m* moon.
CHONGOCHAR *f* civility, politeness.
CHONGOCHARI *m* polite, civil.
CHONN trench.
CHONN MARUNC to dig a trench.
CHONNEM *m* grams.
CHONNEM, VATTONNEM green-peas.
CHOPCO VO CHOPOTTAL p. CHOBCO.
CHOR *m* thief, robber; *dhorianllo chor*, pirate.
CHOR (COTTACHI) ditch, trench.
CHOR-BAIM dangerous well.
CHOR-ZAGO secret place.
CHORBELOLO, -I, -EM fatty.
CHORBEUNC to get fat.
CHORCHORIT brittle, fragile, weak, delicate.
CHORCHORUNC to be brittle, to be fragile.
CHORCO *m* a turner's lathe, a vice.
CHARCUO, -I, -EM thievish, sly, roguish.
CHORI *f* theft, robbery; *udoc vechi chori*, a furrow, trench.

Choriam stealthily quiety, unknowingly.

Chorob *f* fat, fatness, grease.

Choronc (gai) to graze; *ti techoronc*, to blot; *echoronc*, to extend.

Chorou, Charo *m* pasture, (fig) food, nourishment.

Chorounc to lead to the pasture, to graze, to feed cattle.

Chortto petty thief, cheating man.

Chorunc to steal, to rob.

Chorunc collonastanam to cheat, to steal away.

Chorunc doriant to pirate.

Chotran *n* chess, (nant) gratings.

Chotur prudent, careful.

Choturai *f* prudence, carefulness.

Chouc *m* square, cupboard, closet.

Chouc moulding, picture frame.

Choucaxi *f* inquiry, investigation.

Chouconddaunc to make square.

Choucónddo square.

Choucoxi p. **Choucaxi**.

Choucuri monzat four footed animal.

Choucuro, -i, -em quadruped.

Chouda fourteen.

Choudavo, -i, -em fourteenth.

Choug four.

Chougui all four.

Chouio bouio *f* grume, clot.

Chouio bouio zaunc to clot, to curd.

Chounc to see, to observe.

Chound *n* wound.

Choupottiam vochunc to galop.

Chourang a low stool, foot stool.

Chouras *f* all four sides, quadrilateral.

Chouto fourth part, one-quarter.

Chouturo, -i, -em every 4 days; *chouturo zor*, a quartan fever.

Chovatt *m* seat, bench.

Choxilean on all four sides.

Chuc *f* mistake, error, fault.

Chuc corunc to commit a fault or error.

Chuc zaunc p. **Chuconc**.

Chuclee false reports, damaging accusations, intrigues.

Chucleo-khairo tale-bearer.

Chucleo khaunc vo sangonc to play the part of tale-bearer.

Chucmuki disappointment in not meeting one, crossing, divergency.

Chuconc to err, to omit; *vatt chuconc*, to go astray or to loose, the road; *vatter chuconc*, to miss on the road.

Chucônn erroneously.

Chucounc to make one commit a fault, to scape, to avoid.

Chuddet *n* leave of cocoanut tree or palm tree.

Chuddi, chuddo flambeau; *chuddo batacho*, bundle of rice; *panacho chuddo*, pastil of tobacco.

CHUDDO set of glass bangles.
CHUDDTI leaf of palm-tree.
CHUL *f* stove, cooking place.
CHULDON cooking stove.
CHUMBOLL *f* turns of a rope or cloth.
CHUMBUC the loadstone.
CHUN *n* cocoanut scrapings.
CHUNO *m* lime, white-washing.
CHUNO, Cos mortar.
CHUR *f* small pieces or bits.
CHUR CORUNC to make small pieces or bits.
CHURCHURE *m* commiseration, compassion.
CHURCHURE CORUNC VO CHURCHURE DISUNC to have a compassion.
CHURCHUREANIM compassionately.
CHURCHURONC p. CHURCHURE CORUNC.
COBAR CORUNC to finish, to accomplish, to conclude.
COBLAT *m* consent, assent.
COBLAT DIUNC to consent.
COBLEM *n* funnel shaped net.
COBOR Mohammedan grave.
COBRADOR bill-collector.
COBUDOR *m* p. PARVO.
COBUL ZAUNC to consent, to agree.
COBULAT p. COBLAT.
COCARUNC to cluck to crow.
COCAUNC to cluck like hen, to gossip.
COCHARI court, judicial office.
COCHCOCHAUNC to rinse.
COCHOR *n* mule.
COCHRO VO COIR *m* dirt or filth.
CODD *m* burning, ardour.
CODD *n* leprosy ; *codd futtonc*, to get leprosy.
CODDCODO trembling or shivering.
CODDCODUNC to tremble or shiver.
CODDE separate ; *moje codde*, with me; *tuje codde*, with you; *gara codde*, near the house.
CODDEM *n* a bracelet.
CODD-FUTTLOLO leper, leprous person.
CODDI *f* curry.
CODDIO envious, pessimist.
CODDIO resembling a leper.
CODDO (VOGTANCHEA ZADDANCHO) *m* decoction; *coddo orvacho*, cellar.
CODDONC to melt ; *coddonc ragan*, to become very angry.
CODDSAN *f* bitterness.
CODDU bitter; *coddu corunc*, to make bitter; *coddu zaunc*, to become bitter.
CODDVAI *f* bitterness.
CODDVOL *n* side of the body.
CODEL *f* chair ; *codel atanchi*, arm chair; *codel doddchi*, folding chair.
CODEM *m* an earthen baisin.
CODINCH never.
CODULEM small earthen pot.
COENDIR *m* a large rat.
COGUL *f* cuckoo.
COI *f* lobule.
COIFETI a law suit.
COILI *f* potsherd.
COIM VO KEDNAM at what time, when.

Coimbem *n* bucket.
Coimbeunc vo **Colombeunc** to get rusty.
Coimbi, Gorvanchi manger; *coimbi* monzatinc pieunc di-unchi, horsepond; *coimbi naunchi*, bathing tub.
Coimbo fruit-tree yielding plantains.
Coindi *f* a slip knot.
Coipo *m* narcotic.
Coir *m* dirt, coiro caddunc, to sweep the dirt.
Coiti sickle.
Coito *m* kitchen knife or forest knife.
Col *n* shell.
Colcando *m* squill.
Colcolo vo **Culculo** *m* shievering cold.
Colcolunc to tremble.
Colgem *n* bitch.
Coli, Koncli *f* convulsive cough.
Coli female fox.
Coli *f* jackal, vixen.
Collaunc to remove the shell.
Collaxi corunc to join.
Collaxi *f* union or junction.
Colli-launnom fomenter of discords.
Collit attention; *collit corunc* to give notice or warning, to advise.
Collo (ful) bud of a flower.
Collomb mandonc to get rusty.
Collombeunc to rust.
Collonc to know or understand.
Collos *m* top, height, the highest pitch of anything.
Collounc to make known or to advise.
Collpon *n* thinking.
Colo *m* fox, jackal.
Coloi *f* tin.
Coloi caddunc to tin.
Colso *m* coal.
Colsunc to mix.
Colti fire-brand.
Colvollo *m* confusion, disquiet of mind.
Colvont. *n* dancing girl.
Colxeanchi khonn coal-mine.
Combeunc, Comb futtonc to sprout.
Combi *f* hen.
Comblo *m* a young cock.
Combo *m* cock.
Combor, band al eather girdle, belt.
Combreunc to sprout.
Comfor vo **compor** *m* el bow; *comfor marunc*, to elbow.
Comis *n* shirt.
Comounc to make profit, to gain, to earn money.
Comounni profit, gain, earnings.
Compor elbow, joint between wrist and shoulder.
Conc wound on the head.
Conc zaunc to be wounded on the head.
Concari wood-cock.
Conchonc to come off, to separate.
Conchounc to take off, to remove.
Concno *m* native of konkan.
Concno dudi pumpkin.

CONCRI stones broken to small pieces.
CONDD *n* puddle.
CONDDO protection of palm-leafcover against rain used by woman.
CONDDO (MAN) *m* bamboo.
CONDDOLEM *n* small cave.
CONEA virgin, maid.
CONEA-DHAN *f* dowry.
CONFIR *f* coriander.
CONGI *f* sweet potato.
CONGO *m* a snail.
CONGO, -I, -EM intriguer, person fomenting discords.
CONGRO *m* curve, angle.
CONGUEPONN intrigue. [stick.
CONKEM *n* curve or knop of a
CONKER *m* quary-man.
CONN who; *con khobor*, what news; *conn punn*, at least; *conn ansta coun rodlat, some*; *conn conn*, many, some.
CONNCONUNC to stun or to deafen.
CONNEM who, which.
CONNO *m* grain, corn; *conno patticho, the spine, conno tarvacho*, keel of a ship.
CONNOM back-bone.
CONNUIM any body.
CON-ONCH *m* crust.
CONOS VO CONXI ear of corn.
CONOS EUNC to grow an ear.
CONSO *m* corner.
CONSO ĠEUNC to mourn.
CONT rosary.
CONTA *f* tale.
CONTA COXI SANGONC to describe.

CONTREL *n* nich.
CONTRI indigenous, usual.
CONTRI MAL indigenous goods.
CONVALLAI *f* clemency.
CONVALLO *m* gracious.
CONVIT invitation, call.
COOLY carrier, labourer.
COP, RAG, CROD anger, wrath.
COP (SORIACHEM) *n* wine glass.
COPAL *n* fore-head; *copal futtlolo*, unhappy or unfortunate; *copal futtonc*, to split the forehead, to be unfortunate.
COPI *f* pulley or block.
COPI *f* a sample piece.
COPIS kidneys.
COPIT *m* captain.
COPO MARUNC to sew a patch.
COPO VO CUDCO *m* a little piece, a fragment.
COPONC to get angry.
COPOT *m* malice, deceit.
COPTI *f* deceitful, malicious.
COPTTO CADDUNC to take a piece off.
CÕR, *m* a whitlow.
COR colour.
COR (MUZGANCHO) quire of the Church.
CORA CORUNC to stare at.
CORALINA *n* necklace.
CORAUNC to gnaw, to nibble, to pick.
CORBEUNC to mollify by soaking.
CORBOL *m* caramble.
CORCOR grumbling.
CORCORO grumbler.
CORDÃO (BANGARACHO) chain.

Cordo, -i, -em rough; Corco (mar) knock stroke.
Cordunc to grind.
Coreancho paus *m* hail.
Coresm lent.
Corie *m* hail-stones.
Cormeunc to become corrupt, to season.
Cormol (sotrechem) the nut of an umbrella.
Cormott a lot of small fish.
Cornar *m* maker, performer.
Cornel *m* colonel.
Cornet *f* cornet.
Cornim *f* action, doing.
Cornnemcar trumpeter.
Corno *m* trumpet, hunting-horn.
Coro, -i, -em (lugot) crude.
Corod *n* grass.
Corod the thin skin that is between the bark and wood of a tree or grain.
Corond *m* basket.
Corop undeachi crumbs.
Corp Christ Corpus Christi.
Corpaunc to burn.
Corponc to burn.
Corpus child's cap.
Corredor *m* corridor.
Corret fancy pastry roller.
Corvo a piecco of wood etc.
Cortti *f* cocoanut-shell.
Cortub *n* action, deed.
Corunc to make, to perform.
Corunc (gor) to engage a house or to rent a house.
Corun (bhou) specially or principally.
Corve *m* hail-stones.
Cos *m* plaster of the mud.
Coscos *n* poppy-head.
Cosolo, -i, -em what kind or quality.
Cosoloi whatever kind.
Cospot vo cuspot *n* straw.
Cossac launc to test, to verify.
Cossacho fator *m* touch stone.
Cothori, Dhal *n* shield.
Cott *n* fortress.
Cott gavantlem citadel.
Cottem *n* skull, brain pan.
Cottimbir p. Confir.
Cottin hard, strong.
Cottinai difficulty.
Cottri room.
Cottubon *n* scripture.
Cou *m* bud shooting from a palm tree.
Cou *m* tike ; low fellow.
Coub *m* cabbage.
Coucando *m* squill.
Couddi *f* a hedge or fence.
Couddo *m* turtle dove.
Coul *m* a passport or safe conduct.
Couli *f* a small roll taper or a wave.
Coulo *m* a roll; anything in a cylindrical form or wave.
Coulonc to roll or to tie round.
Coutam *n* scenes.
Coutic impressive, beautiful.
Coutuc *n* spectacle.
Covat drill, exercise of body.
Covoto vo Caoto *m* a small cocoanut tree.
Coxtt trouble, labour.
Coxttaonc to work, to labour.

COXTTAUNC to fatigue, to overwork.

COXTTI *m* labourer.

COXTTI CORUNC to fatigue.

COXTTI ZAUNC to get wearied.

CROD VO RAG anger, wrath.

CRODVONT passionate, fretful.

CUACOMBI *f* wood-cock.

CUBDI morose, reticent, reserved.

CUBERT bed-sheet for covering.

CUCOTT malicious.

CUDD *f* body; *cudd garachi*, room; *cudd jeunchi*, dining room; *cudd naunchi*, bath room; *cudd nidchi*, bed-room.

CUDDCO a piece or a bit.

CUDDCO CORUNC to make pieces.

CUDDEA DEVACHI PUZA idolatry.

CUDDEM *n* a hay-stack.

CUDDEPON *n* blindness.

CUD'DO VO ANDLO *m* blind.

CUDDO false; *cuddo deu*, false god.

CUDDO (ZADD) peruvian tree of India.

CUDDOL *f* a weeding hook, pick-axe.

CUDDOU a sort of rabbit.

CUDDOU (MAP) *m* 4 measure.

CUDDTTI *f* mallet.

CUET *f* courage, boldness.

CULCHAO VO DABTI *m* counterpane.

CULCHET *f* hook, clasp.

CULHER *n* spoon.

CULHERAO *m* a big spoon.

CULHERINH *n* a little spoon.

CULL *n* person, individual.

CULLAGAR *n* an orchard.

CULLI (FETI) workmanship make.

CULLI (GERAÇÃO) lineage, race.

CULLI *f* crab or crabfish.

CUL'LO *m* a big crab.

CULOP *n* lock.

CULOP CORNAR lock smith.

CULP fault, guilt.

CULVADDI *m* agriculturer.

CULVADDPON *n* agriculture.

CUMADR *f* she gossip.

CUMADR one's child godmother.

CUMAN *f* she potter.

CUMAO *m* closet, latrines.

CUMAR *m* he potter.

CUMARANCHO DONDO pottery works.

CUMB twenty khandis of grain.

CUMBLEACHEM XET paddy-field, the harvest of which is shared between land-lord and cultivator.

CUMBLLEM part of harvest due to owner of the field.

CUMBLO *m* careya arbora.

CUMBO a pile, heap, accumulation, increase.

CUMER *f* burst thorn bushes.

CUMPADR *m* he gossip.

CUMPADR one's child's godfather. (gossip).

CUMSAR *n* confession.

CUMSAR ZAUNC to confess, to declare.

CUMSODOR *f* confessional.

CUNCARI *m* shout, proclamation.

CUNCHO *m* flag.

CUNCOR cock or hen.

CUNCUDDO louse, of hens.

Cunddi flower-pot.
Cunddo *m* bran.
Cundllem *m* an earthern pot.
Cunhad brother-in-law.
Cuns sharp point or sting; *cuns launc*, to sting, to prick, to tease.
Cunsvar Xmas sweets.
Cunt a grain of cooked rice.
Cuntonc to limp.
Cuntop halting, lameness.
Convent *m* convent.
Gunvo *m* mast.
Cunvor *m* prince.
Cunvory (ostori) princess.
Cuo *m* mast.
Cup vo **Cub** *n* cloud.
Cupi a little bottle.
Cur *m* curate; *cur munxeachi, f* body.
Curarem *n* a small hatchet.
Curcol basket for straining or draining cooked rice.
Curcur cornar one who murmurs, quarrelsome, unsatisfied person.
Curddo,-i, -em blind.
Curmet *f* venereal decease.
Curmuleo burnt rice.
Curmuro zor low fever.
Curnath *f* envious.
Curnathcai *f* envy.
Curnathpon *n* envy.
Curou (padrincho) tonsure.
Curou (padxaikecho) royal crown.
Curpa *f* grace, favour.
Curpevont graceful, gracious.
Current *f* a set of pearls, diamonds etc.
Curu *f* sign.
Curu khursachi sign of the cross.
Cus, Cusi *f* side; *cus davi*, left side; *cus uzvi*, right side.
Cus rottenness, small worms.
Cusco, -ki, -kem evil minded, wicked.
Cuscut a fig or a straw.
Cuslolo, -i, -em rottened.
Cusod rottenness.
Cusomol moisture.
Cusonc to rot.
Cuspidor *m* spitter.
Cusvo *m* womb or uterus.
Cutrem *n* dog.
Cutro *m* dog.
Cutt *f* a blow with knocles.
Cutt (zaddamchi) pieces.
Cuttnem female jump, procuress.
Cuttomb *m* family.
Cutton a jump, procurer.
Cuttorem vo **Mazor** *n* cat.
Cuttoti *f* hammer.
Cutt-ti small wooden hammer.
Cutuleo ticking.
Cutuleo corunc to tickle.
Cutur *m* a turtle cry.
Cutur gallunc to cry like turtle.
Cuvet power, means, tact.
Cuxin separate.
Cuxin caddunc to separate.
Cuxin soronc to be separate.
Cuzinh *n* kitchen.
Cuzinheir *m* cook.
Cuzument *m* decotion.

D

D the fourth letter of the Roman Alphabet.

DA ten (10).

DA ORSANCHO CALL decade.

DAAL *n* a large basket.

DAALI a small basket.

DAAR sharp desire, keen appetite.

DAAR *f* edge, *suriechi daar*, sharp edge of a knife.

DAAR CADDUNC to sharpen.

DABECAR *m* he who prepares skins to carry wine in.

DABO terrace.

DABO *m* a water-bucket, a leather-bottle.

DAC (FOLL) *f* grape.

DAC (ZADD) *n* grape-tree.

DACANCHEM PIC vintage.

DACANCHEM ZADD vine.

DACANCHO MOLLO vineyard.

DACANCHO SORO wine of grapes.

DACLO, -I, -EM small, younger.

DACLO *m* knowledge, manifest.

DACLO LOC the common people.

DACO grapes.

DACOINAR *m* one that shows or points out.

DACOUN *f* pattern, sample, specimen.

DACOUN DIUNC to point out, to prove, to demonstrate.

DACOUNC to show, to present-to, to introduce-to, to guide, to represent.

DACOUNN exhibition, exposition.

DACOUNN DOURUNC to exhibit, to expose.

DACOUNNIM demonstration.

DACTO, -I, -EM p. DACLO.

DACTTO, ZANTTEM HITOR junior, younger.

DACUL VO DAVUL *n* claw, talon, paw, (fig) the hand.

DAD *f* ring-worm.

DADA parent (father), headman.

DADD scarcity, famine.

DADD EUNC VO MARUNC to be scarce, to feel the want of.

DADDAUNC to tread, to beat, to pound, to contuse.

DADDAUNNI *f* act of treading, contusion.

DADDE-DONT larger worms in the stomach.

DADDI *f* jaw.

DADDI BAIM *f* dry well.

DADDI CADDUNC to shave.

DADDI (KHADD) *f* beard.

DADDMAN *f* the jaw-bone.

DADDNAR sender, remitter.

DADDOD *n* eruption, a weal on the flesh (after whipping).

DADDONNEM *n* sending, a present.

DADDONNOM *m* sender.

DADDOP *n* p. Daddonnem.

DADDSONC to burn (the food).

DADDUNC to send, to remit.

DADLEM GADDUM jack ass.

DADLEPONN manliness.

DADLI GANTT fast knot.

DADLO *m* man ; *randd dadlo*, widower.

DADO elder brother.

DADOSPON *n* satisfaction, pleasure, plentifulness.

DADOSPONNIM in a satisfactory manner.
DADOXI satisfied, happy.
DADOXI CORUNC to satisfy, to please.
DADOXI ZAUNC to be satisfied, to be pleased.
DAEM *n* halter.
DAEM, DANVEM left side.
DAG *f* fame, news.
DAG *m* scar, mark, a weal on the flesh.
DAG blot, stain.
DAG DIUNC, DAGUNC to brand.
DAG PODDONC to be rumoured.
DAG PODDONC to blot, to stain.
DAGINNO *m* jewel.
DAGO *m* a piece of thread.
DAI *f* half-yard.
DAI midwife.
DAI VO DALLI *f* bamboo-mat.
DAIJEPONN consaguinity, relationship, use of customary rights.
DAIJI *m* heir, relation.
DAIJIN *f* a female heir or relation.
DAIMB (FOLL) *n* pomegranate.
DAIMB (ZADD) *f* pomegranate-tree.
DAIN *n* dorado, guild head (fish).
DAIZ *n* inheritance.
DAL *f* shield.
DAL-TORVAR sword and shield.
DALAL *m* agent, carrier.
DALALI brokerage.
DALALPONN *n* agency.
DALI *f* bamboo-mat.
DALI *f* lentil.
DALLI *f* bamboo-mat.
DALLIBOND *n* a sword-helt.
DALLIMB *n* pomegranate.
DAMAR pitch, tar.
DAMASC *n* damask.
DAMBUNC to press, to tread.
DAMI *f* epidemy.
DAMONN large needle for sewing thick cloth or canvas.
DAMPNNEM *n* cover.
DAMPUNC to shut, to close, to cover.
DAMUNC p. DAMBUNC.
DAMUN DORUNC to suppress, to withhold.
DAN *n* gift.
DAN DIUNC to give, to bestow; *gor vo ball*, to make over one's goods, by gift.
DANCHEM MEZOP decimal system.
DANCNNEM p. DAMPNNEM.
DANCUNC to overlay, to cover.
DANDDGO,-I,-EM strong, robust.
DANDDI, *f* rack.
DANDDI (MAPACHI) a stick to make even a measure of corn ; strickle.
DANDDI MAPAR VODDUNC to strike with a strickle.
DANDDO *m* the extreme part, the end.
DANDDO (ATANT DORCHO) *m* a cane, a walking stick, a sert of thin slight, stuff.
DANDECAR business man.
DANDO *m* work, occupation.
DANDOL *f* disorder, negligence, misconduct, misunderstanding.
DANDOL confusion, disorder.

DANDOL CORUNC to disturb, to cause disorder.

DANDULGO, -I, -EM disorderly person, negligent.

DANDOLI disorderly, misbehaving.

DANG *n* pace, step, a leap, a jump.

DANG MARUNC to jump or to skip over, to spring.

DANGANNAM large paces or jumps.

DANGAO, -I, -EM long legged.

DANGIRO FIROUNC to proclaim, to publish.

DANGIRO VO DANGRO *m* publication, proclamation, commendation.

DANGULL limb, part of body.

DAN MON *n* contemplation, serious and continued thought.

DAN-MON imagination.

DANNIM *m* to creditor, one who gives, (fig) to be worthy or deserving.

DANNO *m* corn, grain.

DANT *m* tooth.

DANT BANDTA TO *m* dentist.

DANT CADDUNC VO PADDUNC to extract the teeth.

DANT EUNC to teeth.

DANT'PODDO toothless, with broken teeth.

DANT SONDDIO, SONERO having canine teeth.

DANTANCHI PIRAI dentition, time of teething.

DANTANCHO PITTO tooth powder, dentifrice.

DANTEM *n* millstone.

DANTIÓ, -II, -IEM having very large teeth.

DANTO *m* harrow.

DANTO MARUNC to harrow.

DANTONNIM *f* comb.

DANVOL running foot, quick step.

DANVONC to run, to walk fast.

DANVONT rich, very charitable, an alms-giver.

DANVOTT act of running, quickest pace, a race.

DANVOUNC to make one run.

DANVRO, -I, -EM running, quick, (runner).

DAO left, the contrary to right.

DAO, -I, -EM (ANC) tenth.

DAO *m* hatred, enmity.

DAO DORUNC to keep enmity.

DAONN manger.

DAP *f* weariness, fatigue.

DAP EUNC to breathe with difficulty.

DAP MARUNC to be tired, to be fatigued.

DAPEUNC to fatigue.

DAPMAN, OCMAN *m* offence, injury.

DAR *n* door; *fuddlèm dar*, the front door, the principal door.

DAR-RACNNOM porter.

DARACHO VATO hinge.

DARBARI belonging to the counsil of the state.

DARECHO, -I, -EM sharp, keen.

DARNNEM *n* remittance.

DARNNI *f* support, pillar, (fig) help, assistance.

DARNNI *f* present, offering, gift, donation.
DARON *f* current rate, price, value.
DARSHAN respectful homage.
DARU *f* gun-powder.
DARU (SORO) *m* liquor, spirit.
DARU-KHANNEM arsenal, military stores, munition factory.
DARVAZO *m* gate.
DARVONTTO *m* gate, portal.
DARZONNEM *n* a good luck.
DASTECHO, -I, -EM sad, troubled by anxiety, unhappy.
DASTEN MORONC to lose health under weight of cares and anxiety.
DASTI *f* fright, a sudden terror.
DASTI DORUNC to feel afraid.
DATT thick, gross.
DATT ZAUNC to become thick, to condense itself.
DATTAI *f* thickness.
DATTAUNC to thicken, to enlarge to increase.
DATTAUNC (BENCDDAUNC) to frighten, to intimidate.
DATTAUNNIM *f* threat, intimidation.
DATTI p. DATTAI.
DATTONC VO DATTUNC to grow thick to increase, (fig) to be proud.
DATTONNEM *n* condensation.
DATU *m f* metal, ore.
DAU *f* crack.
DAU (CHONNEACHI) *f* lobule.
DAUCUL *n* claw, talon, paw.
DAUCURO, -I, -EM left handed.
DAUDAVIM quickly, hurriedly.
DAULI p. DAUCUL.
DAUM *f* run, course, race.
DAUM MARUNC to run.
DAUNC to keep in order, to arrange.
DAUNDAVIM VOCHUNC to go hurriedly or quickly.
DAUNDDAUNC to make one run, to hurry up, to quicken.
DAUNDDAUNNI *f* haste, speed, hurry, tumult, confusion (fig) pain, trouble, conflict.
DAUNTO, -I, -EM quickly or hurriedly.
DEAN mentality, mental attitude.
DEÃO (DEACN) deacon.
DECON VO DECUN therefore.
DECONC to see, to look, to observe, to view, to consider, to find out, to discover. *Borem deconc*, to desire well; *vaitt deconc*, to detest or to hate; *zosem apnanc decta tosem aplea peleac decchem*, as one loves himself so he should love his neighbour.
DECONNOM shout of reprehension.
DECONNOM MARUNC to reprimand loudly.
DECONUCH only therefore.
DECOR by heart.
DECOR CORUNC to learn by heart, to memorise.
DECOT openly, clearly, knowingly.
DECUNC p. DECONC.
DECUN p. DECON.
DECUNUCH p. DECONUCH.

DECXI cooking pot.
DEDD one and half.
DEDD a person of the mhar caste.
DEDD OZAR *m* one thousand and five hundred (1500).
DEDDI *f* brides-maid.
DEDDIN a female of the mahar caste.
DEDDO *m* the bestman.
DEDDXEM one hundred and fifty (150).
DEFLUS *n* cold.
DEG *f* border, margin, extremity.
DEG DORIACHI sea-shore.
DEG MARUNC to hem.
DEGNODICHI the bank of a river.
DEGRAU *m* degree; (SOPON) *n* stairs.
DEGUECHO, -I, -EM next one, neighbouring.
DEIT owing, in debt.
DEK *f* example, imitation.
DEK DIUNC to give an example.
DEK GEUNC to imitate, to follow.
DEKIVONT exemplary, edifying.
DELEGAD *m* delegate.
DEMAN *n* law-suit.
DEMANCAR *m* caviller, litigious man.
DEMBI *f* point, end.
DEMP *n* pace, step.
DEMP MARUNC to step.
DENCAR *m* p. DENCOR.
DENCAR CADDUNC VO DECARUNC p. dencorunc.
DENCOR roar of a tiger, lion, etc.
DENCOR *m* belching.
DENCOR EUNC to have belching.
DENCOR GALUNC to roar, to rumble, to rustle.
DENCORUNC VO DENCOR CADDUNC to belch(fig) to bluster, to swagger.
DENGALLO, -I, -EM p. dengao.
DENGAO leaping, jumping.
DENNEM *n* debt.
DENNEM *n* gift, donation, present, endowment.
DENNEM ASUNC to have debt.
DENNEMCAR VO DENNEMCARI debter.
DENSO accretion, exaggeration; superfluity.
DENTTO (PANACHO) *m* the stack of an herb.
DER *n* door.
DER brother-in-law (husband's brother.)
DERVONTO *m* p. DARVONTO.
DES *m* fatherland, country.
DESANTOR exile, banishment.
DESANTOR BOVONC to be exiled, to roam or loiter about, to act the vagrant.
DESANTOR CORUNC VO DADDUNC to banish, to exile.
DESANTOR ZAUNC to be banished, to be exiled.
DESANTORI *m* dessantor.
DESPEZ *f* expence.
DESSACHO, -I, -EM public, belonging to a country.
DESSAI nobleman, a man of high rank or position.
DEVA BHAIRO MUNIS atheist.
DEVALLO,-I,-EM divine, heavenly.

DEVOSPONN worship, perfomance of religious duties.

DEVOT devotional visits in Lent to certain places by a party of young man.

DEU *m* God.

DEU BAP God the Father.

DEU PUTR God the Son.

DEU SPIRIT SANT God the Holy Ghost.

DEU BIRANTICHI DUC *f* attrition.

DEU BOREM CORUN thank you.

DEU BORI RAT DIUM Good eveing good night.

DEU BORO DIS DIUM good morning.

DEUCHAR *m* devil, evil spirit.

DEUCHARPONN magic art.

DEUCURPA *f* grace of God, divine grace.

DEULL *n* pagoda, temple.

DEULLI *m* servant of a temple.

DEULLIN *f* a female servant of a temple.

DEUNNEM VO DEUNNIM *n* descent or descending.

DEUNNINDA *f* blasphemy.

DEUNTI declivity, slopy way.

DEUPON *n* divinity.

DEUVOSTON *n* a sacred place, temple.

DEUTA, DEUTI VO DEVI *f* goddess.

DEVAN by God, judicial court.

DEVI *f* goddess.

DEVO, -I, -EM owing.

DEVONC to get down or to climb down.

DEVOS *m* day.

DEVOSPON *n* devotion.

DEVOSTON p. DEUOSTON.

DEXI public, not foreign.

DEXI belonging to a country.

DEZEMBR *m* December.

DEZM tenth's, tithes.

DEZMANCAR *m* tithe collector.

DHOBI washerman.

DHOIRAVONT manly.

DHORM CORUNC to give arms, to take pity, to render a service for God's sake.

DHORM-KHATEM charitable institution.

DHORM-PUTR godson, adopted child.

DHORM-SHASTR religious truth.

DHORMA PORMONNEM religiously.

DHORMA BHAIR GALUNC to excommunicate.

DHOTUR garment of white sheet worn by Hindu males from waist to foot.

DIACN *m* deacon.

DIAMONT VO DIAMANT *f* diamond, precious stone.

DIC VO ROS *m* juice, sap.

DICAO, -I, -EM juicy.

DIDAL *n* thimble.

DIFLO *m* mallet.

DIGAMBOR unmeasured, excessive.

DIGI VO DIRI *f* rampart.

DIGI LAUNC to prop (with forked sticks.)

DIIL loose, large, wide.

DIL mental attitude.

DILAI, E looseness.

DILAUNC to make loose.

Dilguir anxious, troubled by cares.

Dimbi *f* knee.

Dimbi-bor knee-deep.

Dimbi galunc to kneel down.

Dimbi marunc to make genuflection.

Dimbiam vo Dimcuriam cholonc to creep on all four like a cat.

Dimbier ravonc to remain kneeling.

Dinvas *m* acknowledgement, thankfulness.

Dinvassunc tot hank, to express gratitude for a favour.

Dinvaxi grateful, thankful.

Dipcaunc to dazzle, to beguile, to seduce.

Dipcaunem *n* dazzling (fig) blindness.

Dipcounc to get dazzled, to find things exceeding ones expectations.

Dipoc *m* lamp.

Dipti *f* light, that which we see, knowledge, enlightenment.

Diptivont shining, bright.

Dir assistance, help, aid.

Dir, diro diunc to support, to give means to keep up.

Dir diunc to help, to assist.

Diradic valliant, manly, hardy.

Dirbo vo girbo *m* borer, auger.

Dirgam unnecessary or causeless delays.

Dirgam (launc) To delay, to do leisurely.

Diri (gorvanchi) *f* bull-fight.

Diri launc (gorvanchi) to butt, to make the bulls fight.

Diri (medd) *f* pitchfork.

Diri launc to prop with forked sticks.

Dirio launc to cause fights, to excite quarrels.

Dis *m* day.

Dis corunc to celebrate or keep up the date of an event.

Dis, Unet sun ; *jinvaracho dis*, fasting day ; *zolmancho dis*, birthday; *vorsacho dis*, anniversary ; *dis culli*, daily wages.

Dis orsacho anniversary.

Dis zolmacho birthday.

Discont *n* discount.

Disonc vo Disunc to see, to appear, to look; *jivac borem disonam zaunc*, to be in bad health; *churchurre disonc*, to have compassion; *cortubam borim disonam zaunc*, not to be agreeable or pleasing (the actions); *apleam palcanchi duc disonc*, to be sorry for one's sins; *birant disonc*, to be afraid of, to fear; *borem disonc*, to be agreeable or pleasing.

Dispens dispensation, exemption.

Dispens *n* pantry.

Dispenser *m* steward.

Dispotto,-i,-em daily, from day to day.

Dispotto guiras daily bread.

Dissan dis day by day.

Distt *f* sight.

Distt *f* presagement of ill luck,

betwitching by the eye, fascination.
DISTT CADDUNC to remove an ill-luck.
DISTT GALUNC to see, to meet, to visit.
DISTT ZAUNC to have an ill-luck, to be stunedt.
DISTT ZAUNC to suffer from effects of an evil eye.
DISTTI PODDONC to appear, to see.
DISTTICAR hypnotist healing or undoing the effects of evil eye.
DISVODDECAR *m* day-labourer.
DISVODDO *m* daily wages.
DISONNEM appearance, aspect.
DIULI *f* a small lamp.
DIUNC to give, to offer, to present; *viclemdiunc*, to sell; *udar diunc*, to give on credit; *jiv diunc*, to die, (Jesu Christan aplo jiv dilo amche passun, Jesus Christ died for us); to commit suicide, (Pedrun baint jiv dilo, Peter committed, suicide in the well; to love extremely, to boream burgueanc jiv dita, he loves extremely the good boys; *zabab diunc*, to be responsible; *can diunc*, to pay attention, to listen; *tondd dinam zaunc*, not to give a back answer; *vareac diunc*, to winnow (Bat vareac diunc, to winnow the rice.)
DIUNC ADAR to help, to favour.
DIUNC ANIM GUEUNC to exchange.
DIUNC BHAS to promise.
DIUNC DOT to endow.
DIUNC DUC to distress, to oppress.
DIUNC MAN to respect, to honour.
DIUNC PALLO to obey, to execute.
DIUNC PORBEM to congratulate.
DIUNC SOCOT to strengthen; to fortify, to invigorate.
DIUNC SOMZONN to enlighten.
DIUNC SOTHEA to empower, to release, to set free.
DIUNC USNNEM to lend.
DIUNC UZVADD to light up, to enlighten.
DIUNC UZVADDAC to deliver.
DIUNC VOSSONC to allow the use of, the farm.
DIUTTEO PETTOUNC to illuminate.
DIUVAN prime-minister.
DIUTTI *f* torch.
DIVACOR *m* wicked, bad, perverse.
DIVAKOR fearless.
DIVALLI hindu festival in honour of Lakshmi, goddess of wealth.
DIVO *m* lamp.
DIVODD non-poisonous snake.
DOA *m* medecine, remedy.
DOAKHANNO *m* dispensary, hospital.
DOBAJEAN pompously, in a grand manner.
DOBAONN p. DOGVONN.
DOBAONNO *m* threotener, intimidator.

DOBAUNC to threaten, to frighten.

DOBAZO *m* pomp.

DOBI small box, case of small size.

DOBO *m* tinpot.

DOCO *m* blow, stoke, cut.

DOCO a sudden event.

DOCO *m* bunder, quay.

DOCOL *f* manifest, declaration.

DOCOL CORUNC to declare, to make know.

DOCTTI *f* quick clear fire.

DOCTTI (ZORACHI) *f* a slight fever.

DOCTTO *m* a bonifire; pile.

DOCXINN *n* south.

DODD in sound condition. "Dodd bim, seed in good condition."

DODD DORIACHI sea shore.

DODD-DDORIT frightened, in a state of panic.

DODD UDCACHI a measure of water drawn usually from a well. "Add don doddi udoc, fetch two measures of water".

DODDA *f* margin, border.

DODDA FATRANIM BANDUNC to pave the border.

DODDAM quickly, hurriedly.

DODDI *f* a plait or fold, a crumple.

DODDI CORUNC VO DODDUNC to fold, to crumple.

DODDIARO *m* corvina (fish).

DODDO, DOTTO double, twice.

DODDO a measure of weight.

DODDO CAINGACHO a small water melon.

DODDO MAROG *m* a crossway.

DODDODDAM p. doddam.

DODDODDAUNC to frighten.

DODDODDE POLLOUNÇ to witness fearful events.

DODDODDO *m* fright, fear, trembling.

DODDODDUNC to be terrified, to pant, to palpitate. *Tachem calliz azunuim doddoddla,* his heart still palpitates.

DODDOG CADDUNC to suffer, to bear privations.

DODDOG PAUSSACHI shower of rain.

DODDONC to double, to fold, to bow or bend.

DODDPONC to disappear, to hide, not to be seen.

DODDTO, -I, -EM double.

DODDUNC to make double, to fold.

DODDVODDAUNC to hurry up.

DODDVODDO *m* haste, speed, hurry.

DODDVODDUNC to accelerate, to hasten, to press.

DODOG two by two.

DODONC MAROG to cross the ways.

DOÊRIO, -II, -IEM with big eyes.

DOG two.

DÔG *m* heat, warmth.

DOGAIM both.

DOGAM-DOGAM two by two.

DOGD sufferings, afflictions, pain, sorrow.

DOGDOG p. DOGD.

DOG-DOG two by two.

DOGDOGAUNC, to cause suffering, to behave cruelly.

DOGDOGUNC, to suffer, to grieve, to afflict one's self.

DOGDOSORI, unhappy, unfortunate.

DOGLO long indian coat.

DOGO treachery, betrayal.

DOGO-CORNAR treacherous person.

DOGOI, DOGUI, both.

DOGOLBAJI, breach of trust.

DOGONNC, to threaten, to frighten.

DOGOUNNMAR, one who threatens or intimidates.

DOGVONN, *f* a threat

DOGVONNO, *m* threatener.

DOGUI, both.

DOI, *f* cocoanut, shell spoon.

DOIA, *f* compassion, pity.

DOIA CORUNC, to sympathize with, to pity, to be compassionate.

DOIALL VO, DOIALLIC VO, DOIAVONT } compassionate, feeling, charitable, benevolent.

DOIBAR, *n* army.

DOIM, *n* curd.

DOIM, *n* washed clothes.

DOIT, *m* giant.

DOIV, *n* fortune, happiness,

DOIVAO, -I, -EM, fortunate, happy lucky.

DOJA, *f*, elegance, grace.

DOJEA ostentation, vanity.

DOKIN, *n* south

DOL, *f*, cavity, den.

DOL, *m*, a great-drum.

DOLAL, *m* agent, carrier.

DOLALIC VO DOLALKI agency, mediation.

DOL-CAS music using a pair of drums, one large and another small.

DOL-CAS LAUNC to play music, using a pair of drums, a pair of cymbals and a trumpet.

DOLCHO BHAR pendulum.

DOLIO, -I, -EM fat, a person with fat stomach.

DOLKEM POTT stomach like a big drum.

DOLLDIRO p. DOUDIRO.

DOLLE DANCUNC to shut one's eyes.

DOLLE EUNC to get sore-eyes.

DOLLE LAUNC to look at, to fix one's eyes on.

DOLLE MODDUNC to wink.

DOLLI litter, conveyance.

DOLLMAM *f* eye-lids.

DOLLO *m* eye.

DOLLOP *n* grinding, the quantity of corn grinded.

DOLLUNC to grind grain, to reduce grain to dry flour in flour-mill.

DOLONC to rock, to balance.

DOLONC to move to and fro.

DOLONNEM *n* sea-saw, cradle.

DOLOUNC to rock, to lull asleep, (fig) to amuse.

DOLOUNC PAUNNEM to rock the cradle.

DOMAR SIZOUNC to cook on low fire.

DOMBKI threat, repression, forcible insistence.

DOMCAUNC to threaten, to frighten.

DOMDOM *m* aroma, flavour, fragrance.
DOMDOMIT aromatic, odoriferous.
DOMDOMUNC to evaporate sweet smell, scent or odour.
DOMLLO *m* a large ant.
DOMONC to cool down.
DOMOS *m* point, a sharp point or end.
DOMOUNC to cool down forcibly.
DOMPLLO *m* a hole, opening.
DOMPOR knee.
DOMPOR *n* ankle-bone.
DON *n* the paunch, belly.
DON two.
DON, ZOMIN *f* ground, earth.
DON ALONC to have earthquake.
DON (GIRESCAI) *n* wealth, riches.
DON JIVANCHI pregnant, heavy.
DON TONDDANCHO self-contradicting, unreliable.
DONCO *m* leg.
DONCUTTI a spasm, convulsions.
DONDD *m* fine, penalty.
DONDD GALUNC to fine, to punish with a fine.
DONDDEM *n* foolish, silly.
DONDDO cup of leaves pieced together.
DONDDU *n* arch.
DONDDU, TIRCAMTTI bow for throwing arrows. Hoop, anything circular with which something else is bound, particularly casks and barrels.
DONDDUBAL *n* rain-bow.
DONDDVON *f* penance, martyrdom.
DONDECAR business man, trader.
DONDO *m* occupation, labour, business.
DONG *n* stratagem, cheat, trick.
DONG CORUNC to pretend, to deceive, to impose upon.
DONGI, IN a liar, hypocrite, tale-teller.
DONGOR *m* mountain, hill, desert.
DONGOR PULLI *f* a pimple, a little swelling on the eye-lids.
DONGOS sharp, pointed end.
DONGOS act of pushing.
DONGRI *m* one who inhabits in the mountains.
DONGSUNC to excite with repeated strokes.
DONGSUNG to tread upon, to fill up.
DONGUNC to deceive, to impose upon.
DONIAMPONN ownership, dominion over something.
DONIIM both.
DONIM *m* owner, proprietor, master, employer.
DONIN *f* a female owner, proprietress, employer.
DONKI *f* tetanus, spasm.
DONN *n* water after washing the rice.
DONN (AIDON) *n* an earthen vessel like a barrel.
DONORIO, -I, -EM portly or fat person.
DONPAR *m* mid-day,
DONPARAM in the mid-day.
DONS CORUNC VO DONSOUNC to make the water muddy or thick.

DONS(MATIAN MARTAT TI) clapping of fingers on the head.
DONS VO DONSOL (UDOC) *n* muddy water, not clear, obscure, dark.
DONSUNC to excite, to agitate.
DONT *m* a maw worm.
DOPCO *m* stroke, blow, beating.
DOPOTT hard work, tiresome labour.
DOPTTI *f* a rasors'-case.
DOPTTONC to work very hard till one gets tired.
DOPTTUNC to beat, to strike, to hammer.
DOR *f* rate, price, value.
DOR *n* rope; *voddeachem, a low* rope ; *munis*, each man.
DOR *n* a dead bull or cow.
DORBANDI capture.
DORBAR *m* the court of a prince, a court of justice, a tribunal, the assembly of the statesmen.
DORCOL *n* catarrh.
DORI *f* a small rope.
DORIA *m* sea, ocean.
DORIANTLO CHOR pirate.
DORJI *m* tailor.
DORJIN *f* a female tailor.
DORM *m* religion.
DORM-BAP *m* God-father.
DORM-DUV-PUT *f* God child, adopted son or daughter.
DORM-MĂI *f* God-mother.
DORMOPODES *m* sermon.
DORM-PUSTOC *n* sacred scripture, bible.
DORMI VO DORMISTT *m* alms giver, charitable person.
DORMSALL *f* travellers' rest house.
DORN *f* earth, ground.
DORNEM *n* handle.
DORNIM-CAMP *f* earthquake.
DORO (CODDPACHO ETC) *m* vein.
DORO VO DORI cord.
DOROM *m* alms.
DOROM CORUNC to give alms.
DORONC to stick, to adhere, to unite itself; *hat doronc*, to become the hand paralized ; *vachea doronc*, to be unable to speak; *monan doronc*, to remember.
DORONC (URONC) to escape without being damaged or spoiled.
DORUNC to catch, to hold; *paim dorunc*, to beseech a person with great humility ; *golleac dorunc*, to press (for money); *addaum dorunc* to prevent from going, to stop; *jib doru nozo zaunc*, not to be able to hold one's tongue ; *nadd dorunc*, to feel the pulse ; *matear dorun voronc*, to carry on head ; *matear dorunc*, to be very attentive and submissive ; *uclun dorunc*, to elevate; to praise ; *patcacho cantlalo dorunc*, to detest sin ; *patcachi duc orunc*, to be sorry for sin ; *hatant dorunc*, to begin, to commence ; *utrac dorunc*, to find fault with.
DORVODDO hurry, haste.
DORVODDUNC to hurry, to make haste.
DOS *f* hatred, detestation.

Dos (MITTAI) *f* sweet meat.
Dos the quality of a thing.
Dos-NANTLOLO, -I, -EM destitute of its proper quality, worthless, tasteless, useless.
Dosco double-dealing, unrealible.
DOSKEPONN duplicity, unfaithfulness.
DOST friend, sympathetic person.
DOSTI friendship, friendliness.
DOSTUR custom, usage.
DOSTURI commision, brokerage.
DOSUNC to hate, to be troublesome.
DOT dowry, endowment, gift.
DOTTAUNC to threaten, to alarm, to terrify.
DOTT-TTO, -I, -EM double.
DOU (RATCHO) *m* fog.
DOU (SOCAUCHO) *m* dew.
DOU (XINQUELLO) *m* frost.
DOU PODONC to bedew, to drizzle.
DOUDIR *n* misfortune, disgrace.
DOUDIRO, -I, -EM unfortunate, unhappy.
DOUDIRPON *n* misfortune.
DOULLO agitator, critic, intriguer.
DOULLUNC to mix, to turn.
DOULO, VO DOI *f* a large spoon made of cocoanut-shell.
DOULOT wealth, substance, riches.
DOUM DOULLUNC to weaken, to lose firmness or consistency.
DOUNC to grind.
DOUNDOLLIT irresolute, lacking character.
DOUNDOUNC to shake, to exite.
DOUNDOUNEM shake, jerk, alteration.
DOURUNC to keep, to preserve, to save.
DOUSO, -I, -EM whitish,
DOUSO ZAUNC to grow pale.
DOUT *m* ink-stand.
DOUTINTULEM LUGOT *n* pieces of cotton to put into a inkstand.
DOVARNNEM mound built to show the mileage of a road.
DOVE CORUNC to make white, to clean.
DOVIM *f* washed-clothes.
DOVO, -I, -EM white.
DOVORNNEM resting place for carriers, the mound of mileage being used to keep their loads on.
DOVO ZAUNC to be white, to be clean.
DOXA *f* reputation, fame.
DOXA OGDDAUNC to defame, to spoil one's reputation.
DOXIIM in two parts, on both sides, in two halves.
DOXILEAN on both sides.
DOXILO, -I, -EM of both sides.
DOXIR, VAT *f* the wick of a candle.
DRUDD firm.
DRUDDUNC to make firm, to fortify.
DRUSTTAVO *m* apparition, vision.
DRUSTTOCAI *f* enmity, hatred, aversion.

Dú *f* daughter.

Dua prayer, good wishes.

Dua magonc vo corunc to pray̆ for blessings, to praise God.

Duallo vehement desire, whim, longing, a fancy.

Duallo zaunc to have a vehement desire or longing.

Dubai doubtful, dubious, uncertain.

Dubau *m* doubt, hesitation.

Dubau disonc } to doubt, to hesitate, not to believe.
Dubau dorunc }

Dubaua vinn without doubt, certainly.

Dubauan doubtfully.

Dubauonc to have doubt, not to believe.

Dubaxi *m* interpretor.

Dubaxiponn *n* interpretation.

Dubji *f* a woman's under garment of linen.

Dubllo poor, submerged in poverty.

Duc *f* hurt, pain.

Duc *n* sorrow, affliction.

Duc (dolleantlem) *n* tear.

Duc disonc to feel pity.

Ducan *n* liquor shop, tavern.

Ducan assonc to be mourning for a deceased member of one's family.

Ducannem *n* tumour.

Ducatto present to a mourning family of sweets and eatables prepared on a festive occasion.

Duclunc to thrust, to push.

Ducoll, Ducou *m* scarcity, famine.

Ducoll poddonc to have scarcity to have famine; *fullanc ducoll poddonc nam,* there is no scarcity of flowers, *hea gavant ducoll podlolo,* there was famine in this village.

Ducollnem *n* thrust, push.

Ducôn, Ducorni *f* pig.

Ḍucon *n* tavern, petty shop.

Duconc to ache, to be in pain, to sympathise with, to pity.

Duconcar *m* country liquor shopkeeper, tavern keeper, stall keeper.

Ducor *m* pig.

Ducorpon *n* a dirty ungenteel action.

Ducoulolo, -i, -em wounded, suffering from a heavy misfortune.

Ducrachem kharem mas bacon.

Dud *n* milk.

Dud (burgueachem) to wean a child from its mother's milk.

Dud caddunc to milk, to press milk out.

Dud caddunc to draw milk.

Dudar dourunc to feed with milk only.

Dudcan *f* a milk woman.

Dudcan (burgeac dud dita ti) *f* foster dame.

Dud-doxea devastation, waste ravage, damage.

Dud-doxea corunc to waste, to squander.

Duddu *m* money.

Duddvamcan *f* rich moneyed woman.

Duddvancar, *m* rich, moneyed, wealthy person.

Dudi *m* pumpkin.

Dudin *f* pumpkin-tree.

Dudio fat man, one having a protruding belly.

Duduiam roddonc to shed tears.

Duens sickness, illness.

Duent sick, disease, ailing.

Dues hatred, detestation.

Duesunc to hate.

Dukest sorrowful, painful, sad, grievous.

Dull *f* dust raised by the wind, powder.

Dullop pious, merciful.

Dulobai *f* affability, piety, clemency.

Dumaddi confusion, disorder.

Dumaldar *m* persecutor.

Dumallo persecution.

Dumallunc to persecute.

Dumcaunc to box.

Bomco, *m* box.

Dumco marunc p. Dumcaunc.

Dumor a little swelling, especially on a bony part of body, contusion.

Dump incence.

Dumpaunar *m* thuriferary.

Dumpaunc to incence, to perfume.

Dumpaunem *n* thurible.

Dumpel thurible.

Dumxann *n* disorder confusion.

Dunclunc to thrust, to push.

Duncottonc to smoke, to throw vapour.

Dunddaunc to search by turning around, to examine.

Dung *n* tumour contusion.

Dunnem *n* washing.

Dunvor *m* smoke, vapour.

Dunvraunc to throw smoke, perfume.

Dunvri *f* a fog, mist, dimness.

Dunvronc to smoke.

Duont *m* ambiguity.

Duortacho, -i, -em ambiguous.

Dupett double, twice.

Dupett corunc to double, to fold, to bow or bend.

Dupettponn *n* the doubly.

Duput *m* son, descendent.

Dur far, at a long distance.

Durai *f* difficulty, prohibition.

Durai galunc to make difficult, to prohibit.

Durbit *n* telescope.

Durboll, Durbou poor, indigent, weak.

Durbollai *f* poverty, indigence, weakness.

Durbollcai poverty, indigence.

Durbollponn *n* poverty, weakness.

Durdaiv *n* misfortune.

Durgunn *m* vice.

Durgunno, -i, -em vicious.

Durig *n* a fence, a rough wall.

Durpod chorus of a song.

Dusman *m* enemy, adversary, rival.

Dusmancai *f* enmity.

Dusreacho, -i, -em of other, the property of another person.

Dusriim again, once more.

DUSRO, -I, -EM second, next, other.

DUSRO PODDONC to find a competitor.

DUSTT *n* enemy.

DUSTT illness due to a ghostly apparition, effect of a fright.

DUSTTOCAI *f* enmity.

DUSVASI envious.

DUSVASPONN *n* envey, hatred.

DUTOR (CHRISTANVANCHI) elements of the Christian religion.

DUTRO *m* stramonium.

DUUDDI *f* niece, brother's daughter.

DUVES *n* resentment,

DUVES DORUNC to resent, to feel, to know.

DUVOP, DUVUNNEM washing work.

DUVUNC to wash, to clean with water.

E

E the fifth letter of the Roman Alphabet.

EA this.

EA ADIM ere this, before.

EA FUDDEM henceforth.

EANNI *f* huckster-woman, fish woman (fig) a quarrelsome woman.

[illegible] one.

[illegible]RAS heap pile.

[illegible] to unite, to join, to agree.

ECA CALLACHO contemporary.

ECA GAUNCHO fellow countryman.

ECA JINSACHO alike.

ECA ROGTACHO consanguineous.

ECA SANGATACHO associate.

ECA VOGTAR happily.

ECACHE ECVIS ZAUNC to increase and multiply.

ECADEA at times, perhaps.

ECAENNEM entirely, wholly.

ECA-MECACHO, -I, -EM mutual, co-operative.

ECA-MECAR one above the other.

ECA-MONACHO resolute.

ECAN-EOC one by one.

ECANNEM altogether.

ECBACT *m* fast.

ECBACT DORUNC to fast.

ECCADEA VELLA perhaps.

ECDAM once, at one time.

ECDOM at once, quickly, immediately.

ECLO, -I, -EM one, solely.

ECLO ZAUNC to lose a partner.

ECLOCH, -ICH, -ENCH solely, only-one.

ECHO, ACHO, -I, -EM his, her, its.

ECMEKI *f* union, conformity, alliance.

EC-MON resolution, unity, integrity.

ECMULLO-, I, -EM VO } alone single.
ECMUO, -I, -EM }

ECOATAM fast.

ECOATAM DORUNC to fast.

ECODDO, -I, -EM alone, single bare.

ECOLIO, -I, -EM person addicted to solutide and solitary life.

ECONN, ICONN minus one, odd, incomplete.

ECONN-CHALLIS thirty-nine.

Econnis nineteen.
Econn-tis twenty-nine.
Econ-ponnas forty-nine.
Ecott *m* union.
Ecott corunc to join, to unite.
Ecottai *f* meeting.
Ecottaunc to join, to re-unite reconciliation.
Ecras by heaps, without selecting.
Ec-sarkemonn equilibrium.
Ec-sarko equal, even steady.
Ecsonnim fully, entirely.
Ecsuro, -i, -em alone.
Ecsurponn *n* solitude, loneliness.
Ectar union, communion.
Ectar bogtancho communion of saints.
Ecttaim together, unitedly.
Ecttaunc to gather, to amass, to mix.
Ecuch only one.
Ecun in a word, finally.
Ecvadi disagreeable, of one's own mind.
Ec-vis twenty one.
Ecvott p. **Ecott.**
Ec-xem one hundred.
Ecxingallo *m* unicorn.
Edd folly, foolishness.
Eddeponn ways of a fool.
Eddo p. **Veddo.**
Eddonc to rove, to loiter about, to ramble.
Eddonno *m* vagrant, vagabond.
Ednam, Adnandor about this time.
Edo, -i, -em so big, so much.
Edoll a short while.
Edoll porian up to now.
Edoll verian even now.
Edolla this time, presently.
Edou up to now.
Edounc to pretend, to misrepresent, facts frivolously.
Edounni frivolity, pretence.
Edounnom frivolous, flippant.
Eg shooting pain, straining pain in stomach.
Eg marunc to suffer from shooting pains.
Egllaunc vo / **Egllo corunc** } to separate, to desunite.
Egllo, -i, -em separate, desunited.
Egllo soronc to separate, to part, to come off.
Egllo zaunc to be indifferent.
Egllozar *m* separation.
Eh (interjection) oh !
Ei, oi yes, agreed.
Ekebaim in one way.
Ekich she alone.
Ekimeki concord, good understanding.
El *n* creeper, climber.
El trip of load to be carried.
Elcari carrier, labourer.
Eleisaum election, act of voting.
Eleitor voter, elector.
Ell time of misfortune.
Ell sea-shore.
Ell *n* change, hazard.
Ellam bamboo canes.
Ellu *n* cardamon seed.
Ellu *m* thick bamboo.
Em this.
Embaixador ambassador, representative of a state.

EMBARG legal injunction.
EMCONDD *n* hell.
EMPRAS plaster, external, medicine.
EMPRAS LAUNC medicinal application.
EMPREG employment, work.
EMPREGAD employee, servant.
ENDELL castor oil.
ENG *f* embrace.
ENG MARUNC to embrace
ENGIN machine, locomotive.
ENGINER engineer.
ENN *f* joint mother-in-law.
ENNEM *n* coming.
ENNEM this way.
ENNEM deserving, belonging to.
ENNEM credit side of accounts as opposed to debit side of it.
ENNEM, TUCA KITEM *ennem* what does it matter to you.
ENNODDEL castor oil.
ENTOZ, VENTOZ fomentation with cups.
ENTRAD entrance, door-way.
ENTRUZ carnival.
ENTT, VENT unforseen trouble.
ENTUM, ANTUM VO INTUM in this, inside this.
ENVALLEM VO ENVAEM water snake.
EOC one.
EPAR business, profession.
EPARCAR VO EPARI business man.
ER crack, splinter.
ER others "others would do that sort of thing, but I cannot, er corit tosli vost punn mujecodde goddonam."
ER PADDONC to crack.
ERAM LAGUIM with others.
ERAZAR administration.
ERAZARI administrator.
ERDEIR heir.
EREM poop, stern.
EREUNC to crack.
ERONN the tree yielding castor oil.
EROZ heretic person.
ERVADOS fennel.
ERVAM 3 days ago.
ERVELAR herbalist, skilled in herbal treatment of diseases.
ES victory, triumph.
ES KENSANCHI a style of dressing the hair.
ES VORONC to win, to gain victory.
ESCAD stair-case, ladder.
ESCAND scandle.
ESCOL school.
ESCOLACHE DUDDU school-fee.
ESCOLACHO BURGO school boy, student.
ESCOTT escort.
ESCOU brush.
ESCRIVÃO writer, clerk.
ESPOLET cap of the gun.
ESTANS desk.
ESTEÇÃO, DACTTO SERMÃO homily.
ESTICEN station, place of stopping.
ESTREBILH chorus of song.
ETOL stole.
EUCHU scorpion.
EUDI jew.
EUGUI performar of wonders of the Yoga philosophy.

EUL *n* wolf.

EUNC to come ; *oncaro eunc*, to nauseate, to have vomittings ; *zor eunc*, to get fever ; *monan eunc*, to recollect ; *colomb eunc*, to get rusty ; *fodd eunc*, to get boil ; rogot eunc, to drop blood ; *varem eunc*, to blow the wind ; *ainc eunc*, to sneeze ; *borti eunc*, to overflow, *sucti eunc*, to dry the water ; *dolle eunc*, to get sore eyes ; *tachem naum maca enam*, I do not remember his name.

EUROPACHO, -I, -EM European.

EUROPI CHAL CHOLONNC to follow European manners, to Europeanise.

EUZONC VO EUZUNC to think, to imagine.

EUZONN resolution, determination.

EUZONNEM thought, imagination.

EVANGEL the gospel, holy Scriptures.

EVASTA *f* desaster, misfortune.

EVECHEM PAP original sin.

EVOI certainly, yes.

EXCOMUNNAO VACHUNC to excommunicate.

EXEM in this way.

EXTEIPAR from time to time.

EZAM CORNAR examiner.

EZAM CORUNC to examine, to test.

EZMAN hostess, mistress of the house.

EZMANI host, master of the house.

F

F the sixth letter of the Roman Alphabet.

FABL, FABLAM fable, fables.

FABRIQUEIR church warden.

FABULAR book of fables.

FACANDDAI *f* play, jest.

FACANDDI *m* buffoon, jester.

FACANN *n* jest, mock, derision.

FACANN CORUNC to jest, to joke.

FADD wound.

FADDCO piece of cloth.

FADDEM *n* even.

FADDO *m* a piece of cloth.

FAFAUNC to cudgel.

FAFDDONNEM *n* act of shaking off, rejecting.

FAFDDUNC to shake off, to toss.

FAFOR *n* a blow, a spurn.

FAFOR MARUNC to give a blow.

FAFSONNEM injury caused with claws or nails.

FAFSUNC to bruise with claws

FAI beech-tree.

FAI *f* a strip of cloth ; *comsachi fai*, frill.

FAIDO *m* advantage, gain.

FAKIR religious mendicant, a poor man.

FAL sarcastic allusion.

FAL strip.

FALANT talkative, loquacious.

FALEA to morrow.

FALEACHO, -I, -EM of to-morrow.

FALEM *n* to-morrow.

FALEM ZAUNC to dawn, to arrive at break of day.

FALLO *m* tear, rent.

FALLONC VO FALLUNC to tear, [to cut.

Fals untrue, false.
Falsidad untruth, falsity.
Falt act of missing, being found less or in fault.
Faltur unnecessary or undesirable person or thing, a stranger, odds and ends.
Faltur bail woman of ill fame.
Faltur burguem bastard child.
Faltur-dadlo man of no respectable standing in society.
Famad celebrated, famous.
Famanchem bonder flag hoisted to announce a forth comming festival, a person of cheap or undesirable popularity.
Famil *f* family.
Fanc fame, renown.
Fanc renown, notoriety.
Fancarunc to spread out, to expand.
Fancaunc to diffuse itself, to reflect.
Fanconc to reflect.
Fancounc to diffuse, to publish, to divulge.
Fanfarrão boaster, vainglorious person.
Fanki *f* fame, renown.
Fanteailem noketr aurora, morning star.
Fantem *n* dawn.
Fanti, Panti, *f* tresses, braid (of hair).
Fanti galunc to braid, to make into tresses (the hair).
Fantto *m* shoot.
Fantto futtonc to shoot forth or branch.
Fanttonc to spread out.
Fanttonc to tear, to cut asunder.
Fanus lantern, lamp.
Fao *m* a strip of cloth.
Faó deserving.
Fao zaunc to deserve, to merit
Fapaunc to beat, to strike.
Far *m* shot ; a blow ; a stroke.
Far *m* once, one time.
Far marunc to shoot, to burn fireworks.
Far vogot much time.
Far zaunc to explode.
Fara time, "guelolom tea fara Joao bettlo maca, at the time I went John met me."
Faram humorous dialogue.
Faraunc to entangle, to grasp, to seize.
Faraunc(tanduu) to clean the rice.
Faraz(mhar) a person of mhar caste.
Faric corunc to pay, to satisfy, to settle.
Faricponn *n* payment, satisfaction.
Faricponn corunc to atone.
Farizen pharisee.
Far-mar skirmish, conflict, causing to exchange blows.
Farmas medical dispensary.
Faro *m* a stich, a sewing with a needle.
Faro doddto *m* double stich.
Faronc to be entangled, to be caught.
Fars comic play, humorous scene.

FAS *m* knot.
FAS GALUNC to tie a knot.
FASAUNC to catch in a springe, to tie.
FASCAM *n* entanglements, knots.
FASCAM MANDDUNC to entrap.
FASONN *n* escarification.
FASONNAM MARUNC to scarify.
FASSI execution of the criminal sentenced to be hanged.
FASSI gibbet, gallows.
FASSI MARUNC to hang.
FATI slice, piece.
FATOR *m* stone.
FATOR CANTOINAR sculptor.
FATOR (FONDAVELLO) tomb-stone.
FATOR VANTTUNCHI grinding stone.
FATOR ZAUNC to become stone.
FATOR-DOVI marble-stone.
FATRANCHI KHONN quarry.
FATRAUNC to throw stones.
FATT, *f* the back.
FATT CORUNC to turn round.
FATTA-FATT immediately behind.
FATTA-FATT VOCHUNC to go behind, to follow.
FATTIM behind.
FATTIM GALUNC to leave behind.
FATTIM SORONC to turn back.
FATTIM URONC to remain behind.
FATTLO, -I, -EM of behind, previous.
FATTOC way to a public road.
FATURLI *f* pebble.
FAUNC to cut, to tear.
FAÜNC to dissect, to carry out a surgical operation.
FAVO deserving.
FAVO CORUNC to permit.
FAVO THEA BHAIR extra.
FAVO ZAUNC to merit, to be deserving.
FAVONC to deserve, to merit.
FAXI *f* gibbet, gallows.
FAXI DINAR *m* the public executioner, hangman.
FAXI DIUNC to hang.
FAZEND revenue office.
FEBADDO,-I, -EM mocker, jester.
FEBAEO *f* mockery, jests.
FEDDI turn of play, the time of playing.
FEDDOP *n* shearing.
FEDDUNC to clip, to shear.
FELL *m* play.
FELLONC to play.
FENNIM alcohol, high grade of country liquor.
FENNO SABUACHO lather.
FENNOM *m* froth, foam.
FENNOM CADDUNC to throw froth.
FENNOM EUNC to foam, to froth.
FENNOM KELLEANCHO bunch of plantains.
FER *f* market.
FER *f* a course, races.
FER (TUTT) *m* difference.
FER MARUNC to run quickly.
FERIAD *m* holy-day.
FERMENT poultice, application of external medicine.
FERO *m* act of going round, a round about way.
FERO MARUNC to go round, to go from one place to another and come back.

Ferr tailor's iron for ironing clothes.

Ferr marunc to iron clothes.

Fest feast, religious festivity.

Festacar gay and frivolous person, merry-maker.

Festachem Miss high Mass of the festival day.

Feti the making of an article, the design of a manufature, charge for making.

Feti galunc to adorn, to beautify.

Fetiancar *m* calumniator, slanderer.

Fetio *f* calumny, slander.

Fevrer *m* February.

Fiador one standing or offering personal security for another.

Fians security of acceptable kind.

Fidalg *m* gentleman.

Fielam *n* buckles.

Fikir *n* care, risk.

Fikir assonc to be careful.

Fikrecho, -i, -em anxious careful.

Filli (darachi) *f* latch.

Filli (donkeachi) *f* juncture, junction.

Fillo *m* nail.

Filo *m* tulle.

Filoz a kind of home made fritters.

Filsão authorised mark or stamp of approval on weights and measures.

Filzofi philosophy, mode of reasoning out facts.

Fint *n* ribbon.

Fi-onn *f* whistle.

Firiad *f* complaint, accusation.

Firiad corunc to file a suit.

Firiadcar *m* plaintiff.

Firingui European, commonly subjects of Portugal.

Firnem *n* turn, turning.

Fironc to go about, to walk.

Fironc ginean to loose one's senses.

Firounc to make one go about.

Firounc goddo to ride.

Firoy marunc to ride (on horseback).

Fiscanddi deceitful ; roguish.

Fiscann deceit, act of cheating.

Fiscottonc to be disappointed in an attempt; to lose one's troubles.

Fistul *n* fistula.

Fitis magic spell.

Fitisponn magic art.

Fitrunc to deceive, to cheat.

Fitser *m* wizard.

Fittounc to pay up the debt, to settle accounts.

Fitur *m* deceiver, cheater.

Fiturai *f* deceit.

Fituri cunning, seductive.

Fiturpon *f* deceit, illusion.

Fobor *f* news.

Foc, Focam husks of caju nuts.

Foc, Focam sprouts of caju-nuts.

Focot only, solely.

Fodd *m* blister.

Fodd caddunc to blister.

Fodd eunc to swell, to puff up.

Fodd (roi) *f* small pieces.

FODD XETACHEM a part or piece marked by ridge in a paddy-field.
FODDAFODD *f* acute pain.
FODDAM *n* poles.
FODDCAUNC to whip, to flog.
FODDCO *m* stroke, blow.
FODD-FODDNNEM *n* struggle, convulsive movement.
FODDFODDUNC to struggle.
FODDKI *f* alum.
FODDNI act of breaking.
FODDOP rock, boulder.
FODDOP *n* act of breaking.
FODDUNC to break, *tocli fod-dunc*, to have head-ache.
FOEM *n* plank.
FOFAUNC to heat, to give blows.
FOFEUNC to become inflamed.
FOFOLL (MADDI) *f* beetle nut-tree.
FOFOLL *n* beetle nut.
FOFOLL (ZADD) *f* beetle nut-tree.
FOG fire, fire-works.
FOGAC VOCHONC to be defeated, to lose heavily.
FOGUEIR manufacturer of artificial fire-works.
FOI *f* small plank.
FOIDA *m* advantage, gain.
FOJET CORUNC to swindle, to cheat.
FOJET ZAUNC to be cheated or swindled.
FOJENT VO FOJET *f* trick, swindling.
FOL *f* a sheet of paper.
FOLDORAI prodigality, extravagance.
FOLER *m* light-house.
FOLINH *n* tin plates.
FOLL *m* fruit, advantage, gain.
FOLL CADDUNC to profit, to employ usefully.
FOLLADIC fruitful, advantageous.
FOLLANOM, -I, -EM certain person, or thing not mentioned but understood to be one alluded to.
FOLLAR *m* refection, light food.
FOLLEM *n* board.
FOLLI p. FOI.
FOLLI slate.
FOLLONNIM *f* comb.
FOLO leaf.
FOND *m* grave, sepulchre.
FOND CADDUNC VO / FOND MARUNC } to dig a grave.
FONDD allusion to an undesirable matter.
FONDD DIUNC to emprove the taste of curries by an additional operation.
FONDDAR APLEA MATI VODDUNC to fill one's own grave, to furner one's own person ends.
FODDONC to dig.
FONFAEM *n* small wooden bridge.
FONNO *m* bunch.
FONT *f* cautery.
FONTIO, -I, -EM canterised person.
FONTT *f* (PAIANCHI) the heel.
FONTT *f* (MOCHEANCHI) a heel piece.
FONTTAUNC to kick.
FOR *n* (ANGAILEANCHO) lining.

For *f* (bainchi) bottom.
For *m* (garacho) ceiling.
For hot, strong, severe.
Forem true, not wrong, certainly.
Forem *n* a hoe.
Forem corunc to attest, to certify.
Forem corun dacounc to prove, to demonstrate.
Forforounc to speak much.
Forforunc (divo) to crepitate, to crackle.
Forforunc (munis) to speak unreasonably.
Formaunc to draw a sentence, to order.
Formonn *n* sentence, order, mandate.
Forn *n* bakery, oven.
Foro measure of 16 pailies for measuring grain.
Foro, -i, -em true, reliable, truthful.
Foroz *f* itches.
Forpunc to scratch.
Forzonc to cause an itching, tickling.
Fossonc to be disappointed.
Fossounnim disappointment.
Fott *f* lie, falsehood.
Fott marunc to cheat, to deceive.
Fottacri small shots.
Fottas small air-gun of bamboo tree.
Fottco *m* blow, stroke.
Fottfottem sounding instrument.
Fottki *f* alum.
Fottkiro, -i, -em liar, deceiver.
Fottounc to cheat, to deceive.
Fou *m* p. foll.
Fou (batache) toasted rice.
Fou caddunc p. foll caddunc.
Fouz *f* army.
Fozno *m* mortar.
Fozno marunc to fire a mortar.
Fozot *f* injury, dishonour.
Fozot corunc to dishonour.
Frad *m* friar.
Fraz phrase, expression.
Fret *f* freight.
Fronh *f* pillow-case.
Frontal *n* alter-piece.
Frut *n* fruit,
Fud *f* the breech.
Fuddam in future.
Fuddar *m* future time to come.
Fuddea mucar in sight.
Fuddeant near, close by.
Fuddem before, olden time.
Fuddem sorunc to advance, to improve.
Fuddlean in front.
Fuddlem dar *n* principal door.
Fuddlo, -i, -em of front, or behind.
Fug *f* ferment, leaven.
Fug *f* swelling, (fig) pride, vanity.
Fugaum *m* chicken pox.
Fuglolo, -i, -em swollen.
Fugon *f* swelling, pride.
Fugonc to be swollen, to be soacked or drenched.
Fugot galunc to soak.
Fugounc to drench, to soak, (fig) to frighten.
Fugounn unreasonable complaint, loving complaints.

FUGUICHO PITTO baking powder.
FUL *n* flower.
FUL (DOLLEANTLEM) albugo.
FULANCHO GONS *m* nosegay.
FULANCHO JELO wreath of flowers.
FULANCHO MOLLO garden of flower plants.
FULGO, -I, -EM dandy.
FULLEM VOROS next year.
FULLODAR *n* front door, principal door.
FULLOLO, -I, -EM blossomed.
FULONC to flourish, to blossom, to flower; *loumfulonc*, to make the (hair) stand on end, to make one shudder; *doria fulonc*, to become the sea stormy.
FULOUNC to flourish, to blossom, to influence, to encourage; *sotri fulounc*, te open an umbrella; *xidd fulounc*, to hoist the sail; *kens fulounc*, not to comb the hair.
FUMADOR smoker.
FUNC *f* puff.
FUNC MARUNC p. FUNCUNC.
FUNCA *f* fame, publication, notice.
FUNCH fennel.
FUNCNNI blowing pipe.
FUNCOT free, gratuitously, unjustly.
FUNCOTCHO, -I, -EM without, paying for.
FUNCUNC to puff, to blow.
FUND *m* fund.
FUNKEA free, gratuitous.
FUNKEACHO,-I,-EM free, without paying for it.
FUNEL *n* funnel.
FUNTT *f* pitch-fork.
FUNTTONC p. FUTTONC.
FURSOD *f* time, leisure.
FURSOD DIUNC to give time.
FURSOD GEUNC to take rest.
FURXEM *n* viper.
FUSCAUNC to crack, to encourage, to fight.
FUSCAUNC to breathe hard, to belch, to smoke excessively.
FUSCO *m* crack, puff.
FUSCO MARUNC to crack, to puff.
FUSFUSSONC to whisper.
FUSLAN *f* inducement.
FUSLAUNC to induce, to influence.
FUSLAUNNIM *f* inducement, influence.
FUTFUTONC to whisper, to speak in a low voice.
FUTT *f* crack, rent.
FUTTANAM EUNC to swell so as to make a boil burst.
FUTTONC to break, to burst, to germinate, to shoot; *tachem sodanch toclem futtam*, he is always unfortunate; *dolle futtonc*, to be blind or envious; *can futtonc*, to become deaf.
FUXAL happy.
FUXALPON *n* happiness.
FUXI *f* pleasure, wish, desire.

G

G the seventh letter of the Roman Alphabet.
GAAN *f* bad smell.
GAAN EUNC to stink, to get bad [smell.
GAANTT *m* mountain, hill.

GAB pregnancy.
GABA VOCHONC to become pregnant.
GABO *m* any thick, uneven thread.
GABOI VO / GABOLLI *f* } spawn, roe.
GABRAUNC to cause spasm, to make one perplexed.
GABRO, -I, -EM perplexed, shaky, puzzled.
GABRO ZAUNC / VO GABRONC } to hesitate, to be perplexed.
GABSOTTONC to miscarry.
GADD *n* hard, not giving way.
GADDECAR owner or driver of a car.
GADDGO *m* earthen pot.
GADDI (MUNIS) *m* sorcerer.
GADDI *f* carriage.
GADDI ANCARNAR *m* coachman.
GADDI BAINCHI wooden pulley of a well.
GADDIEPON *n* sorcery, witch craft enchantment.
GADDIN *f* sorceress.
GADDIVALO cart-driver, owner of a cart or carriage.
GADDO *m* cart.
GADDUM *n* ass, (pig) stupid fellow.
GADDUM RODDONC to bray.
GADI *f* grocer s shop, tavern, a public house.
GAGA VOCHONC to stammer.
GAGIO *m* stammerer.
GAGOR *f* pot.
GAGRO *m* a woman's petticoat.
GAGRO-KIMÃO **Girl's petticoat and skirt.**
GAGURAI *f* fear, alarm.
GAGURONC to be frightened.
GAI cow.
GAI, GAVO *m* wound.
GAI PECOUNC to heal wounds or sores.
GAIAN *n* song.
GAIAN CORUNC to sing.
GAICEM MAS beef.
GAICHEM ORDDEA SORXILEM MAS brisket.
GAINDDOLI *f* guts, intestines.
GAINDDOU *m* an earthworm.
GAIEN p. GAIAN.
GAIR (XENNACHI) *f* dung-hill.
GAIRUM *n* calf.
GAL *m* face, cheek.
GALÃO gold or silver lace.
GALE whiskers.
GALIO DADLO whiskered man.
GALL, GAU *f* imprecation, curse, abuse.
GALL MARUNC VO / GALLI SOVONC } to curse, to abuse to scold.
GALLUNC to sift, to strain, to filter.
GALMUNN gland.
GALMUNNAM EUNC to suffer from mumps or swelling of glands.
GALOMBO *m* very small prawns.
GALUNC to put in, to put into, to impute; *panti galunc*, to twist; *varem galunc*, to fan; *copalac mirio galunc*, to contract one's forehead; *khot galunc*, to dirty; *dimbi galunc*, to kneel down; *moche galunc*, to put on shoes; *angaulim galunc*, to dress.

GALUNC to put, to thrust.
GALUNC DONDD to punish with fine.
GALUNC GHARA BHAIR to evict.
GAM *m* sweat, perspiration.
GAMAEM *n* rash blotches.
GAMANCHO LOTT profuse, perspiration.
GAMEUNC to sweat, to perspire.
GAMNNI *f* pregnant.
GAN *n* a pawn.
GAN DOURUNC to pawn, to mortgage.
GANGONN pomp, ostentation.
GANH *m* interest.
GANNAR *m* singer.
GANNARIN *f* songstress.
GANNECAR owner of oil press.
GANNEM *n* singing.
GANNENCAR *m* owner of a mill.
GANNERO, -I, -EM stinking.
GANNOM *m* a mill.
GANNONC to stink.
GANNERDO uncleanly; stinking.
GANNEREM shrubs grown in filthy places.
GANNO oil press.
GANPOTR *n* a mortgage paper.
GANPOTR CORUNC to write a mortgage paper.
GANS *m* bite.
GANS GEUNC to stick.
GANS MARUNC to bite.
GANS MARUNC POTTAN biting pains in the stomach.
GANSNNEM *n* rubbing, friction.
GANSUNC to rub, to chafe, to scour.
GANTON act of bringing together.
GANTONN *f* enfilade.
GANTT *f* bell.
GANTT *f* knot; *nisor gantt*, loose knot.
GANTT money, amount of savings.
GANTT MARNAR *m* bell ringer.
GANTT MARUNC to tie.
GANTT MARUNC to ring the bell.
GANTT SODDUNC to untie, to loosen.
GANTTCAR trader in imports from and exports to hilly.
GANTTICHI REPIC peal of the bell.
GANTTICHI TORR belfry.
GANTTANCAR *m* manufacturer of bells.
GANTTAUNC to tie, to fasten.
GANTTI *f* side of a hill, ascent, rising.
GANTTLI *f* hand-bell.
GANTTVON mountaineer, hilly.
GANVA BHAIRO CORUNC to deport, to banish.
GANZ *f* a weal on the flesh, scratching.
GANZIL *m* drone.
GANZO *m* a bird's maw, the throat.
GAO *m* wound, cut.
GAONC to find, to meet.
GAR *n* lizard.
GAR (CORVO) ice; *thond-thond-gar*, as cold as ice, very cold.
GARANNEM household.
GARANNEM *n* accusation.
GARANNEM CORUNC VO GALUNC to accuse.
GARANNENDICAR *m* accuser, plaintiff.

GARODDI *m* conjuror. [eyes.
GARXE DOLLE other than black
GAS, MOSAGOT *f* work, trouble.
GAS GEUNC to work hard.
GAT *m* treachery, perfidiousness.
GAT CORUNC to betray, to deceive.
GATKI perfidious, treacherous.
GATMARO treacherous, perfidious.
GATTNNO *m* miller.
GAU *f* abuse, curse.
GAUM *m* village.
GAUMGORO,-I,-EM of the country, not foreign.
GAUMPON *n* metting of community.
GAUNC to sing.
GAUNC p. GALLUNC.
GAUNCAR villager, member of village community.
GAUNCHI CHALL custom of the country.
GAUNCHO, -I, -EM indigenous.
GAUNCHO MUNIS countryman.
GAUNTTI indigenous.
GAUNVARINI *f* female singer.
GAVET drawer of a chest or table, etc.
GAVETANCHO DP' chest of drawers.
GAZ *m* echo, sound.
GAZONC to sound, to echo.
GAZOR *m* carrot.
GEDDEM *n* odd.
GELL VO GEU *m* space between the fingers.
GELOLO, -I, -EM past, old.
GENNAR *m* receiver.
GENNEM *n* debt, reception, approbation.
GEUNC to accept, to receive; *victem geunc*, to buy; *zuzon geunc*, to conquer; *pallam geunc*, to become strong or firm; *bud geunc*, to consult; *dek geunc*, to imitate; *gòttai geunc*, to take courage; *rinn geunc*, to borrow money; *jiu geunc*, to kill; to assassinate; *can geunc*, to take forcibly; *udar geunc*, to buy on credit; *nogol geunc*, to buy on cash payment; *gangeunc*, to rest, to fall upon; *voddoum geunc*, to bend down; *usnnem geunc*, to borrow.
GID *m* vulture.
GID (POD) *n* song, canticle.
GIDDGEM *n* hawk.
GILLONC, GILLUNC to swallow.
GIM VO GIMALL *m* summer.
GINDI *f* water basin.
GINEAN *n* understanding, intelligence, comprehention.
GIONC to swallow, to devour.
GIR *m* vacuum.
GIRAIC *n* custom, extraction.
GIRAN *n* eclipse.
GIRAS *m* food, nourishment.
GIRASUNC to devour.
GIRBO *m* auger, drill.
GIRDDO *m* dwarf.
GIREST *m* rich, opulent.
GIREST ZAUNC to enrich.
GIRESTAI *f* riches, opulence.
GIRGIREM *n* a wheel full of fire works.
GIRO glutinous.

GIROP *m* crum, kernel of a walnut.

GITA *f* song, canticle.

GIUNC to swallow.

GOBOR *m* ash, powder.

GOBOR CORUNC to reduce to powder, to make ashes.

GOBRO,-I,-EM (rong), grey colour.

GOBRO *m* (masoli), a sort of seafish.

GOD lap. "Avoin dorla burgueac aple godin, the mother holds the child on her lap.

GÔD dock; vapor godin assa, the steamer is in the dock.

GODD sweet, delicious.

GODD indian sugar, jaggery.

GODD KELLEANCHO bunch of plaintains.

GODD PICO AMBO sweet ripe mango.

GODD VO GODDAEM *n* cluster of figs.

GODDAULIM sprouting cajunuts.

GODDBODD disturbed state, noisy proceedings.

GODDBODD CORUNC to disturb, to misbehave, to create disorder.

GODDBODDO, -I, -EM hasty, uncertain, wanting mental balance.

GODDCAN woman selling Indian sugar.

GODDE *m* horse.

GODDEANC NAL MARNAR farrier.

GODDECOST liquorice.

GODDEM MUT *n* diabetes.

GODDE-PAUL *n* maiden hair.

GODDESUAR *m* mounted soldier, cavalry.

GODDEVALO *m* groom.

GODDEZAVEM *n* liquorice.

GODDGODD thundering noise, clatter; *tum kileac goddgodd cortai?* why do you make a noise? *goddgoddo·anim paus borochbor ela*, the thunder and rain come together.

GODDGODD CORUNC to make a noise.

GODDGODD ZAUNC to have a noise.

GODDGODDIT quickly, hurriedly.

GODDGODDO *m* thunder.

GODDGODDO MARUNC VO GODODDUNC to thunder.

GODDGODDUNC to thunder.

GODDI *f* mare; *goddi vogot*, moment, time; *lugtachi goddi*, fold; *dosichi goddi*, sweetness.

GODDI CORUNC to fold.

GODDIAL *n* watch.

GODDIBOR a moment.

GODDIE-GODDIE frequently, very often.

GODDIEC perhaps.

GODDKEM *n* colt.

GODD-MOUM as sweet as honey.

GODDNAR MUZGANCHO composer.

GODDNNAR *m* inventor, manufacturer.

GODDNNI *f* happening, occurrence.

GODDO, GODDI (KHELLAN) playing partners.

GODDONC to happen, to occur, to come about. *Mojea lagim*

ti vost goddonam, I cannot do that thing; *hem moje piddec goddonam,* this is not conducive to my health.

GODDOP *n* invention, building.

GODDPI *m* inventor, manufacturer.

GODDSAN *f* sweetness.

GODDSONC to unite, to establish intimate relations.

GODDSUNC to weld to unite.

GODDULO colt, foal.

GODDUNC to invent, to construct, to build.

GODDVAI *f* sweetness.

GODDVONN *f* juncture, junction.

GODDVON *n*(GODDEANCHI) *f* stables.

GODDXEM *n* sweet.

GODRI mattress, bed-cushin.

GOFAN embracing.

GOFAN GUEUNC to embrace, to hold close, to one's bosom.

GOFIN *f* sling.

GOFLOT unexpected difficulty.

GOGON *n* heaven, firmament.

GOINDDO *m* entrance of a hedge.

GOIR obscure, not clear.

GOIRUMI SUAT sooty place.

GOL *m* valley.

GOLL *m* gallows.

GOLL stupid, foolish.

GOLL DIUNC to hang one's self, to commit suicide.

GOLLAR MARTA to hangman.

GOLLAR MARUNC to hang.

GOLLAXERO *m* sarsaparilla.

GOLLBOLL *m* tumult, noise.

GOLLBOLL CORUNC to raise a tumult.

GOLLCHI BAJI *f* portulaca, purslain.

GOLL-GOLL *m* gargle.

GOLL-GOLL CORUNC to gargle.

GOLLGOLLIT loose, lax.

GOLLGOLLONC to decay, to demoralise.

GOLLI lane, narrow path.

GOLLIO stupid, block head.

GOLLO throat.

GOLLO DIUNC to offer one's life.

GOLLONC to leak.

GOLLONC to get loose, to fall down, to move.

GOLLOUNC to remove, to make use, of; to remember, to think.

GOM *n* gum.

GOMAR CORUNC to iron.

GOMONC to know, to understand, to comprehend.

GOMOT *f* fun, raillery.

GOMOT CORBAR entertainer.

GOMOT CORUNC to make a fun, to amuse one's self.

GOMOTCAR comedian, clown.

GOMOTI humorous, entertaining.

GOMOUNC to inform, to make one understand.

GONCUNC to bark, (fig) to vociferate.

GOND *f* prison, trap.

GONDACHEM ZADD *n* sandal.

GONDD TANDUANCHO bag of rice.

GONDDO *m* tassel; *callzacho gondo,* heart.

GONDIC SAMPDONC to fall in a trap, to be in difficulties.

GONDOF *m* sulphur, brimstone.

GONDOLL *m* confusion.

GONDOLLONC to be confused.

Gondou *m* confusion, disorder.

Gondou corunc vo gondvonc to confound, to jumble, to throw into confusion and disorder.

Gongurlo *m* beetle.

Gonkunc to growl.

Gonn eagle.

Gonn *f* kite.

Gonn (kens) thick, close.

Gonnit *n* calculation, number.

Gontt mouthful of liquid.

Gonntti *f* muster, review.

Gonntti corunc to muster, to review, to count.

Gons *m* bunch.

Gons (moddkechi) soot.

Gont marunc to sip, to suck.

Gontt *n* house ; *burge follear gonttam cortat anim keuttat*, boys make houses on board and play.

Gontt *m* gulp, swallow, draught.

Gontt borunc to gargle.

Gontter *m* nest.

Gontter corunc to make a nest.

Gontto *m* spider's web.

Gonttunc to drink,to swallow.

Gonvlli *m* shepherd.

Gonvoll *m* tent.

Gonxe *m* aphthous ulceration, sore.

Gop *m* breast, bosom.

Gop false news, misleading report.

Gopan dorunc to sit embracing a loved person.

Gopi liar, pretender, deceiver.

Gor *n* house.

Gor chaonc to be in agony.

Gorabo *m* family.

Gorantti a hook.

Gorb *m* conception.

Gorb samballunc vo dorunc to conceive, to be pregnant.

Gorbest *f* pregnant, heavy.

Gorbest zaunc to conceive, to be pregnant.

Gorbi *f* area, space.

Gorbpat *m* abortion.

Gorcan *f* mistress, of the house, wife.

Gorcar *m* master of the house, husband.

Gorcho, -i, -em belonging to a household.

Gordar *n* residence, dwelling.

Gordi density of crowding people.

Gordon throat, fat throat.

Gorennim *f* snoring.

Gorennim caddunc vo goreunc to snore.

Gorgarunc to grunt.

Gorgor *m* agony.

Gori *f* fishing, hook, angle.

Gorib poor, meek, mild.

Goribponn poverty, meekness.

Gorjecho, -i, -em necessary, needful, not free.

Gorjelolo, -i, -em vo gorjevont necessitous, needy.

Gormeche dis hot season.

Gormi *f* heat.

Gornal *m* grenade.

Gorni *f* residence, dwelling.

Goro, -i, -em white.

GORO *m* a big angle, a big fishing, hook.
GORO *m* (ponsacho), jack fruit grain.
GORODPOKI *m* crane.
GOROINAR *m* angler.
GOROUNC to angle.
GOROZ *f* necessity, need.
GOROZ *f* whistling or hissing sound.
GOROZ GALUNC to whistle.
GORTTON ruin, destruction.
GORUAM *n* cattle.
GORUM *n* bull or cow.
GORV *n* pride.
GORVAM *n* cattle.
GORVASO domesticated.
GORVAXI inhabitant, resident.
GORVI proud,
GORVIDAR proud, arrogant.
GORVODO *m* family.
GORVOT household requisites including furniture.
GORVOTI *f* furniture.
GOSCON ringworm.
GOSCOSO *m* water-fall.
GOSCOXEANCHO PAUS heavy rain fall.
GOST taste, appetite, desire.
GOSTT tale, anecdote.
GOSTTEO SANGNAR talker, idler.
GOT state, condition.
GOTT strong, robust, hard, difficult.
GOTTAI *f* strength, courage.
GOTTAI DIUNC to encourage, to animate.
GOTTALO confusion, disharmony.
GOTTEUNC (GORUM) to sit, to rest a while.
GOTTO *m* (gorvancho)stable,*gotto bocddeancho,* sheep-fold.
GOTTO *m* (batacho) grain.
GOTTOTTONN *n* ruin, ruined edifice.
GOTTRI ASSONC to possess means or money.
GOTTRI CAPSACHI bale of cotton.
GOU p. GOLL.
GOU *m* husband, consort.
GOU *m* (zalliecho) cavity of a net.
GOUCARIN *f* a married woman.
GOUGOO shaky.
GOUGOU CORUNC to gargle.
GOUGOUNC (TANTIM) to grow addled.
GOUM *m* wheat.
GOUMLLI *m* shepherd.
GOUNDDO mason.
GOUNTTO, GOUNTTI neck.
GOUVACHI BAIL married woman.
GOUXI *f* flying, fish.
GOVAI *f* evidence.
GOVAI (sacxedar) witness.
GOVAI DIUNC to depose, give evidence.
GOVET *n* drawer.
GOVO-REDDO *m* wild buffalo.
GOZ (ZOC) *m* ell.
GOZ *n* sucker of a pump.
GOZAL *f* conversation, talk.
GOZAL CORUNC to talk, to converse.
GOZCORN *n* tetter.
GOZOR *m* carrot.
GRAD *f* railing.
GRAMMAT grammar.

GRANSSANCHO humorous, entertaining.
GRANTH *m* book.
GRAS *m* food, nourishment.
GRAS CORUNC to behave in amorous manner, to amuse.
GRAVAT *m* neck-tie.
GRAX *n* blacking.
GREST rich, opulent.
GRESTAI *f* riches, wealth.
GRINALD *m* garland, chaplet, crown.
GRUT *m* paste.
GU *m* dung.
GUARD *m* guard.
GUARDANAP *m* napkin.
GUBO (FUZILACHO) *m* tinder.
GUBO (PACRUM) *m* the horned owl.
GUDAUM *m* celler, warehouse.
GUDD *n* enigma.
GUDD clue to a secret.
GUDD (CUNCDDANCHO) *m* coop.
GUDD DUCRANCHO pig-sty.
GUDDI *f* cork.
GUDDI MARUNC XINXEAC to cork the bottle.
GUDDODDAUNC to tread, to put under feet.
GUDDONC to be trodden.
GUDDU-LASSAUM intrigue, dishonest course of action.
GUELO, -I, -EM past, preceding.
GUERR war, battle, conflict.
GUERREIR warrior, quarrelsome person.
GUERRIST warrior, combatant.
GUINEANA BHAIR PODDONC to lose senses.
GUINEANA VINN senselessly.
GUIR a little opening to get in.
GUIRAIC customer.
GUIRESTANCHO,-I,-EM belonging or suitable to wealthy people.
GUIROB pulp of fruit.
GUIT GAUNC to sing songs, to sing hymns.
GUL, -I tokens of a game.
GULAB *n* bramble, thorn, bush.
GULABACHEM FUL *f* rose.
GULABACHEM ZADD *n* rose-tree.
GULABI rosy, rose-coloured.
GULAM *m* slave, captive, in subjection.
GULAM CORUNC to enslave.
GULAMPONN *n* slavery, captivity.
GULLA NALLICHO shell.
GULLANCAR sickly, unhealthy.
GULLI (ARMACHI ETC) *f* bullet.
GULLI (PITTACHI) *f* ball.
GULLI (SUTACHI) *f* reel.
GULLO *m* ball.
GULLOMB, GULLBI bowl of metal.
GULLOMDDAUNC to suffocate.
GULLOMDDI *f* suffocation.
GUM silent, quiet.
GUMCO, -KI, -KEM silent, reserved, noiseless.
GUMKEPON *n* taciturnity.
GUMOT *m* country drum.
GUNDDEM *n* a small bundle of thread.
GUNDDO *m* stone.
GUNEAUM *m* fault, error.
GUNEAUNCAR *m* guilty.
GUNGULI vegetable coral.
GUNJI *f* vegetable coral of India.
GUNJI (ZAD) *f* a coral-tree of India.

Gunn *m* virtue, effect, inclination; *voclac boro gunn poddlo,* the medecine had a good effect; *to burgo boream gunnancho,* that boy is virtuous; *Pedruc vaill gunn asal,* Peter has got had habits.
Gunnadic virtuous, civil, polite.
Gunnem coil of coir rope.
Gunnest *m* virtuous, polite.
Gunnoddicai *f* good creation.
Gunsunno *m* small mill stone.
Gunttarunc to wrap.
Gunttcunc to harrow.
Guntti *f* marble, seed.
Gunttnom pestle.
Guntto *m* harrow.
Guntunc to thread, to string, to range in a file, to link or connect.
Gunvoll *f* giddiness.
Gunvoll eunc to be giddy.
Gunvonc to move.
Gupit secret, private.
Guptacho, -i, -em secret.
Guptest confidencial, private.
Guptestai *f* secrecy.
Gupto, -i, -em reserved, secret.
Gurddi cork, stopper.
Gurddo large cork or stopper.
Gurddo marunc to gag, to stop flowing liquid.
Gurgulet *n* watering pot.
Gurgulo *m* spider, common weaver.
Gurmeunc to snarl.
Gurn teacher, person respected for his learning.
Guru *m* priest.
Gurut *m* putty.
Gurvachar pregnancy.
Gurvar pregnant.
Gurvarpon *n* pregnancy.
Gus a kind of duck.
Gusmoddonc to be suffocated, to be choked.
Guspaunc to disturb, to perlex.
Gusponc to be troubled, to be perplexed.
Guspottaunc to asphyxiate, to suffocate.
Gussonc to secure admission, to enter as an unbidden guest.
Gutt *m* secret.
Guttlaunc to wrap up.
Guttli *f* parcel, bundle, packet.
Guttlo *m* bundle.
Guttlonc to be wraped up.
Guttmell *m* counsel, advice, resolution.
Guttmell corunc to hold a meeting to resolve.
Guzaronc to pass in silence.
Guzarunc to make one pass in silence.
Guzran corunc to live within one's means.
Guzraunc to live within ones means, to pull on frugally.

H

H the eight letter of the Roman Alphabet.
Ha! sigh of relief.
Ha, ha, ha, peals of laughter.
Habilidad ability.
Hac shout, a loud call.
Hafddonozo toslo, -i, -em impalpable.

HAIRANN perturbation, weariness.
HAIRANN ZAUNC to be much troubled.
HALAUNNI gesture.
HALF-CASTE Eurasian, person of mixed parentage.
HAMAL porter, domestic servant.
HAMALDOSTO mortar and pestle.
HAMBOG deceit.
HAMBOGUI MUNIS cheat, rascal.
HAMLETT omlette.
HANDAH seats on back of an elephant for two or three persons.
HANSO laugh, laughter.
HANSONC to laugh, to ridicule.
HARCOR obstacle, impediment.
HARMAN harmonium.
HARVO green, immature.
HAT hand.
HAT LAGONC NAM TOSLEM intact.
HATACHEM CAM manual labour.
HATAN DORCHO PANTTULO hand basket.
HAT-BOROUP handwriting.
HATPAIKI manual skill.
HAVALDAR sepoy sergeant.
HAVALO time of agreement, an instalment payableas agreed,
HAVALO DIUNC to accept terms of paying a debt, to promise.
HAVO oven.
HAVO NOLLEANCHO oven for baking tiles.
HAZAR thousand.
HAZRAVONT possessing thousands, wealthy.
HAZRAVONT ZAUNC to become wealthy.
HERANS inheritance.
HERDER *m* heir.
HEROZ heretic person, one holding independent views, especially in religion.
HERVELAR herbalist, physician skilled in herbal treatment of diseases.
HEVOI yes, certainly.
HINDD herd, flock.
HINDLO hammock.
HIPOTEC *n* mortgage.
HISS CORUNC to tease, to belittle.
HISTOR history.
HISTOR BOROINAR historian.
Ho, -I, -EM this one.
Ho, HO, HO ! peal of laughter.
HOLCO mean, low, petty.
HOLKEPONN acts betraying mean and low qualities.
HONR honour, high esteem.
HOR *n* hour.
HORACHE HORA once in an hour, from hour to hour.
HORT *n* garden.
HORTELAUM *m* mint.
HOSPIS an asylum for sick persons, travellers and other people needing rest-house.
HOSPITAL *n* hospital.
HOSPITAL (PIXEANCHEM) lunatic asylum.
HOSTORI DOIRAVONT heroine.
HOTEL inn, boarding and lodging house.
HOTI elephant.
HU *f* louse.

HUCUM order, permission.
HUCUM CORUNC to order, to command.
HUCUM DIUNC to permit, to allow.
HULL-HULLO imprudent, restless.
HURLU foolish.
HURUS temporary fair on festive occasion.

I

I the ninth letter of the Roman Alphabet.
IAD *f* rememberance, recollection.
IAD CORUNC to draw attention to, to remind.
IAD ZAUNC to remember, to recollect.
IAJ voyage, travel.
IAJ interest, gain, profit earned by lending money.
IANTHRO *m* machine.
IANTOR official inventory of the orphans' property.
IBAD *m* perdition, ruin.
IBAD CORUNC to ruin, to destroy.
IBADDI spendrift, waster.
IBADDUNC to waste, to spend.
IC *n* poison.
IC GALUNC to poison.
ICAO, -I, -EM poisonous.
ICAR *m* poison.
ICARONC to get poison (into a wound etc.)
ICDDE this side, here.
ICDDE TICDDE in different places.
ICHAR question.
ICHAR CORUNC to question, to ask.
ICHARNAR *m* questioner, inquirer.
ICHARUNK to question, to interrogate.
ICLLAB suffering.
ICLLAB CORUNC to make one suffer.
ICMOT *f* ability, capacity.
ICMOT CORUNC to devise means.
ICMOTI ingenious, clever.
ICONDD odd, incomplete.
ICOU odd, separate.
ICRA eleven (11)
ICRAO, -I, -EM eleventh.
ICRECAR, IN salesman or saleswoman.
ICRIT bought, purchased.
ICTI PIDDA GUEUNC to buy unnecessary troubles, to suffer for the sake of godness.
ICTO, -I, -EM p. ICRIT.
ICTO DIUNC to sell.
ICTO GEUNC to buy, to purchase.
ICUNC to sell.
ID mohammedan festival.
ID life, life-time.
IḊ waste, distruction.
ID LAUNC to waste, to spend.
IDAD age, period of live-time.
IDDCON GUEUNC to remain hanging.
IDDCOUNC to adle.
IDDI indian cigarette.
IDDO set of glass bangles, bridal set of glass bangles.
IDEA *f* ability, art.
IDEAVONT ingenious.

IDOU destruction, waste, loss.
IDOU ZAUNC to lose heavily, to suffer from a serious calamity.
IDUO, -I, -EM VO IDVAXI waster, spendrift.
IDVAS *m* waste, ruin.
IEC *f* & *n* one.
IEC SATTIM altogether, once for all.
IECAR, IEC, one above the other.
IECBAT *m* fasting.
IECBAT DORUNC to fast.
IECBUD *f* agreement, mind, opinion.
IEDO, -I, -EM so great, s, magnitude, size, bulk.
IEKI-MEKI *f* reconciliation.
IELAM sort, lottery.
IEOC one.
IERVAM the other day, the day after to, morrow.
IES *f* victory, honour.
IES VORUNC to have a victory, to gain.
IEUNC an animal to be delivered from its offspring.
IEZ *f* interest, gain.
IFERN hell.
IFONAR ZAUNC to be vexed.
IGAR vicar, parish priest.
IGROZ *f* church.
IGROZ-MATH *f* Holy See.
IJEA pain, dhysical ailment.
IJI RACONC to watch, to do watchman's duty.
IJIN engine, machine.
ILAZ resource, means.
ILDOZ aged person, old in years.
ILO, -I, -EM small, little, short.
ILOSO, -I, -EM small; *maca chod naca, iloso puro,* I don't want much, a little will do.
ILUD velvet cloth.
IMAJ image, *imaj khursa voir,* crucifix.
IMAN faith, full confidence.
IMAZ KHURSACHI crucifix.
IMTTEPON meanness, avarice, stinginess, niggardliness.
IMTTEPON CORUNC to give with meanness.
IMTTEUNC to sob often, to hiccup.
IMTTI, *f* sob hiccup.
IMTTI CADDUNC p. imtteunc.
IMTTO, -I, -EM stingy, miser.
INAM *m* reward, recompense.
INAM DIUNC to reward.
INCHAR CORUNC to enquire.
INCHEAN p. angachean.
INCHU *m* scorpion.
INCHUN CADUNC to select.
INCHUNC to pick up, to collect.
INDD *m* flock; *gorvancho indd,* flock of cattle; *ducrancho indd,* a herd of pigs; *sunneancho indd,* pack of dogs; *uttancho indd,* a drove of camels.
INDDLO hammock.
INDU Hindu, Indian of the original Hindu family.
INDULJENS *n* indulgence.
INDUO *m* see-saw.
INDUO (PACRUM) p. KIRKIRO.
INDUR *m* rat.
INDUSTAN India.
INDUSTANI indian, urdu language.
ING *m* assafoetida.
INGA here.
INGA THAN from this place.

Ingachea *n* from here.
Inglez Englishman, english language, english.
Ingllo *m* burning coal.
Ingllo, -i, -em naked.
Ingllo corunc to make naked, to undress.
Inimig enemy, hostile person.
Innanim carpenter.
Innannim *m* black-smith.
Innanpon carpentry.
Innannpon *n* work of black smith.
Inniam p. **icdde.**
Innim *f* tresses.
Innim galunc to make into tress, to braid, to interlace.
Innsan *f* reprehension, rebuke.
Innsan caddunc to reprehend, to rebuke, to scold.
Innsunc to reprehend, to rebuke.
Innunc to weave.
Inter *m* funeral.
Interracho carbari undertaker.
Intruz carnival.
Intum p. **Antun.**
Invanche dis cold season, winter.
Invej envy, jealousy.
Inventar legal proceedings for safeguarding minor's interest.
Ipotec mortgage.
Iprit *n* wonder, miracle.
Iprit disonc to marvel, to wonder.
Ir hard part or stalk of palm-leaf.
Iração mental disturbance.
Irar zaunc to lose one's common sense, to be perplexed.
Irgonc to melt, to dissolve.
Irmandade confraternity, sodality, brotherhood.
Irmão brother, member of a confraternity.
Irmit chapel.
Irnem chisel.
Iroddo *m* half day.
Ironc to dissolve, to melt.
Irvo rong green colour.
Is twenty.
Is corunc to tease, to despise.
Is lagonc to be vicious.
Iscad stair-case, movable ladder.
Iscad *f* stairs.
Iscator *f* carpenter's level.
Iscol school.
Iscolicho burgo school-boy, student.
Iscou brush.
Iscou roomy, capable of affording accommodation.
Iscou distant, separate, brush.
Iscuttunc to unsew, to separate.
Ismião excommunication, anathema.
Ismol alms, charitable help.
Ismol magnar beggar.
Isor *f* forgetfulness, want of memory.
Isor poddonc to fôrget, not to remember.
Ispa chair countless.
Ispachem sarkeponn accuracy.

ISPACHI XICOUNN accountancy.
ISPACHO CARCUNN accountant, book-keeper.
ISPAD *f* sword.
ISRAUNC to make one forget, to distract.
ISRONC, ISRUNC to forget.
ISTICEN station, place of stopping.
ISTIL fashion, custom, style in.
ISTOR history, narrative.
ISTOR BOROINAR historian.
ISTT *m* friend.
ISTTIN female friend.
ISTTOGOT *f* friendship.
ISTU fire.
ISVAS *m* confidence, reliance.
ISVAS DORUNC to trust, to rely.
ISVAS SODDUNC to give up hopé.
ISVASONC to confide.
ISVON *m* (masolli) sawfish.
ISWAR god, Highest Spirit.
ITCO, -I, -EM so much.
ITKEA BITOR VO.
ITKEA MODEM VO.
ITKEA MONNOSAR VO.
ITKEARI VO.
ITLEA BITOR VO.
ITLEA MODEM VO.
ITLEA MUNNOSOR VO.
ITLEARI in the meantime, with this.
ITLO, -I, -EM so much, this much and no more.
ITLOCH so much only.
ITT *f* qualm, any thing that provokes vomitting.
ITT DISONC to be disgusted, to cause vomitting.
ITT (MATIECHO) *m* brick.
ITTECAR *m* brick-maker.
ITTEUNC to be disgusted, to cause vomitting.
IUM KHAUNC to feel cold, to suffer from cold weather.
IUNDONC to rove or loiter about.
IUNDONNO, -I, -EM vagrant.
IVAUNC to look, to observe.
IXEC rare, unusual.
IXOP *m* account.
IXOP CHUCOUNC to settle an account.
IXOP CORUNC to make an account, to sum up.
IXOPDAR VO ~~IXOPI~~ reckoner, accountant.
IZ lightning.
IZ PODDONC to experience the shock or discharge of lightning.
IZAI *f* trellis, grate.
IZAR trousers, breeches.
IZDDO eunuch.
IZDDO hermaphrodite.
IZIPEL *n* erysipelas.
IZIT DIUNC to visit, to go and meet.
IZMIT *n* wonder, miracle.
IZODD rain blowing inside in stormy weather.
IZOT honour, self-respect.
IZOT CADDUNC to defame, to deride.
IZZONC to fizzle out.

J

J the tenth letter of the Roman Alphabet.
JA-JA enough, get away.

Jabab reply, answer.

Jaban speech, reply.

Jadu *m* charm, bewitching.

Jaducar vo Jaduvalo *m* sorcerer, bewitcher.

Jadveshi misanthrope.

Jagronn wakefulness, alertness, vigil.

Jagronn corunc to keep night watch, to be vigilant.

Jagrut rabonc to remain awake.

Jaguir village lands held in perpetuity for services rendered to the state.

Jaguirdar holder or owner of village lands.

Jajmim *n* jasmin.

Jaket jacket, coat.

Jal fishing net.

Jalli net-work.

Jamachem morttel bottle of jam.

Jamacho dobo tin of jam.

Jamat community.

Jamat borunc to convene communal meeting.

Jamb act of yawning.

Jambeunc to yawn.

Jambo caddunc to yawn, to feel extremely lazy.

Jamin security.

Jamin raonc to offer one's security for another person.

Jamindar holder or owner of large landed estates.

Janer *n* January.

Janot dandy.

Janvan young man.

Japaniz japanese.

Japão Japan.

Jar *n* jar.

Jardal *m* appricot.

Jast *f* injury, offence.

Jast marunc to offend, to abuse.

Jasti much, more.

Jasti excessive, superfluous.

Jastivont injurious, offensive.

Jat an Indian caste.

Jatnai care, diligence.

Jatra fair, hindu festival attracting devotees and people buying and selling.

Jaz ship, sailing vessel.

Jebordosti compulsion, unjust use of force.

Jednam when, at the time.

Jeit demeanour, style of behaviour.

Jel *m* see-saw.

Jeldi quickly.

Jele mallunc to put on garlands of flowers, to adorn.

Jelec coat.

Jelec mottvem jerkin.

Jeli *f* jelly.

Jelo *m* garland.

Jelo guntunc to make a garland.

Jelonc to swing to and fro.

Jelounc to make one swing to and fro.

Jelso entertainment.

Jem *f* sleep, sleepiness.

Jemelolo, -i, -em sleepy.

Jemeunc to fall asleep, to feel sleepy, to grow torpid.

Jenjurtem *n* twilight.

Jenzronc to rub against a thing, to touch slightly.

JEON *n* dinner, food.
JEOS heat, steam.
JEOS CORUNC to boil, to heat.
JEH poison.
JLRBOND *m* whip, lash given with a whip, (fig) calamity, affliction.
JERBOND DIUNC VO MARUNC to whip, to lash.
JERIPURANAVALO hawker of oddgoods.
JERN wife, married woman.
JERNAM when, at the time of.
JERUL surely, without doubt.
JERURI immediate, urgent.
JESUIT jesuit, member of the Society of Jesus,cunningman.
JEUNC to dine, to eat food; *pez jeunc*, to drink canji; *dud jeunc*, to suck milk.
JEUNNACAR boarder.
JEUNNAM DIUNC to receive boarders.
JEVONN dinner, meal.
JEVONN SANJECHEM supper.
JIB *f* tongue.
JIBLI tongue, languet, reed-stop (of an organ).
JIBOTTO, -I, -EM talkative, tattling.
JIC-JIC lustre, shine, polish.
JICNAR *m* winner, conqueror.
JICNEM *n* victory.
JICON DORUNC to catch, to pick up, to grasp.
JICONC to gain, to win.
JIEUNC to live, to exist.
JIIL *m* boy, baby.
JIL VO.
JILCUTT *fn* thicket, wood, forest.
JIN *n* the pommel of a saddle.
JIN genie, ghost.
JIN GALUNC (GODDEAC) to saddle.
JIN MARUNC to sacrifice one's live, to endure troubles.
JIN SANDDUNC to faint, to die.
JINGI *f* moveable property, furniture.
JINN *f* life.
JINNOM (ZADD) *m* an elder-tree.
JINOS kind, sort.
JINSAMPORIM in different ways, variously.
JINSAVAR of different kinds.
JINNT *f* ~~giddiness~~, fainting fit.
JINNT MARUNC to faint, to be giddy.
JINUAR fast.
JIO, -I, -EM alive.
JIO ASUNC to be alive, to live.
JIO MARUNC to kill,to assassinate.
JIO ZAUNC to rise from the dead, to come to life again.
JIREM *n* cumin.
JIRON *f* digestion.
JIRONC to digest, to consume, to lower; *udoc jironc*, to absorb the water; *kensolli jironc*, to dissolve the tumour.
JIRONNC to cause assimilation, to possess power of digestion.
JIS a piece of chalk.
JITO p. JIO.
JITROP *n* vegetable.
JIU *m* life, soul, vigour.
JIU ASONC to be alive.
JIU BORONC to reanimate, to regain the strength.

Jiu caddunc to kill.

Jiu diunc to commit suicide.

Jiu diunc to love extremely.

Jiu (folleac fatrac) *m* vein.

Jiu geunc to assassinate, to murder.

Jiu vochunc to expire, to die, to feel acute pain.

Jivann *n* a living creature.

Jivar uttonc to disregard ones life, to be self-denying.

Jivessim marunc to kill, to murder.

Jivim marunc to kill.

Jivit *n* life.

Jivo, -i, -em alive. *jivo unddo,* fresh bread.

Jivont alive.

Jivont zaunc to come to life again.

Jivontponn *n* resurrection.

Johnachi bud instinct.

Jomin the ground, soil, land.

Jompoi marunc to jump for something high up.

Jon right to a share in the profits of a village community.

Jondlo millet.

Jonncar holder of a share and rights as a member of a village community.

Jor strength, power.

Jovai foolishness.

Jovai munis a fool.

Jovar mosquito.

Jovarichem bhirem swarm of mosquitos.

Judi *f* coat.

Juiz *m* judge.

Juiz paz *m* justice of the peace.

Julh *m* July.

Juna, -i, -em old, worn-out.

Junh *m* June.

Jubileu jubilee.

Judev jew, hebrew.

Jugari gambler.

Jugari gor gambling house.

Julo hammock.

Julonc to swing to and fro.

Jumbor chandelier.

Jun ripe, matured.

Juncott nearly old, not young.

Jur *m* interest.

Jutto, -i, -em false, untrue.

Juvari millet.

K

K the eleventh letter of the Roman Alphabet.

Kabudar dove.

Kac *f* armpit.

Kadd *n* beard.

Kadd corunc to shave.

Kadd doriachi *f* harbour, riverside.

Kaddai *f* wooden sleeper.

Kaddio bearded.

Kaddki *f* chin.

Kailean from below.

Kailo, -i, -em of below.

Kal below, under, subject to.

Kala below.

Kalte maninchio, -i, -em hanging down the head, sorrowful.

Kaltepon *n* inferiority, lowness, abjective, humility.

Kalto, -i, -em low, inferior, humble.

KALTO CORUNC to lower, to make one humble.

KALTO GALUNC to lower, to subjugate, to put under; *kalti-man galunc*, to hang down the head.

KALTO ZAUNC to fall, to sink, to stoop.

KAMBLI *f* a peace of partition made of timber.

KAMBO *m* column.

KAMP *n* cut, stroke.

KAMPAUNC to give strokes or cuts.

KANC *f* arm-pit.

KANCUNC to cough.

KAND *m* shoulder.

KAND MARUNC to put on shoulder, to undertake to do.

KANDO *m* branch.

KANGO,-I,-EM a great eater, glutton.

KANN *n* eatables, sweets.

KANNAR *m* a great eater.

KANNAVOLL *f* an inn, boarding house.

KANNERO, -I, -EM a great eater, glutton.

KANTTAVO abhorrence, disgust.

KANTTECOR *f* aloe.

KANTTI *f* brambles.

KAONN *f* manger.

KAPRI *m* negro.

KAR *m* dye.

KAR salty, full of salt.

KAREM *n* salt-fish.

KARO,-I,-EM salted; *karem udoc*, salt water; *kari masolli*, salt-fish.

KARVI *m* fisherman.

KARVIN *f* fisher-woman.

KAST *f* punishment.

KATCULEO tickling.

KATCULI *f* nettle.

KATIR on account of, *devakatir*, fot the love of God.

KATT *f* bedstead.

KATTLEM *n* bedstead.

KATTMUA scrofula.

KATTODD *n* mud, mire.

KATTODDAUNC to splash, to dirt, to cover with mud.

KATTODDONC to be defiled.

KATTONN *n* mud, mire.

KAUNC to eat; *ium kaunc*, to feel cold, *tachem mon taca kata;* his conscience pricks him; *to kileac tacho jiv khata?* why does he trouble him? *sogli rat maca bicon katat*, whole night the bugs bite me; *caetanan moie duddu kelel*, cætano has misappropriated my money.

KAUNNIM *f* manger.

KAXA legitimate, own, true,

KAZ caju-tree.

KAZU caju-fruit.

KAZULO *m* butter-fly.

KAZUR *m* date.

KAZUR MADD *m* date-tree.

KEBADDAM *n* fun, mockery, jest.

KEBADDAM CORUNC to make a fun, to jest, to mock.

KEDDEM *n* monument, edifice.

KEDDEM BANDUNC to build a monument.

KEDDOLL p. KEDOU.

KEDDOLLCHO,-I,-EM of short time.

KEDEA VELLA when, at what time.
KEDIM when.
KEDINCH never, at no time.
KEDNAM VO KEDONAM when.
KEDO, -I, -EM of what size, how big.
KEDOU a short time back.
KEEM *n* plantain.
KEIJ cheese.
KEIMBO *m* plantain-tree.
KEL *n* hook.
KELDAUNC to parody, to imitate.
KELDAUNNI parody, mimicry.
KELDEM *n* female monkey.
KELDO *m* monkey.
KELKEN *n* hook.
KELL *m* play.
KELLAD *f* phthisis.
KELLEANCHO GODD bunch of plaintains.
KELLEM *n* plantain.
KELLGODDO, -I, -EM player, gambler.
KELLIO,-I,-EM player, gambler.
KELLONC to play, to amuse, to gamble.
KELLOUNC to amuse, to make one play.
KELLOUNC to entertain a guest.
KELLOUNNEM entertainment.
KELLUNC p. KELLONC.
KEM *f* embrace.
KEMP *n* precious stone; *tambddem kemp*, ruby; *pachvem kemp*, emerald; *olldduvem kemp*, topaz.
KENCH *f* crush.
KENCHONC to be crushed.
KENCHUNC to crush, to press.
KENDD *n* flame, (fig) passion, love.
KENDDNAR *m* derider, mocker, jester.
KENDDNI mockery, insult, complaint of ingratitude.
KENDDNIM *n* mockery, jest, derision.
KENDDUNC to despise, to mock, to deride.
KENS *m* hair.
KENSAR VO KENSAREM *n* stork.
KENSOI VO KENSOLLI *f* furuncle, boil.
KENSOR *f* Indian saffron.
KEONC to play, to amuse; *anson kellon to dis caddla*, he passes his time in amusements; *xiranim rogot keula*, blood circulates in the veins.
KEPO deaf.
KEPO extravagant, capricious.
KERIT separate, different, except, exclusive.
KERIT CADDUNC to remove, to put aside.
KERIT CORUNC to separate, to exclude.
KERIT DOURUNC to exempt from.
KERNAM when.
KERNANCH never.
KESTTAEO *f* jests, derisions.
KETH *n* war, battle.
KETRI *m* warrior.
KETT *f* a throng.
KEU *m* play, amusement.
KEUGODDI *m* gamester.
KEUNC to entertain.

KEVAD *f* consumption, phthisis.
KEVADCAR, RIN consumptive person.
KHACUNC, KHOCUNC to spit, to cough.
KHADD CORUNC to call at a port.
KHADD-MEXEANCHO bearded man.
KHADDO absence,failure of ones duty.
KHALI MOT levity, frivolity of an empty mind.
KHALTEPONNIM respectfully, humbly.
KHAMP palate.
KHANKE MARUNC to hold between armpit and waist.
KHAPURLEM negress.
KHARANTTI small hoe.
KHARAP CORUNC to tire one's patience.
KHARCON dry date.
KHARNO mortar.
KHARONNIM salt water.
KHARSAN saltish taste.
KHAS one's own.
KHATT EUNC OV MELLONC to discover loss or shortage.
KHATTARO bullock-cart.
KHEDD chalky soil.
KHEDDEM rural place.
KHEDDO GANV rural village.
KHELL KHUXAL RAUCHO pastime.
KHELL THOCAUNNECHO jugglery.
KHELLACHEM CLUB sporting club.
KHELLACHEM GOR gambling house.
KHELLONC THOCOUNNEM ADARUN to play tricks by sleight of hand,to practice imposture.
KHENGADDI gambler, player.
KHEP a trip of carrying.
KHEPO number of trips to and fro.
KHEUGADDI THOCOUNCHO juggler.
KHISCAN GALUNC to pocket.
KHOBORDDAR beware.
KHOBORDDAR fit, courageous, active.
KHOCO packing case.
KHODDI SUDRAUNC to educate, to reform.
KHODDIO defective, faulty.
KHODDO GALUNC to hand cuff.
KHODON CORUNC to agitate, to disturb.
KHODOUNC to stir, to turn over.
KHOLCO bottom part of sailing vessel.
KHOLI room.
KHON liquid part of pickle.
KHONCLI cougn; expectoration.
KHONCLI EUNC to cough.
KHONCLO fluid thrown out by coughing.
KHONDDNIM labour of digging.
KHONN part, division, drawer.
KHONONC to lose," coc dis khonlo, one day is lost."
KHONTT MARUNC to kick.
KHONTTAUNC to kick off.
KHOPONC to finish, to sell out.
KHOPONN funeral rites.
KHOR depth, profundity.
KHOR ADDUNC to bring something as a proof from the depth.

KHOR ZAUNC (KHORO, -I, -EM to justify one's self. [rude.
KHORKHOS harsh, exacting,
KHORO ZAUNC to justify one's self.
KHOROS EUNC to be exhausted by fatigue, to brethe hard.
KHOTT loss, shortage.
KHOTTI CORUNC to delay, to be detained.
KHOTTPOTT CORUNC to struggle for making one's view point acceptable.
KHOTTPOTTI person striving to gain his object.
KHOUNTTEUNC to become rancid.
KHOXALPONN *n* joy gladness.
KHUD personally, very truly.
KHUDA God.
KHUNN CORUNC to commit murder.
KHURDDO CORUNC to cash, to convert paper money into cash.
KHURSACHI CURU sign of the cross.
KHUS pleased, contented, joyful.
KHUZULO small water-pot.
KI or, ho *ki* to, this or that.
KI that. *Pedrun sanglem ki apun Goiam velam munn.* Peter said that he would go to Goa.
KIAUNC to nail.
KICHDDAUNC VO KICHDDOUNC to scoff, to rail at.
KIDDO *m* maggot, worm; *onloscornacho kiddo*, remorse of conscience.
KIL playful pinch in touching a friend's new garment.
KILL *f* bolt.
KILLAILOLO, -I, -EM nailed.
KILLAILOLO CADDUNC to unnail, to unplait.
KILLAUNC to nail, to knock or drive in.
KILLI *f* bolt.
KILLI (PAIANCHI) *n* ankle.
KILLO *m* nail.
KILLO MARUNC to nail, to drive in a nail.
KILO *m* fort, fortress.
KIM. p. KI.
KIMAR ZAUNC to experience keen annoyance.
KIMOT *f* value, price.
KIMUS *n* musquitto.
KINARI border, end of anything
KINN *n* corn.
KINN *m* moment, instant; *kinna bitor*, in an instant, instantly.
KINTTI *f* dog-louse.
KINVANTTO fit of anger.
KINVONCH shriek, piercing cry.
KIO *m* nail.
KIONCH *f* shout, cry, shriek.
KIONCH MARUNC to shriek, to cry.
KIONN *n* ulcer, wound.
KIR *m* parrot.
KIR, GUR sweet canjee of new rice.
KIR ZAUNC. To behave like others, to lose one's own commonesnse.
KIRA-SARKO, -I, -EM person speaking as tutored or influenced by his surroundings.

KIRANGLLI VO KIRANGOLLI the smallest finger.

KIRCOLL p. KIRCOU.

KIRCOLLPON *n* lowliness, insignificance.

KIRCOU retail, insignificant, abject; *kircou vicunc*, to sell retail; *kircou vost*, insignificant, thing.

KIRCOUPON p. KIRCOLLPON.

KIRD anger, fit of wrath.

KIRDAN ULOUNC to speak angrily.

KIRDONC to cry out angrily.

KIREM *n* (pacrum) a sea mew.

KIRI LAGONC to suffer from a chronic disease.

KIRKI *n* window, opening.

KIRKIRO (PACRUM) *n* king fisher.

KIRLO *m* bud, germ.

KIRLONC to germinate, to sprout.

KIRLUNC DANT to grind the teeth.

KIRMEM *n* cold.

KIRMUZI *n* purple, rock-shell.

KIRN *n* ray.

KIROD *m* anger, wrath.

KIROD EUNC to be angry.

KIRODVONT passionate, furious.

KIRONC to be melted, to dissolve.

KIRONTT *f* tike.

KIROUNC to dissolve.

KIRPON weak, feeble.

KIRTI *f* fame, renown.

KIRTIVONT famous, renowned.

KISO *m* pocket.

KISOR *n* straw, fiber.

KISOUNC to card.

KISULL *f* (atiar), *f* plane.

KISULL VO KISUU *f* scraping, shavings.

KISUU CADDUNC VO KISUU MARUNC to scrape, to shave, to rasp.

KIT respect, good name.

KIT UBOUNC to dishonour, to defame.

KITCO, -KI, -KEM, VO KITLO, -I, -EM how munch.

KITEA VO KITEAC because, for what.

KITEM what; *kitem corn vo kitem corun*, how, in what way.

KITT *f* spark of fire.

KITT (LOCONDDACHI) *f* dross of metals: *callo kitt*, very black; *tondd callem corunc*, to make a sour face.

KITTOLEM *n* funel.

KIUCULLO VO KIUCUO a small bell.

KIUM *m* anger, wrath.

KIUM EUNC to be angry, to fret.

KIUM-ABORIT full of anger, furious, raging.

KIUNCHONC to cry, to shriek.

KOBAR grave of a Mohammedan.

KOBODDAR courage ! bravo.

KOBOR *f* news.

KOBOR CADDUNC to inquire, to investigate.

KOBOR DIUNC to inform, to announce.

KOBRASTAN Mohammedan graveyard.

KOBREM *n* dry cocoanut-kernel.

KOCNEANCHEM DIUL *n* pagoda.

KODD *f* (munxeachi) custom, habit.

Kodd *f* defect, fault.
Kodd caddunc to find fault with, to criticise.
Kodde sacor *f* sugar candy.
Koddo *m* manacles.
Kodd-ddo *m* head, (fig) bad scholar.
Koddoll muddy, thick.
Koddollai *f* muddiness.
Koddollaunc (udoc) to disturb the water or make it muddy.
Koddop *n* rock.
Koddu *m* chalk.
Koi *f* rivulet, canal for watering.
Koim where; *tum koim asloi?* where were you? *to koim gela?* where has he gone? *to koim koim bounta,* he wanders in different places.
Koim-koincho,-i,-em of various places.
Koim ec nam no where exist.
Koim than vo / Koim sann vo / Koim sottiam } from where.
Koinch nam no where exist.
Koinchean from what side.
Koincho,-i,-em from where, of what part.
Kol deep.
Kolai *f* deepness, profundity.
Kolaunc to sink deeper.
Kolaxi sailor.
Koli *f* dry leaf.
Kolio corunc to gather dry leaves.
Koll, kou *m* brine, a pickle made of salt and water.
Koll *f* hood; *maleac gali koll,* put the hood on the head.
Koll *f* covering.
Kollboll *m* tumult, noise.
Kollbollunc to raise a tumult.
Kolli fisherman.
Kol-lunc to eat after removing the shell.
Kolo *m* leaf.
Komis *n* shirt.
Komp *f* hut.
Kompem *n* roof of the mouth.
Komptti *f* a small hut.
Kon *n* bakery.
Koncarunc to cough, to spit, to expectorate.
Konchatti thrusting.
Konchoilolo, -i, -em inlaid work.
Konchounc to fix, to inlay wood or stone.
Koncli *f* cough; *coli koncli,* convulsive cough.
Koncli eunc vo / Koncunc } to cough.
Kondd *m* pond, tank.
Kondd *m* agreement, contract.
Kondd corunc to regulate, to adjust, to accord.
Kondd galunc to pay the rent, to pay the agreed amount.
Kondd marun geunc to buy in a lot.
Konddonc to dig.
Konddpi *m* delver, ploughman.
Kondduncp. Kondd corunc.
Konddvo *m* puddle.
Konn (masoli marchi) *f* a wickerbasket.
Konn *f* mine, cavity.

KONN *m* drawer; *kille konn assal tea mezac?* how many drawers have that table?
KONN MARUNC to sink a shaft.
KONNONC to dig.
KONNONOM *m* mortar.
KONNOP *n* digging.
KONNOPOTTI impertinence.
KONNOPOTTI CORUNC VO / KONNOPOTTI LAGONC } to tease, to annoy, to weary.
KONNPOTTICHO, -I, -EM troublesome, vexatious, intrusive, improper, impertinent.
KÔNT *f* affliction, sorrow, sadness.
KONT (PAIANCHI) *f* heel.
KONTOUNC to afflict, to grieve.
KONVOTT *n* rancid, rusty, (fig) old, of bad taste.
KONVTTAN *f* rustiness, rankness, (fig) oldness, bad taste.
KONZIR *n* dagger.
KONZIR MARUNC to stab with a dagger.
KOP (GIRAIC) *m* sale.
KOP ZAUNC VO / KOPONC } to have a good sale.
KOPOUNC to sell, to dispose of.
KOR hot, intense; *kor udoc,* hot water; *kor uzo,* intense fire.
KOR rigorous, severe, hard.
KOR CORUNC to make hot.
KORAI *f* heat.
KORAI *f* rigour, severity. *Ea munsubdarachi korai zabor,* the rigour of this judge is very great.
KORAP tired, weak, feeble.
KORAP ZAUNC to tire, to fatigue, to get tired.

KORCH *m* expenses, cost.
KORCHANDDI *f* (MASOLI) a river fish.
KORCHIC spendrift.
KORCHUNC to spend, to waste.
KORDDO *m* list, inventary.
KORDDO dull, not clever.
KOREDI *f* price, value.
KOREM truth, certainty.
KOREM *n* (MASOLECHEM ETC.) a rough skin.
KOREM (AUT) *n* mattock, hoe.
KOREM CORUNC to verify, to ascertain.
KOREPONN *n* certainty, truthfulness.
KOREPONN DIUNC to assure, to assert.
KORKORIT harsh, rough, rugged.
KORKORITAI *f* roughness, harshness, austerity.
KORO, -I, -EM truthful.
KORODD *n* baldness.
KORODD PODDONC to become baldheaded.
KORODDO *m* curry, comb.
KORODDO VODDUNC (GODDEACHER) to curry, to comb.
KOROZ *f* itches, itching *Pedruc koroz zalea,* Peter has got itches; *unnam udcan mojea angachi koroz geli,* the itching of my body passed with hot water.
KORPUNC to scratch, to stimulate.
KORPUNC VO / KORPUN CADDUNC } to scrape, to shave.
KORSAN GALUNC to put one to expenses.

Korsaunc to make one tired.
Korvattaunc to scrape, to gather together.
Korvoddi scraping, the thing scraped.
Korvoddunc p. **Korvattaunc.**
Korvont *f* saw.
Korvontcar *m* sawyer.
Korxelolo, -i, -em tired fatigued.
Korxeunc to be tired, to be fatigued.
Korzunc to feel itching sensation.
Korzuvallo, -i, -em itchy.
Kot *n* stain, blot.
Kotaunc to stain, to blot.
Kotem *n* title, account.
Koti *f* lease, hiring, renting.
Kotkotaunc to boil.
Kotkoto *m* boiling.
Kotkoto eunc vo / **Kotkotonc vo** / **Kotkotunc** } to boil.
Kotounc to defile one's self, to follow ill courses.
Kotoulolo, -i, -em stained, spotted.
Kott *f* heel.
Kottai *f* wickedness.
Kottar *n* warn house.
Kottarli milleped.
Kottaunc to kick.
Kot-tem *n* shell.
Kotteponn *n* wickedness.
Kotti *f* delay, fault, error.
Kotto, -i, -em bad, wicked; *kotto rupia*, bad rupee, not genuine.
Kottpott *m* quarrel, fight.
Kou *m* brine, pickle made of salt and water.
Koubaunc to divert, to be occupied in.
Koullam *n* scales.
Koullaunc to scale fish.
Kounc to fix in a place.
Kounttan *f* rustiness, rankness.
Kountteunc to get rancid.
Kovat drill, exercise.
Koxal happy, contented.
Koxal corunc to make one happy or contented.
Koxal zaunc to be glad-of, to rejoice with (persons) over or at (it).
Koxali *f* present, gift.
Koxi *f* will, desire, pleasure, happiness.
Koxi bogunc to take pleasure in, to be pleased with.
Kozno *m* mortar.
Kozno marunc to fire a mortar.
Kubdi reserved, morose, silent.
Kubo *m* ankle.
Kudd do change, small coins.
Kudd do corunc to change, to exchange.
Kulli vo Kullo p. **Kotto.**
Kullo foolish, mad.
Kumsodor confessional.
Kunn *f* sign, mark.
Kunnailolo, -i, -em appointed, remarkable.
Kunnam corunc, vo / **Kunnam galunc** } to mark out, to make distinguishing signs.

KUNNI *m* criminal.
KUNT XITACHEM grain of cooked rice.
KUNTTI *f* a prop, a hand-spike, lever.
KUNTTO *m* prop, support.
KUNTTO (DANTEACHO) *m* a mill-clack.
KUNVO *m* mast.
KUNVOR (FEMALE) princess.
KUNVOR (MALE) prince.
KUP much, plenty.
KUR *m* pedicle, support.
KURDO *m* change.
KURIS *m* cross.
KUTT-TI small wooden hammer.
KUXAL happy, contented.
KUXAL CORUNC to make one happy or contented.
KUXAL ZAUNC to be happy, to be satisfied.
KUXALI *f* joy, happiness.
KUXI *f* will, pleasure, desire.
KUZO *m* a narrow mouthed vessel.

L

L the twelfth letter of the Roman Alphabet.
LÃ wool ; *lanch m lugott*, woolen cloth.
LAB *m* usury, interest.
LAB VO EOC one.
LAB ZAUNC to gain in business, to succeed in an undertaking.
LABONC to gain.
LAC *f* sealing-wax.
LAC *m* one hundred thousand.
LAC (CURLECHI) *f* spawn; milt.
LACANCHO, -I, -EM worth lakhs of rupees.
LACOTTO *m* letter, charter.
LACPOTI possessor of wealth worth lakhs of rupees.
LADAINH litany.
LADD excessive love, over-indulgence.
LADDCO *m* wild-boar.
LADDCO common name given, to man burning artificial fireworks.
LADDCO ZAUNC to become a pet, to be made much of.
LADDU ball or balls of sweet meat.
LADDUANCAR person selling balls of sweet-meat.
LADI pavement of masonry-work.
LADI GALUNC to pave with stones, tiles, or bricks.
LAG flattery, adulation.
LAG *m* flattering, coaxing.
LAG MARUNC to be a pretender, to mislead by false profession.
LAG-BAG *m* treatment, manner, address, behaviour.
LAGCHO, -I, -EM from, of, for, by; *moje lagcho*, from me.
LAGIM near, close by; *to moje lagim uloinam*, he does not speak with me, *tumim dogui lagim vochat*, both of you go together.
LAG-MARO jester, making fun, amusing, person.
LAGONC to stick, to adhere; *sor lagonc*, to get drunk or intoxicated, char *dis lagonc*, to take

4 days; *kan borem lagonc*, to taste the eatables well; *masoli maca bori lagonam*, I do not like fish; *Pedr cal than chacrec laglo*, Peter has been employed since yesterday; *Forsuc deuchar lagla*, Francis is possessed of devil; *pixem lagonc*, to become a fool; *zor lagonc*, to suffer from fever; *maca zobor cont lagli*, I was very sorry; *buc lagonc*, to feel hungry; *hi suri lagla*, this knife is sharp; *cantlo lagonc*, to get hurt by a thorn; *golleac ardd lagonc*, to have a bone sticking in the throat; *faleam chondrimanc giran lagtelem*, to-morrow will be the eclipse of the moon; *tujim utram mojea callzac laglim*, your words made a great impression on me; *to tuca soiro lagla?* is he your relation? *hem ocl tuca lagta*, this spectacle suits you.

LAGSAR near, about, almost.

LAGSILO,-I,-EM near, next, neighbour.

LAGSIM close, near.

LAGUIM EUNC to approach.

LAGUIO, LAGOVO false pretender, an unreliable person.

LAICAR smart person, one resembling a lawyer.

LAL red colour.

LAL a kind of precious stone.

LALA (FUL) *m* tulip.

LALA ZAUNC to be dead drunk.

LALATT *n* head.

LALCHI fond of unlawful gain.

LALEUNC to crave, to desire strongly.

LALL *f* saliva.

LALLIO,-I,-EM drivelling, slabbering.

LALUS bribe, illicit demand for money.

LAMB long, tall.

LAMBAI *f* length.

LAMBAI CORUNC to delay, to waste time on a trifling affair.

LAMBELO,-I,-EM long, extended.

LAMBI p. LAMBAI.

LAMBONC to hang, to suspend one's self.

LANBOUNC to hang.

LAMBRETI *f* nosegays.

LAMBTO a parasite, hanger-on.

LAMPITT unprincipled, mischievous.

LAMPLÃO lantern, lamp.

LAMPT sanctuary lamp.

LAN small, young.

LAN CORUNC to humble, to debase.

LAN RINNACHI insolvency.

LAN VODD CORUNC to support, to bring up, to feed.

LAN VODD ZAUNC to be supported, to be fed.

LAN ZAUNC to condescend.

LANCA illumination.

LANCA PETTOUNC to illuminate in festive style.

LANCDDI IMAJ wooden image.

LANCUDD *n* timber, wood.

LANDDO destitute person.

LANDGO *m* wolf.

LANS bid at an auction sale.

LANS, BALO lance, dart.

LANS BANGARACHO necklace.

LANS CORNAR bidder.

LANS CORUNC to bid at an auction sale.

LANS GALUNC to wear a gold necklace, also to bid at an auction sale.

LANVICAI humility, meekness.

LANVICAI GUEUNC to behave humbly or with humility.

LAN-VODD children, family.

LAOP *n* plantation, application.

LAPIS pencil.

LAR *n* wave.

LAR (VODDLEM) *n* huge wave.

LARACHO COULLO the roll of a sea-wave.

LARANJ orange.

LARAR LAR wave on wave.

LARINJ orange-tree.

LAS burning pain, torment.

LAS DIUNC to give cause for one's sufferings.

LASSONC to burn, to be destroyed by fire.

LATT *f* an instrument to draw water from a well.

LATT *f* kick.

LATT *n* dung of a horse.

LATT CANDDCHEM peeler.

LATTNEM pastry roller, rolling-pin.

LATTODD blow, slap.

LATTUDOC CADDCHEM pumping wheel.

LATTUNC to sell off, to dispose.

LAU *f* saliva.

LAUN DIUNC to denounce, to accuse.

LAUNC to plant, to touch, to apply etc; *zadd launc*, to plant a tree; *mateac al launc*, to touch the head (by hand); *vocot launc*, to apply medicine; *khast launc*, to punish; *uzo launc*, to set fire; *dio launc*, to light a lamp; *ixop launc*, to keep an account; *batti launc*, to distil; *bangar cosac launc*, to assay gold; *moddem matiec launc*, to bury the dead; *masoli mittac launc*, to salt the fish; *rundniac cantliam launc*, to add fuel in a stove; *burgeac je on launc*, to feed a child; *corunc launc*, to order to do; *vattec launc*, to waste; *kernam than looclaita?* how long has he been using a spectacle ? *tujim battam lailim?* have you inscribed your property ?

LAUNC COHI to intrigue, to foment disorders.

LAUNDDAI *f* intrigue, a tale-bearing.

LAUNDDEPONN *n* an act of tale-bearing(in order to set people at variance.)

LAUNDDO, -I, -EM intriguing, intriguer.

LAUNDEPONN CORUNCVO } to intrigue.
LAUNDEPONN SANGONC }

LAUNNIM *f* inscription.

LAUNNIM, PAUNNIM *f* triennal auction-sale of the property of a community.

LAUO, -I, -EM drivelling, slabbering.

LAUPI *m* planter.

Laupin *f* female planter.
Lec *m* account, reckoning, report.
Leconc to reckon one's self.
Leconc to be related to.
Lecram children, offspring.
Lecunc to count, to reckon; *connanc conn lekinam* one does not care for another.
Lef (**masoli**) *f* limpet.
Lef *m* unction.
Lef caddunc to anoint, to consecrate.
Lefddaunc vo / **Lefddunc** } to apply, anything improperly.
Legit till, untill, even.
Leilão auction sale.
Leilão corunc to sell by auction.
Lencrum child, an infant.
Lendd pig-dung.
Lenddaunc to mock, jeer.
Lenddauni mockery.
Lenki *f* a little girl.
Lens handkerchief.
Lenvonc to lick.
Lep *m* application, exterior medicine.
Lep *f* sole fish.
Lep plaster, application for external use.
Letrad pleader, lawyer.
Letradponn legal profession.
Leunc to write.
Leunc to lick.
Leunttepon *n* greediness, eagerness to eat.
Leuntto, -i, -em greedy.
Lic (**mateantli**) nit.
Licor (**soro**) *m* liquor.
Lig *n* buckle.
Likitt *n* dross. of metals.
Limb *m* limbo.
Limbi (**zadd**) *m* lemon-tree.
Limbo *m* lemon.
Limonad *n* lemonade.
Lin humble, obscure.
Lingis *n* sausage.
Lingudd *m* willow.
Linponn *n* humility.
Linponnim humbly, modestly.
Linttuvaen by humility.
Linttuvai *f* humility.
Lipnnem *n* hiding.
Lipon raonc to waylay, to lay an ambush.
Liponc to hide, to conceal.
Lipounc to hide, to conceal.
Liptem unknowingly, secretly.
Lipto,-i,-em hidden, concealed.
Lissaum lesson, instruction.
Lissaum corunc to study, to learn.
Lissaun diunc to repeat before teacher what is learnt.
Liunar reader, literate.
Liunc to write, to scribe.
Liunnem *n* writing.
Livr (**borouncho**) copy-book.
Livr victolo book-seller.
Livr xapnar printer, publisher, author of a book also.
Livrac cap galtato *m* book-binder.
Livrari *f* library.
Lob *m* cassock, sotan.
Lob *m* avarice, ambition.
Lobad false, wicked.
Lobaddi *m* a cheater, deceiver.

LOBADDI CORUNC to cheat, to deceive, to fraud.

LOBADDPONN fraud, deceit.

LOBDONC to court, to woo.

LOBDDONNEM *n* courtship, love intrigue.

LOBI avaricious, ambitious.

LOC *m* people, nation.

LOCHCOR *n* army, troops.

LOCHCORI *m* soldier.

LOCHEAND *n* calumny.

LOCHEAND GALUNC to calumniate, to slander.

LOCHEANDDI *m* calumniater, slanderer.

LOCLOC lustre, brilliance.

LOCLOKIT shining, brilliant.

LOCLOLO, -I, -EM bent, inclined.

LOCONC to incline, to bend; *hem zadd loclam,* this tree is bent; *to soro pion locta,* he is drunk.

LOCONC to walk with unsteady feet, to miss footing.

LOCOND *n* iron.

LOCONDACHI KILL *f* bolt.

LOCONDDI made of iron.

LOCOUNC to incline, to bend.

LOCSONC to slip, to miss-footing.

LOCTTO, -I, -EM not sharp.

LODDAI *f* fight, battle.

LODDGO fighter, fit to combat.

LODDO *m* knock, stroke, beating.

LODDO DIUNC to beat, to hammer.

LODDONC to fight, to combat, to be engaged in a campaign of opposition, to oppose an adversary.

LOFANGO, -I, -EM wicked person.

LOFOR unprincipled person.

LOFORPONN illicit mode of life.

LOGDDEPON *n* halting, lameness.

LOGN *n* wedding, marriage.

LOGOM *f* bridle.

LOGOM GALUNC to bridle, to refrain.

LOI *f* file, line.

LOIS *n* ware.

LOIS CAZARACHEM sets of glassware, table requisites and goods taken on hire.

LOIS MATIECHEM earthen ware.

LOJ VO POSRO *m* shop.

LOJA *f* shame.

LOJA DISONC to be ashamed of.

LOJER *m* shop keeper.

LOJEUNC to be ashamed of.

LOJEVONT bashful, timid, inexperienced, modest.

LOJIST bashful, shameful, disgraceful.

LOKIC *f* fame, dawn of popularity.

LOKITO *m* letter.

LOMON *n* multitude.

LOMPOTTO dishonest, shameful.

LONCH bribe, corruption.

LONCH GALUNC to bribe, to currupt.

LONCH GEUNC to be bribed, to be corrupted.

LONCHEM *n* pickle.

LONCHEO extortioner.

LONDDGO lame, halt.

LONDDO multitude, a crowd.

LONGDDO, -I, -EM crippled, maimed.

LONIM *n* butter.

LONLAG soft deceitful manners.
LONV MENREANCHI fleece.
LOO *m* weal on the flesh after whipping, contusion.
LOO (GANTICHO) clapper of a bell.
LOO (PACRUM) quail.
LOO (XENNACHO) dung-cake.
LOONC to be defiled, to get dirty.
LOONG (ANTUNNAR) to whirl, to revolve, to turn round.
LOONG *m* an iron instrument for breaking stones.
LOONG (CALAFUR) *n* clove.
LOOUNC to defile, to dirty.
LOPTUCAI *f* luxury, concupicence.
LOR NIDESHI drowsiness.
LOS *f* asthma.
LOSCOR *n* army troops.
LOSIO, -I, -EM asthmatic.
LOSUN *f* garlick.
LOTT *n* flood, violent current.
LOTT-FOL razor-strap.
LOTTIC *f* lie, falsehood.
LOTTICPONN p. LOTTIC.
LOTTKI GOVAI false witness.
LOTTLOLO,-I,-EM pushed, thrusted, inserted.
LOTTNNI *f* push, thrust.
LOTTONC to go forcibly, to enter; *uddoc lotta*, the water runs.
LOTTUNC to push, to thrust, to put inside.
LOU in a low voice.
LOU CORUNC to lighten, to lessen.
LOUCONC to shake, to reel, to totter.
LOULLOLO, -I, -EM dirtied.
LOULOUNC to be pleasant, to be delightful.
LOULOUNC to be full bloom, to look fresh and beautiful.
LOULOVIT pleasant, delightful.
LOULOVITAI amenity.
LOUM *f* hair.
LOUM FUTTONC to get hair.
LOUM-EIRIO, -I, -EM hairy.
LOUNKO, -I, -EM reeling, tottering, fickle.
LOUTO, -I, -EM stationary, slow, unprogressive.
LOUVAD assessor, appraiser.
LÕV CATRUNC to fleece, to shear.
LOVONC to remain grovelling, to be stationary.
LOVOT PODDONC to delay, to move slowly.
LOVOT VOCHONC to go on grovelling, to creep.
LOZ *f* shame.
LOZ CORUNC to put to shame.
LOZ DISONC to be ashamed.
LOZ ZAUNC to undergo shame or ignominy.
LOZONC to be ashamed, to be bashful.
LOZOUNC to make one ashamed.
LOZUNC p. LOZONC.
LOZ NARLANCHEM store-room for storing cocoanuts.
LOZ-UBOUNNO,-I,-EM shameless.
LUAN in a low voice.
LUAN softly, gently.
LUCHCHEPONN dishonesty, roguery.
LUCHCHO, -I, -EM sly rogue, dishonest.
LUDDBEPONN stammering.

LUDDBEUNC to stammer.
LUDDBO, -I, -EM stammerer.
LUDDI *f* agility.
LUGOT *n* cloth.
LUGOTT INNUNC to weave cloth.
LUGTTACHI GUIRNI weaving mill.
LUGTTACHO TANNOM weaving [loom.
LULLI exercise.
LUMBONC to wash anus.
LUNCHLOLO, -I, -EM sucked.
LUNCHNAR *m* sucker.
LUNCHNEM sucking.
LUNCHONC to suck, to draw.
LUNDD *n* trunk without head.
LUNDDO, -I, -EM naked, mutilated.
LUNTTO, -I, -EM naked.
LUNVUNI labour of reaping, place of reaping a harvest.
LUONC to mow, to reap.
LURAUM *m* rolong.
LUSCAN *n* damage, loss.
LUSCAN CORUNC to damage, to give loss.
LUSCAN EUNC to suffer loss.
LUSCANN BORUNC to make up a loss, to compensate for a loss.
LUT *f* hysterics.
LUT MARUNC to suffer hysterics.
LUTI *f* spittle.
LUTI GALLUNC to spit.
LUTT *f* booty.
LUTT CORUNC to rob, to plunder. to carry a daylight robbery.
LUTT ZAUNC to witness or hear about a place being pillage.
LUTTCHI,-EM,-O, plunderer, robber, freebooter.
LUTTNAR *m* robber, plunderer.
LUTTUNC to sack, to pillage.
LUUNCHE DIS harvest time.
LUUNLELO mowing.
LUUNNIM *f* the harvest.
LUUNPI VO IN reaper, mower.

M

M the thirteenth letter of the Roman Alphabet.
MĀ mother.
MAA great, much.
MAAL big, great.
MAAL province; *stary maal*, province of Satary.
MACA for me, to me.
MACHIL *n* palanquin.
MACN machine, engine.
MACN CHOLOINAR engine driver.
MACN INNUNCHEM weaving machene.
MACN SIUVONCHEM sewing machine.
MACN VOZON UCLUNCHEM crane.
MACODD *n* monkey.
MADD *m* occoanut-tree.
MADDI *f* betelnut-tree.
MADDOILOLO, -I, -EM troddem.
MADDOUNC to tread, to trample under one's feet.
MADIEM an indian drum, played with both hands on right and left sides of it. Its body is made of fine earth.
MADON delirium.
MADON ULOINAR delirious person.
MADR *f* nun.
MADROPEL mother-of-pearl.
MADUR delicate, tender.

MADURAI *f* delicacy.
MAE *f* mother.
MAERO *m* wife's parents, house.
MAF pardon, forgiveness.
MAF CORUNC to pardon, to forgive.
MAF ZAUNC to be pardoned.
MAG *m* track, sign, token.
MAG LAGONC to leave a track or sign.
MAG (MASOLLI MARCHO) fishing net.
MAGAM formerly.
MAGELO mine.
MAGILDAR back door of a house.
MAGIR afterwards, behind.
MAGIRLO, -I, -EM previous, successor.
MAGNAR petitioner, beggar.
MAGNNEANCHO invocation.
MAGNNEM prayer, petition.
MAGO parting of the hair.
MAGONC to ask, to request, to pray.
MAGONC BOLLAN to demand, to extort.
MAGONC LANVICAIEN to entreat, to request humbly, to pray.
MAGONC SOTHEN to claim, to demand.
MAGUIR GODDON EUNC to ensue.
MAHARAJ respectful title or greeting.
MAHARAJAH king of kings.
MAHATMA great soul.
MAHDI female of an animal.
MAI *f* story.
MAI MUINOM month of May.
MAI-BAP parents.
MAIECHEM GOR storyed house.
MAIFOLL *n* wallnut.
MAIFOU ZADD gall nut tree.
MAJEAN I; *majean nezo*, i cannot do.
MAJI, -EM, -O mine.
MAL property, goods.
MAL cargo, merchandise, goods,
MAL ADDUN DOVORLOLO stock of goods.
MAL BHAIR GANVAN DADDUNC to export goods.
MAL BHAIR GAUNCHO ADDUNC to import goods.
MAL BORUNC to pack goods.
MAL CHODDOUNC to deliver goods for being carried.
MAL DEVOUNC to unload goods, to take delivery of goods arriving.
MALCREAD ill-bred.
MALCREADPON ill-breeding.
MALDISAUM curse, malediction.
MALDUELAN scurvy.
MALEM *n* bee hive.
MALEM swarm.
MALEM GANZILANCHEM hornets' rest.
MALGODDI DUU *f* first born daughter.
MALGODDO *m* big, elder.
MALGODDO PUT *m* first born son.
MALGODDPONN primordial.
MALI *m* match maker.
MALIN *f* female match maker.
MALLI *m* gardener.
MALLIE SOCOL downstairs.
MALLIE VOIR upstairs.
MALLO *f* storey.
MALLO loft.

Malloi *f* floor, story.

Mallunc to deck the head; *fulam mallunc*, to adorn the head with flowers ; *bangar mallunc*, to adorn the head with jewels.

Mallund *n* amphisbena.

Malo, Mali male match maker.

Malti *f* bowl.

Maluc person of little sense.

Mam *m* maternal uncle.

Mami *f* aunt (wife of maternal uncle).

Man *f* nape of the head.

Man *m* honour, respect.

Man *f* bamboo.

Man bogunc to be respected, to gain popularity.

Man caddunc to offend, to dishonour.

Man diunc to honour, to respect, to pay homage.

Man ubounc to defame.

Manā elder sister, elderly female respected as sister.

Manadic respectable, honourable.

Manaim *m* grown up man, cooly.

Manculo, -i, -em beautiful, elegant, well formed.

Manculponn *n* finessness, beauty, elegance.

Mand *m* circle ; *chondrimanc mandd poddla*, the moon has got a circle.

Mandad order, permit.

Mandd *f* covering, lid.

Mandd *m* stall, shop.

Manddaen slowly, at leisure.

Manddai leisure, delay.

Manddeli *m* stall-keeper (of cloth.

Manddem *n* fatness.

Manddi *f* legs.

Manddki *f* frog.

Manddki (masoli) *f* cuttle-fish.

Manddolo *m* carpet snake.

Manddonc to create, form; *tantian pilo manddunc*, to form a chicken in an egg.

Manddop *n* order, disposition.

Manddos *n* Indian sweet.

Mandduc *m* frog.

Mandduns to put in order ; *zall manddunc*, to set a net.

Manddvol settlement.

Manddvol corunc to settle a dispute business.

Mandon earthen pot for canjee.

Mandonc to please, to be pleasing, to gratify.

Mandpotri *f* worm-wood.

Mandri *f* bamboo mat.

Mangan *n* sleeves.

Mangem *n* alligator.

Mangor a big hut.

Manh caprice, freak.

Manhi pormonem whimsically.

Manhicho, -i, -em capricious, whimsical, freakish.

Manil *n* swan.

Maninc *n* amethyst.

Maninchem bett *n* ground where bamboo trees are grown.

Manki *f* frog.

Manki zaddavoili *f* cater-piller.

Manos *f* snare, gin.

Manos hood-gate, wood-work automatically opening at low or ebbing tide, and closing to stop the flow of water at high tides.

Manounc to be agreeable, to give respect.

Manpotri *f* worm-wood.

Manpulli *f* cancer.

Mansuguecho, -i, -em respectable person, a well-behaving. individual.

Mansuguen decently, courteously.

Mansugui etiquette, civility.

Mansugui corunc to entertain guests decently.

Mant *m* mantle.

Mantaro *m* old man.

Mantarpon *n* old age.

Mantri hypnotist, skilled in the mantric science.

Manus *m* man; *devacho manus*, minister of God.

Manzori *f* cluster, bunch.

Maoddo vo **Maonddo** } house of father-in-law.

Maonn p. **maullon.**

Map p. **maf.**

Map corunc to measure, to make an account.

Map (doriachem) chart.

Map (sounsarachem) *n* map.

Map (mezchem) *n* measure.

Mapatoc *n* mortal sin.

Mapeli vo **Mapi** one that measures.

Mapunc to measure.

Mar *m* beating.

Mar diunc to beat, to punish.

Marad male.

Maraja emperor, great king.

Mara-mar *f* strife, fight.

Marcar *m* murderer, ferocious.

Marecar *m* murderous, inhuman.

Marfim *f* ivory.

Margai *f* dearness, scarcity.

Margi *m* one that sells at dear price.

Margi (vattsur) traveller.

Maric an exclamation of disgust, filthy.

Marin *f* wife of a mhaar.

Marinheir *m* mariner, sailor.

Marmore marble stone.

Marog dear, precious, valuable; *marog uzo*, very dear.

Marog *m* road, way, street.

Marot cunning person, mischief-maker.

Marsacho muinom month of march.

Mart (ruc) *f* myrth.

Maru *m* devil, demon.

Marunc to beat; *cull marunc*, to give a knock; jivo marunc, to kill, to assassinate; *apun apnanc jivo marunc*, to commit suicide; *gollar marunc*, to hang; *fator marunc*, to throw stone, to extract stones from a pit; *masolli marunc*, to fish; *xir marunc*, to be bled; *mor marunc*, to coin; *fol marunc*, to tell a lie, to deceive; *urmalachi deg marunc*, to hem handkerchief; *tarvantodd marunc*, to arrive a ship at a port; *xins marunc*, to behead; *hem* *khan tondar marta*, this eatable cause loathing; *jint marunc*, to faint, to feel giddy; *canos marunc*, to file ; *gans marunc*, to bite; *san marunc*, to sweep; *anga borem varem marta*, there is a good breeze here, *gant marunc*, to ring a bell, to tie, to make a knot; *cuddco marunc*, to mend, to patch; *tonnkean marunc*, to cudgel; *galli marunc*, to curse; *zaddacheo talleo marunc*, to trim.

MAS *n* flesh; *bazlelem mas*, roast meat; *bocrechem mas*, mutton; *ducrachem mas*, pork; *gaichem mas*, beef; *toulelem mas*, fried meat; *ucorlelem mas*, boiled meat.

MASALL fleshy, pulpy.

MASALO *m* curry-stuff.

MASOLLCAN *f* fisher woman.

MASOLLCAR *m* fisher man.

MASOLLI *f* fish.

MAT extention.

MAT EUNC VO MATONC to be fat, to be fleshy (fig) to be proud.

MAT top, height, the highest pitch of anything.

MAT VO GOZAL *f* conversation.

MATARI *f* old woman.

MATARO *m* old man.

MATARPONN old age, imbecility and peevishness of old age.

MATEM *n* head; *tachia mattear ek ojem asa*, he carries a load on his head.

MATEM MARUNC to shoulder up an enterprise.

MATI *f* earth, land, soil, ground

MATI CHICOTT *n* clay, potter's earth.

MATIEC LAUNC to bury.

MATLOLO, -I, -EM fat, fleshy.

MATO *m* p. MATARO.

MATONC to be fat, to be fleshy.

MATONC to display healthy growth, to become prosperous.

MATOUNC to faten, to make fleshy.

MATR a little.

MATRE p. MATARO.

MATRI VO MATARI *f* old woman.

MATRISO, -XI, -XEM p. Matso, -XI, -XEM.

MATRO VO MATARO *m* old man.

MATTOU *m* pavilion, a curtain hanging in the form of a tent.

MAU (GAIACHI) *f* cicatrice, scar

MAULLI *f* cobweb.

MAULLING(FOLL) *n* cedrat, cyder.

MAULLING (ZADD) *f* cedrat-tree.

MAULLO *m* maternal uncle.

MAULLONN VO MAUONN *f* aunt or father's sister.

MAUM father-in-law.

MAUXI *f* aunt.

MAUXI BAU *m* he cousin.

MAUXI BOIN *f* she cousin.

MAVOLLONC to wither, to fade; *dis mavolla*, the sun was set.

MAZAR in the middle, centre.

MAZCANDDO the fore finger.

MAZLIM *n* muslin.

MAZO, -I, -EM p. MOZO, -JĨ, -JEM.

MAZOR *n* cat.

MAZOLL middling, ordinary.

MAZRACHEM POR kitten.

Mecllaunc to separate, to loosen.

Mecllo, -i, -em disunited, separated, loosen.

Mecllo corunc to separate, to detach.

Mecllo zaunc to be separated.

Medd *f* prop, lever, handspike.

Meddem *n* socket, any hollow thing or place which receives or hold something else.

Mei *m* stockings, socks.

Meitt cooks' assistant, kitchen mate.

Melar corunc to sweeten with sugar.

Mell meeting, mixture.

Mellai vo Mellaunnim *f* mixture.

Mellit corunc to profit, to gain.

Melloc *m* dirt.

Mellonc to find, to meet, to visit.

Mellounc to mix, to gain.

Mellunc p. **Mellonc.**

Melolo, -i, -em dead.

Mendduri *f* ewe.

Menddro *m* ram.

Menddur *f* lamb.

Mendu *m* brains.

Mengo, -i, -em melancholic, meditative, thoughtful.

Menn *n* wax.

Mennachi vat wax-candle.

Mennachim baulim wax-figures.

Menncar *m* dealer in wax.

Menncapodd *n* wax cloth.

Meo, -i, -em dirty.

Meonc to get dirty, to be defiled.

Meonc p. **Mellonc.**

Meounc to dirty, to stain.

Mer *f* limit.

Mer, Mero ridges in a paddy-field.

Mer launc to build a ridge.

Mercad market.

Mercador merchant.

Mercasi *f* commerce.

Mereli *m* neighbour.

Merend *n* luncheon.

Mergol a dish of cooked vegetables.

Merri *f* p. **Mendri.**

Merro *m* sheep.

Merrum *n* stag, deer.

Mett *m* place where soldiers are stationed.

Mettan *f* hemming.

Mettan marunc to hem.

Mettio *f* fennugreek.

Mettunc to hem.

Meulolo, -i, -em met, found.

Meulolo, -i, -em dirtied, stained.

Meunni *f* sister in-law.

Meunno *m* brother-in-law.

Mez *n* table; *cusichem mez,* side table; *jeunamchem mez,* dinner table; *borounchem mez,* writing table; *varculem mez,* round table.

Mezi sarko, -ki, -kem measurable.

Mezlolo, -i, -em counted

Mezop *n* measurement, measuring.

Mezop corunc to count, to measure.

Mezpi *m* measurer; *gaum mezpi*, surveyor of land.

Mezunc to count, to measure; *taca con mezta*, who cares for him.

Mhar person of Mhar caste.

Mharancho,-i,-em belonging to Mhar caste.

Mharodd locality of Mhar people.

Mijas *f* boasting, pride.

Mijas corunc to boast.

Minot *f* work, labour, toil.

Minot geunc to work, to toil.

Minoti hard-working, laborious.

Minut *m* minute.

Miol (zad) *n* milk-bush.

Miras *n* farm, property.

Mirasdar *m* farmer, proprieter.

Miri (cagdachi) *f* plait or fold.

Miri (poleachi) plait or fold.

Miri (vistidagi) *f* crumple, plait.

Miriam *n* black-peppers.

Mirim *n* curry stuff.

Mirim vanttunc to grind curry stuff.

Mirio signs or furrows of age, sickness or sorrow on the human face.

Mirio poleancheo dimples.

Mirio (zad) *m* sterculia fetida.

Mirmironc to burn.

Mirounc to rejoice, to be glad.

Mirsang *f* chilly.

Mirsang (zad) *f* chilly plant.

Mirvel *f* pepper-plant.

Mis *n* mass; *voddlem mis*, high mass; *ductem mis*, low mass.

Misal *n* missal.

Misalli *n* mixture.

Missallonc to mix, to join.

Misallunc to mix, to blend.

Misaunc p. misallunc.

Misson corunc to blend, to mix.

Mister *m* mystery.

Mistin *f* mistress, teacher.

Mistir *m* master, teacher.

Mistis eurasian, anglo-indian, person of mixed parentage.

Mitt *n* salt.

Mitt marunc to preserve, to salt.

Mittcan *f* female dealer in salt.

Mittcar *m* dealer in salt, salter.

Mittai *f* sweets.

Mitti *f* crack of the tongue.

Mitti marunc to make noise by the tongue.

Mittmittaunc, dolle to twinkle, to wink.

Mixallo vo / **Mixao** } one that has big mustaches.

Mixi *f* mustache.

Mizricaum *m* basil-gentle, sweet basil.

Moa *f* the gum.

Moall *f* soft, tender, kind.

Moall corunc to soften, to mellow.

Moall zaunc to soften down, to get mild, to be temperate.

Moancho mus *m* a bee.

Moaunc to soften, to move to compassion.

Moche *m* shoes.

Moche xiunta-to cobbler.

Mochi *m* shoe-maker.
Mocto *m* country liquor shop, tavern.
Mocto, -i, -em just sufficient.
Mocun caddunc to knock down.
Mocunc to aim, to examine attentively.
Mod concupiscence, ardour of sexual instincts.
Modd *n* tempest, storm.
Modd *f* plait, fold.
Modd *f* change; *tuje lagim rupiachi modd asa?* have you got change of a rupee?
Modd *f* impediment, obstacle.
Moddco large earthen pot.
Moddcor broken, unfit.
Moddcull vo / **Moddcuu** } a pitch-fork
Modd-decar *m* stimulated, incited.
Modd-di *f* a goad, stimulation.
Moddean rat *f* midnight.
Moddem *n* corpse, dead body.
Moddki *f* pot.
Moddlolo, -i, -em broken.
Moddonc to break; *jeunnachi ruch moddonc*, not to have any appetite for food; *taca vochunc chear dis moddle*, he took 4 days to go; *to saucar moddlo*, that merchant failed; *sonvoim moddonc*, to discontinue one's habit; *doria moddonc* to become the sea stormy; *laram moddonc*, to rise up waves in the sea.
Moddop *n* breakage.
Moddtel *n* bottle.
Moddunc to break; *boddi moddunc*, to break a stick; *rupoi moddunc*, to change a rupee; *tannem zaile duddu moddle fest corunc*, he spent a lot to celebrate the feast; *dolle moddunc*, to wink; *soiric moddunc*, to break a marriage engagement; *uler moddunc*, not to keep one's word, *upordes moddunc*, transgress the law; *khoni moddunc*, to change one's mind, to persuade.
Moddvoll *m* washer-man.
Moddvon *f* washer-woman.
Moddxi *f* indigestion.
Modecat vo / **Modecot vo** / **Modem** } in the middle, centre.
Medenchean through the midst.
Modencho, -i, -em middle.
Modest *m* arbitrator.
Modestai *f* free and uncontrolled will and pleasure, expedient.
Modeunc to be inflamed by sexual passions.
Modi fashions, new styles.
Modi corunc to adopt new fashions, to like new styles of living.
Modiam middling, ordinary.
Modiamai *f* mediocrity.
Modian midnight.
Modlean through the middle.
Modlo, -i, -em middle, centre.
Modon *f* God-mother.
Modun middling, ordinary.
Modur delicate, tender, too nice.

MODURAEN delicately.
MODURAI *f* delicacy, daintiness.
MOEM *n* mask.
MOENCAR *m* masquerade, mummery.
MOG *n* jug.
MOG *m* love.
MOG mug, a cup of metal.
MOG CORUNC to love.
MOGACHO, -I, -EM loving, affectionate.
MOGALL kind, affectionate, courteous.
MOG-CORNAR lover.
MOGELO, -I, -EM my, mine.
MOGREM *n* michaelmas daisy.
MOGREPONN moreseness, silent opposition.
MOGRO, -I, -EM reserved, displeasing, heedless.
MOI *f* hind, deer.
MOIA *f* love, affection.
MOIDON *n* plain, field.
MOILLO obscure.
MOIMAS *m* esteem, appreciation.
MOINOM *m* month.
MOIR mahomedan.
MOJEAN I; *mojean corum nozo*, I cannot do.
MOKI *f* sight, (of a gun).
MOL *n* price value; *uneh mol*, very dear; *uncha molacho*, valuable, precious: *unneam molacho*, cheap, ordinary, common.
MOLADIC precious, valuable.
MOLAM *n* springs.
MOLAUNC to bargain, to settle price.
MOLL *n* humour, moisture.
MOLLE-POLLE sweet cakes, flattering conversation. "João molle-polle sangonc uxar. John is sweet talker or smart in flattering.
MOLLO *m* orchard, garden.
MOLLO garden, orchard.
MOLLO, -I, -EM sweet, delightful.
MOLLO FULLANCHO flower-garden.
MOLLO NARL sweet cocoanut.
MOLLOB *n* firmament.
MOLLOP *n* grinding, thrashing, corn.
MOLLOP VO MOUNIM thrashing of corn.
MOL-LUC *f* epilepsy.
MOLLUNC to thrash corn.
MOLOMB *n* ointment.
MON *n* death.
MON *n* intention, mind.
MONA *n* suspension, suspence, amazement.
MONA CORUNC to suspend, to amaze, to astonish.
MONA EUNC VO MONANC EUNC to please, to be pleasing.
MONA ZAUNC to be suspended, to be quiet.
MONCONTICHO,-I,-EM VO MONKONTIVONT } melancholic.
MONCOTT *n* wrist.
MONEPONN *n* dumbness.
MONJECAR entertainer, an amusing fellow.
MONKONTI melancholy, sadness.
MONNI *f* a pair of beads.
MONNOI VO MUNNI *f* a stool.
MONNONC VO MUNNONC to say, to repeat, to recite.

MONNONEM VO ODD convulsion.
MONO, -I, -EM dumb.
MONO ZAUNC to become dumb.
MONSUBDAR *m* judge.
MONSUBI *f* justice, right, equity.
MONSUNC to determine, to decide, to decree.
MONTR VO VIST *m* friend.
MONUS *m* p. MANUS.
MONUXEPON p. MANUXEPONN.
MONUXEPON GUEUNC to become man, to take human form.
MONVAR man-of-war.
MONZAT irrational animals.
MONZATINCHO ZOMO menagery.
MO-OP *n* grinding.
MO-OP, PITTACHEM kneading of flour.
MOR *m* peacock.
MOR *f* stamp, mark, coin.
MOR CORUNC to seal, to close.
MOR MARUNC to stamp, to make a mark.
MOR MARUNC DUDVANC to coin money.
MORANG straw-berry.
MORAULO *m* a prop, a shade for a house.
MORDI courage, manhood.
MOREM (ZADDACHEM) *n* cancer of a tree.
MORGI *f* hen.
MORI *f* sea-lamprey.
MORIAD *f* modesty.
MORIAD VO, MORIADI VO, MORIADIC } modest, moderate.
MORL, MORLAM stalks of palm-tree.
MORLONNI *f* strong cold.
MORLUC *f* epilepsy.
MORLUCAR, IR, IN epileptic.
MORN *n* death, end of life.
MORNACHI GANTT passing bell.
MORNANDIC deadly.
MORO *m* shark.
MOROD man, husband.
MORONC to die, to perish, to terminate, to end.
MORONN *n* death.
MORTICAR *m* murderer, criminal.
MORUNC p. MORONC.
MORVON *f* washer-woman
MORVOU *m* washerman.
MOS *f* she buffalo.
MOSCORECAR, IN jester.
MOSCORI *f* mockery, fun.
MOSCORI CORUNC to joke with, to jest at.
MOSOR *m* obstinacy, stubborness.
MOSOR CORUNC to be stubborn, to be obstinate; most lascivious misbehaviour, intemperance.
MOSTIPONN *n* ebriety, drunkenness.
MOSTO, -I, -EM intoxicated, [drunk.
MOSTR *n* sample.
MOSTUNC to tread upon.
MOT *f* understanding, reason.
MOTIM *n* pearl.
MOTIPROCAS understanding, reason.
MOTIVONT rational.
MOTTO, -I, -EM fat.
MOT-TOMODDO, -I, -EM in a dying condition.
MOTTVO, -I, -EM short, dwarf.

MOU soft, tender; *mou masoli*, fish beginning to rot.
MOU CORUNC to soften.
MOUBOTT, *f* cloudy.
MOUBOTT ZAUNC to grow cloudy.
MOUBOTTONC to become cloudy.
MOUL preserve of fish or meat.
MOULLI *f* bundle, faggot, sheaf.
MOULLI VAREACHI *f* a puff of wind.
MOU-LLO *m* kernel of a walnut.
MOULLOLO,-I,-EM thrashed, frequented; *moulleli vatt*, beaten track; *moullelem pitt*, kneaded flour; *moulleleo cazu*, pressed or squeezed caju.
MOUM *n* honey.
MOUNC to squeeze, to press.
MOUNNIM thrashing (corn).
MOUPONN *n* softness, tenderness.
MOUSUD *f* screw.
MOUSUD ORNUNCHEM AUT screwdriver.
MOUZ *f* amusement, diversion.
MOVALL soft, tender.
MOVALLONC to feel compasion or pity.
MOVALLPON *n* tenderness, kindnes.
MOVEM *n* mask.
MOZO, -I, -EM my, mine.
MOZORECAR, IN day-labourer.
MOZOT *f* help, assistance, protection.
MOZOT CORUNC VO / MOZOT DIUNC } to give help, to assist.
MOZOTIVONT *n* protector, helper.
MOZUR tender, soft, delicate.
MOZURAI *f* tenderness, delicacy.
MOZURI wages, labourer's due.
MUC mouth, opening.
MUC *n* feature, face.
MUCAR in front, next, near.
MUCAVELEAN ahead.
MUCAVELO, -I, -EM of above, of next.
MUCTI *f* glory, honour.
MUCTI FOUZ salvation army.
MUCTIDAR glorifier.
MUCTIVONT glorious, blessed.
MUCUTT *m* crown.
MUD *n* suit of clothes.
MUD-DUNC to squeez, to press.
MUDDASO *m* turban.
MUDDCUU *f* hook.
MUDDI *f* a pack, bale.
MUDDI BANDUNC to make a pack.
MUDDIALLO, -I, -EM curled.
MUDDO *m* p. muddi.
MUDDO (SARNICHO) the end or the extreme part of a broom.
MUDI *f* ring; *mudi cazarachi*, wedding-ring.
MUDLAN from the beginning.
MUDOL beginning, starting work.
MUI *f* ant.
MUIEUNC to prick (like the stinging of ants), to benumb.
MUINOM *m* month.
MUINOM (CAZARACHO) return of bridal pair to the bride's house.
MUKELI *m* chief, leader, head.
MULAM guilding.
MULAM DIUNC to guild.

Mulat *m* negro.
Mull, mund *n* stem, origin.
Mullcho, -i, -em original, radical.
Mullim *f* at the foot.
Mullo *m* raddish.
Mumkeponn *n* taciturnity, silence.
Mumko, -ki, -kem taciturn, [silent.
Muncar one that lives in the property of another person without paying.
Mund *n* stem.
Mund root, origin.
Munddai stupidity.
Munddo mutilated.
Munddonc to shut, to close, to lock up.
Munddou (dolleanchi) *f* eye ball; *dovi munddou dolleanchi*, socket.
Munddounc to shut, to close.
Mundou (tantiacho) *f* yellow of an egg.
Mundro marking-iron.
Mungil bitter.
Munglar *m* tuesday.
Mungos *n* weasel.
Munis *m* man.
Munni saying, proverb.
Munniari *m* minister; *devacho munniari*, priest.
Munnoim *f* stool.
Munnonc to speak, to utter.
Munsubdar *m* one that executes justice strictly.
Munxeponn *n* human nature.
Munz *f* girdle.
Muo *m* raddish.
Mur *f* seddiment, dregs, dross.
Murc imprudent.
Murcponn *n* imprudence.
Mureant near, in front, close by.
Murgottonc to smile at.
Murmi fator soft red stone.
Murmuro *m* embers.
Murom
Muromb foddunc to break rocks by using gunpowder.
Murut *m* beginning, principal, first cause.
Murut poddonc vo galunc to begin, to start, to open.
Mus *m* fly; *mus moancho*, bee.
Muscachio sango horse-raddish.
Muscor *n* face, feature.
Muscott p. **Muscor.**
Musing *m* horse-tree.
Musmusunc to burn, to heat up.
Musoll vo musou pestle.
Mustaiki *f* household, furniture.
Mut *n* urine.
Mutonc to piss, to make water.
Mutrem *n* percupine-flesh.
Mutt *f* box; *mutt ostuchi*, handle.
Muttaunc to box, to give blows.
Muttincho khell boxing sport.
Mutri public urinal.
Mutunc p. **Mutonc.**
Muxi mockadoes, the first end or fag end of a web, the loose threads of the end of a wrap.
Muzeu *m* museum.
Muzg vo Vazontri musician.
Myassi proud, insolent.

N

N the fourteenth letter of the Roman Alphabet.

NAB *m* turnip.

NABAB nawab, a prince or noble in a Mohammedan state.

NABI prophet, seer.

NAC *n* nose.

NAC CATORLOLO cut off nose, (fig) shameless.

NAC CATRO,-I,-EM behaving shamelessly.

NAC CATRUNC to cut off the nose (fig) to disgrace.

NACA ZAUNC to object,to refuse.

NACARO, -I, -EM over-hasty for possessing things desired or becoming available, greedy.

NACARONC to seek eagerly, to take advantage of a favourable chance with unseemly haste.

NACH *m* dance, ball.

NACHINEM *m* nachinim, elensine.

NACHONC to dance.

NACHOP *n* dance, ball.

NACHPI *m* dancer, stage, dancer.

NACHPIN *f* woman dancer, dancing girl.

NACHREM SOUNG dancing seem, dancing girl.

NACHRO, -I, -EM dancer.

NACOTTO *m* a big nose.

NACSAUNC to scratch with nails.

NACTTEO, -I, -EM long-nosed.

NACUTT VO
NACXI } *f* nail.

NAD *m* sound, echo.

NAD enthusiasm,

NADAN enthusiastically, in high spirits, whole-heartedly.

NADD *f* pulse.

NADD *f* deceit, error, mistake.

NADD BANDUNC to use charms against evils.

NADD DORUNC to feel the pulse.

NADD DUCHARACHI evil temptation.

NADDGO, -I, -EM cunning, deceiful.

NADDI *f* the breech.

NADDO false, deceiver.

NADDO juggler's pole.

NADDLOLO spel-bound.

NADDONC to be deceived, to be cheated.

NADDUNC to deceive, to cheat, to mislead.

NADELOLO, -I, -EM enthusiastic, high-spirited.

NADEUNC to feel or become enthusiastic, to be lively.

NAG *m* cobra snake.

NAGDDEPONN *n* nakedness.

NAGDDO, -I, -EM naked.

NAGDDO CORUNC to strip one's clothes, to make naked.

NAGDDO ZAUNC to strip of clothes,to lose one's possessions.

NAGONN *f* robbery, plunder.

NAGOULOLO ZAUNC to feel keenly one's disappointments.

NAGOUNC to rob, to plunder.

NAICUT *n* dropsy.

NAIM *m* barber.

NAKESTIM causelessly.

NAKIAM through the nose, nasal.

NAL *m* cocoanut.
NAL BANDUNC to shoe a horse.
NAL (GODDIACHO) horse-shoe.
NALCAR, NALSHETT owner of dealer, in cocoanuts.
NALL *f* cannon.
NALLICHO GULLO shell.
NALO stream of water.
NAM no, without; *aum dinam*, i do not give; *nam coutam to gelo*, he went away without knowing.
NAM CORUNC to cancel, to destroy.
NAM TOR VO / NAM ZALEAR } if not; *kellim add nam zalear ambe add*, bring plantains if not bring mangoes.
NAM ZAUNC to disappear.
NAMAZ worship, religious devotion.
NANA grandfather.
NANAMPORIM differently.
NANAMPORINCHO, -I, -EM different; miscellaneous.
NANAPORIM in a negative manner.
NANATTEM GUINEAN mind imbued with pessimism.
NANATTO, -I, -EM pessimistical.
NANCAR negative.
NANGOR *m* plough.
NANGOR plough.
NANGOR GALUNC to cast anchor.
NANGOR (TARVACHO) *m* anchor.
NANGORLELEM(TARUM)come to an anchor.
NANGORLOLO, -I, -EM ploughed, cultivated.
NANGORNIM VO / NANGRONN } *f* ploughing.
NANGRI ploughman, tiller.
NANGRUNC VO COSUNC to plough, to cultivate.
NANI grandmother.
NANN *n* bath.
NANNAMCAR p. NANCAR.
NANNEM *m* coin, money.
NANNIM *f* bath room, washing place.
NANN'OUNC to bathe, to wash.
NANVANCHO,-I,-EM well-known.
NANV-NANTLOLO, -I, -EM obscure, unknown.
NARELPUNOM cocoanut day of Hindus.
NARI *f* woman, wife.
NARING orange.
NARINGIN *f* orange-tree.
NARL *m* cocoanut.
NARLI vo COTTI *f* cocoanut shell.
NARU *m* guinea, worm.
NAS *m* damage, perdition.
NASONC to spoil, to be damaged.
NASONC not to have.
NASTO breakfast.
NAT *f* grand-daughter.
NAT, ZAUIM *m* a grand son-in-law.
NATAL *n* christmas.
NATALANCHEM VESPR *n* christmas eve.
NATRAM grand children.
NATSUN *f* a grand-daughter-in law.
NATTAC disappearance.
NATTAC CORUNC to disappear
NATTAC ZAUNC to disappear.
NATTCAI VO NATTUCAI envy, spite.

NATTCAIECHO, -I, -EM Envious.
NATTOC threatical play, a form of public amusement.
NATU *m* a grand-son.
NATUC *n* owl.
NAU *f* gun, cannon.
NAU MARUNC to fire a cannon.
NAUM *n* name.
NAUM ANNEM CORUNC to defa-[me.
NAUM ASTO, -I, -EM famous.
NAUM NASTO,-I,-EM anonymous.
NAUM OSTEM fame, renown.
NAUMCHEM AIDON *n* bathing-tub.
NAUNC to bath.
NAVADDLOLO,-I,-EM celebrated, famous.
NAVADDUNC to honour, to make famous.
NAVANNOGO,-I,-EM celebrated, famous.
NAVET *f* navet.
NAVIM *m* barber.
NAXIVONT hurtful, injurious, prejudicial.
NAZAR gift of homage to a prince.
NAZUC fine, beautiful.
NAZUCAI *f* beauty, fineness, handsomeness, prettiness, loveliness, neatness.
NEA law suit, (fig) contest.
NEA CORUNC to sue at law, to seek for a place.
NEALLI VO NEELI *m* caviller, litigious man.
NEAN VO NOEAN again, once more.
NEDCUCHAR *m* envy, spite.
NEDCUCHAR DORUNC to be envious, to be spiteful.
NEDCUCHARI, *m* one that is envious.
NE-EM feast of harvest.
NE-EM VO NOEM new, fresh.
NEGAR ZAOP denial.
NEGR African (male).
NEGRIN female African.
NEGU deluge, flood.
NEKETR *n* star.
NEKETR ORLEM *n* planet.
NEM *n* hole, ditch, pit.
NEM *f* nomination.
NEM *m* rule.
NEM CADDUNC VO NEM MARUNC } to sink a ditch.
NEM DIUNC to ostracise formally a member of society, to excommunicate.
NEMANC to sink, to go below the surface of the ground.
NEMDAR determinator.
NEMIT *n* cause, motive, ground.
NEMIT DIUNC to cause, to make, to produce.
NEMOS resolved, hold, fixed, definite.
NEMOUNC to shake, to weaken, to ruin; *lem gor nemlem*, that house collapsed; *mazo paim te zomninl nemlo*, my leg sunk in that ground.
NEMUNC to determine, to fix, to resolve.
NENNAR ignorant.
NENNARPONN *n* ignorance.
NENNO *m* p. NENNAR.
NENNO ZAUNC to be ignorant, not to know, to be unacquainted with.
NENNTTO, -I, -EM p. NENNAR.

NENNTTUVAI *f* humility.

NENTTO, -I, -EM guileless, innocent.

NEO,-I,-EM vo NOVO,-I, -EM new.

NER cockles, weeds.

NERV *n* nerves.

NERVANCHI PIDDA hysteria.

NERVOZ nervous.

NESLOLO, -I, -EM dressed.

NESON VO NESOUNIM garment, vestiment.

NESONC to dress.

NESSON CADDUNC to undress, to take out (one's clothes).

NESTTO,-I,-EM p. NOSTTO,-i,-em.

NESTTURAIEN cruely, rigorously.

NESTTURONC to become cruel.

NETT *m* impulse, energy.

NETT *m* ornament, apparel, decoration.

NETT DIUNC VO NETT MARUNC to give impulse.

NETTACHO,-I,-EM energetic, impulsive.

NETTOUNC to trim one's self, to adorn, to deck.

NETTOUNC to decorate, to trim, to adorn; *tica bangaran nettoili*, she is adorned with jewels.

NETTRO the eye, sight, aspect, look.

NETTUNC p. NETTONC.

NEUREO a kind of sweets, fritters.

NEVASSÃO novelty.

NEVIDAD good news, tidings of much joy.

NEXTTO *m* p. NOXTTO.

NIALL *m* reflection.

NIALL CORUNC VO NIALLUNC to consider, to reflect, to redound.

NIB *n* cause, motive.

NIB excuse, futile plea.

NIB DIUNC to give an excuse.

NIBANCHO,-I,-EM insincere, finding excuses.

NIBAO quietness, calmness.

NIBAUNC to still, to appease, to calm, to repose.

NIBOR hard; *ho fator nibor*, this stone is hard; *Lourens nibor*, Lourence is cruel; *ho soro chodd nibor*, this liquor is very strong; *nibor nibor fator*, very hard.

NIBOR CORUNC to harden.

NIBOR ZAUNC to grow harsh or hard or firm.

NIBRAUNC VO NIBRAI hardness, toughness, solidity (fig) rudeness harshness, inhumanity, resistance.

NICA marriage-tie.

NICANDDO unnecessary, useless.

NICAUNC to undo, to take, to pieces, to dismount.

NICHEU *m* resolution, purpose.

NICHEU CORUNC to resolve.

NICHINTAI *f* convenience.

NICHOL chaste, pure.

NICLAMPONN *n* chastity, purity.

NICLAUNC p. NICAUNC.

NICOUNC to be dislocated, to come asunder.

NICTO,-I,-EM NOW, at the present moment.

NID *f* sleep.
NID NAM ZAUNC to remain sleepless.
NIDAN tender, kind, affable.
NIDAUNC to put to sleep.
NIDEST sleepy.
NIDLOLO, -I, -EM sleepy, asleep.
NIDONC to sleep, to take a nap.
NIDSURO, -I, -EM sleepy, drowsy.
NIGUT perfect.
NIGUT CORUNC to repair, to perfect, to improve, to finish.
NIGUTAEN perfectly, completely.
NIGUTAI *f* perfection, faultlessness beauty, grace.
NIKADDIO beardless.
NIKIPINNEM sepulture, burying.
NIKIPIONC to bury.
NILAM *n* ballast, lastage.
NILL *m* indigo, anil.
NILLO *m* bangle.
NIM, NOI no.
NIM ALMUNDDAI *f* trick, wile, prank.
NIMALMUNDDO, -I, -EM restless uneasy, turbulent, noisy.
NIMANNEM lastly, finally.
NIMANNO, -I, -EM last, final, end.
NIMBI lime-tree.
NIMBU *m* lime, *sacor nimbu*, orange.
NIMGONNEM *n* question, interrogation.
NIMGUNC to question, to ask, to interrogate.
NIMIM *n* half.
NIMIT *n* cause, motive, pretext, excuse.
NIMNNO last, final.
NIMUC *m* moment, instant.
NIND *f* murmur.
NINDA *f* murmuring, back biting.
NINDA CORUNC to murmur, to grumble.
NINDEST *m* murmurer, back biter.
NINDUNC to suffer, to bear.
NIO *m* bangle.
NIOL *f* milk-weed.
NIOLL VO NIS *m* canji water.
NIOLL VO NIVOLL clear, pure.
NIONÇ to cool; *tacho rag niulo*, his anger is cooled down.
NIONNI *f* the harvest, the harvest time.
NIOUNC to cool.
NIPZONC to be born, to come into life, to grow, to spring, to come forth, to rise, to break out.
NIRADAR abundonment.
NIRADAR CORUNC to abundon.
NIRADARI one that abundons.
NIRANCAR *m* incorporeal.
NIRASONC to abolish, to revoke.
NIRAXA desparation, hopelessness.
NIRAXI desparate.
NIRBAG misfortune, unhappiness, adversity.
NIRBAGI unfortunate, unhappy.
NIRCAMI idle, not occupied, unfortunate.
NIRDANI unfortunate.

NIRDAR VO NIRDARAI evidence.
NIRDARI evident.
NIRDUC insensibility, cruelty.
NIRDUCO, -KI, -KEM callous, insensible.
NIRFOLL unfruitful, fruitless.
NIRMOLL VO NIRMOLLI desentry.
NIRMOLL VO NITOLL clean, pure.
NIRMOLLONC VO NITOLLONC to purify.
NIRMOLLPONN neatness, cleanliness.
NIRMOLLUNC VO NITOLL CORUNC, to clear, to purify.
NIRMONN *n* permission.
NIRMONN destiny.
NIRMUNC to permit, to allow, to consent.
NIRMUNC to be destined.
NIRO sweet and pure juice.
NIROGOT useless.
NIRONTOR indifference.
NIROP licence, permission.
NIROP DIUNC to permit, to give leave.
NIROPAD innocence.
NIROPADI innocent.
NIROPUNC p. NIROP DIUNC.
NIROZER immortal.
NIROZERI immortality.
NIRPUTRAI sterility, barreness.
NIRPUTRI sterile, barren.
NIRVICAR antidote.
NIRVONDAR courageous, bold, intrepid.
NIRVONIM brave, courageous.
NIRVONN courage, boldness.
NIS *m* land-mark.
NIS AND MER NAM unlimited.
NIS (PEZECHO) *m* canji water.
NISON *f* ladder.
NISORTI *f* precipice.
NISRONC to slip down, to lose foothold.
NISSONTONN ruin, downfall.
NISSOR the state of being slippery.
NISSOR-GANTT slip-knot.
NISSORDI, -EM -O, slippery.
NISTEM fish.
NISTTUR cruel, *nisturai*, cruelity, inhumanity.
NIT *f* justice.
NITIDAR *m* magistrate.
NITIVONT *m* severe, that executes justice strictly.
NITOL clean, pure.
NITOLAI *f* neatness, cleanliness.
NITOLCAI VO NITOLPONN } p. NITOLAI.
NITT right, straight, just.
NITTAUNC to straighten.
NITTIER GALUNC to arrange, to dispose, to regulate, to order.
NITU *f* spitle.
NITU GALUNC to spit.
NIU (RONG) *m* blue.
NIU RAMPONC to dye, to become coloured.
NIUNNEM *n* dish-clout.
NIULLAUNC to make a drunkard sober.
NIULLONC to become sober, calm or cool.
NIURONC to be saved, to escape.
NIURONG *f* prickly-pear.
NIVADDO *m* decision judgment.
NIVADDUNC to decide, to judge, to resolve.

NIVARONN defence, salvation.
NIVARUNC to save, to deliver from.
NIVOLL clean, pure.
NIVOLL ÇORUNC VO } to purify,
NIVOLLUNC } to clarify.
NIVOUNC to cool.
NIVRAUNC p. NIVARUNC.
NIXANDCAR *m* one that signs subscriber.
NIXANN CORUNC to sign.
NIXANNI *f* signature, sign.
NIXANNI *f* sign, mark.
NIXEM *n* boiled rice water.
NIZ legitimate, true.
NIZ *m* land-mark.
NIZ CADDUNC to remove a land-mark.
NIZ GALUNC to set up a land-mark.
NOCLLO ZAUNC not to know, to be unacquainted with, to be ignorant of.
NOCTIR *n* star.
NOCXETR p. NOCTIR.
NOCXI *f* decoration, carving.
NOCXI SOMDIRACHI chart.
NOCXI SOUNSARACHI map of the world.
NOD *f* river.
NODAR PODDONC to see, to perceive.
NODD *f* obstacle, difficulty.
NODDGO, -I, -EM full of obstacles.
NODDNIM *f* weeding.
NODDONC to weed.
NODOR *f* sight, look.
NODOR BANDUNC to deceive, to cheat.
NODOR BOND ZAUNĈ to loose sight, to become blind.
NOFA *f* gain, profit.
NOFA CORUNC to make a profit.
NOG *m* piece.
NOGOR *n* city.
NOGOT (DUDDU) cash.
NOGOT FARIC CORUNC to pay cash down.
NOI ninety.
NOIM *f* river; *dacli noim*, rivulet.
NOLBOTO, -I, -EM addicted to omina-nation, superstitious.
ṆOLL pipe.
NOLL GOTTARACHO drain-pipe.
NOLL UDCACHO water-pipe.
NOLLI *f* pipe, conduit.
NOLLO *m* tile.
NOM no.
NOMAN hail.
NOMBAR return.
NOMOSCAR hail.
NOMOSCAR CORUNC to adore, to salute.
NOMPOIT disappearance.
NOMPOIT CORUNC to make disappear.
NOMPOIT ZAUNC to disappear.
NONDONC to prosper, to be happy.
NONNDDOIO *m* brother-in-law.
NONNIM *f* weeding.
NONNOND *f* sistter-in-law (husband's sister).
NOPUNSOC neuter.
NOR *m* passage, freight.
NOR male of a fowl.
NOROC bad smell, stinking.
NOROM soft, tender.

NOROM CORUNC to soften, to modify.

NOROM PODDONC to be spiritless.

NORT *f* north.

NORTI DUDDUANCHEO promissory notes of money.

NOS nerve, nerves.

NOSTO breakfast.

NOU *m* pipe.

NOULANCHO, -I, -EM surprising, amusing.

NOUREACHO DEDDO best man.

NOURI bride.

NOURO *m* bridegroom.

NOURO-OHOCOL bridal pair.

NOVEAN again, once more.

NOVEMBER *m* november.

NOVGOTIM newly, again.

NOVIDAD news, new fruit of the season.

NOVO, -I, -EM new, fresh.

NOVOL *n* wonder, miracle, novelty.

NOXIB *n* fortune, luck.

NOXTT *n* misfortune, damage, loss.

NOXTTO, -I, -EM wicked, bad.

NUL null, void.

NUM no.

NUMR number.

NUR light, brightness.

NUSTEM *n* fish.

O

O the fifteenth letter of the Roman Alphabet.

O ! ah !

O ANI TO MUNIS this and that man.

O VO TO either.

OB GATACKO,-I,-EM treacherous.

OBAGI unhappy, unfortunate.

OBAVART bad faith.

OBGAT treason, perfidy.

OBGAT CORUNC to betray.

OBGATI traitor.

OBLAT gifts or collection of gifts to a patron saint.

OBOLL cowardness, weakness.

OBOLLI coward, weak, not courageous.

OBORVONSEAN desperately, hopelesly.

OBORVONSO, desparation, hopelesness.

OBR workmanship, work.

OBREIR skilled workman.

OBRIGAÇÃO obligation, duty.

OBRIGAD thankful, thanks.

OBRIGAD compelled, obliged.

OBUDIPONN foolishness, sillyness.

OBUDIVONT foolish, silly, ignorant.

OCANT p. ACANT.

OCANTAUNC p. ACANTAUNC.

OCAR depot, stor e-house.

OCAR ZOLLVACHI depot of firewood.

OCASIÃO occasion, function.

OCHIRCAEN cautiously, carefully.

OCHIRCAA caution, carefulness.

OCHNNEM VO / OCHNNIM } going, march, journey.

OCHONC to go; *cholon ochonc*, to go on foot; *goddian ochonc*, to ride; *sansponn ochonc*, to go by feeling; *londdantlean rogot cohonc*, to vomit blood; *gaiachem rogot ochonc*, to bleed a wound, *tacho zor ochonam*, his fever does not leave him; *to uloitanam luddbo oita*, he stammers whilst speaking.

OCHORIEM *n* miracle, wonder.

OCHUNC p. OCHONC,

OCL *n* spectacle,

OCLANCAR optician.

OCLEGUER in the bride's house.

OCLER PODDONC to do things foolishly.

OCMAN *m* offence, affront.

OCMANI offensive, insulting.

OCOL *f* bride; *ti ocol sundor*, that bride is beautiful.

OCOL (GINEAN) intelligence, understanding, sense; *te bailec ocol nam*, that woman has no sense.

OCOL-NOURO bridal pair.

OCONDD solid, firm.

OCONDDO *m* thumb.

OCONDIT eternal.

OÇOT medecine, remedy.

OCRA eleven.

OCTI medicinal.

OCTI medical practitioner.

OCXER *n* letter.

OD half.

ODD *f* convulsion.

ODD great, lofty, principal.

ODD banyan-tree of India.

ODD MARUNC to have convulsions.

ODDA *f* bet.

ODDA MARUNC to bet.

ODDAN greatness, impressive power ?

ODDANLO,-I,-EM belonging to a high-class people, or family.

ODDAODD *f* emulation.

ODDAODD DORUNC to emulate.

ODDAODDCAR *m* emulary, rival.

ODDAODDIN with emulation.

ODDCHON *f* pressure, attack, urgency.

ODDCHUNC to press, to attack.

ODDCUNC to inquire, to recognize.

ODDCUNC to greet, to speak first words on meeting an acquaintance.

ODDE *m* myrombolans.

ODDECAR boatman.

ODDEM *n* breast.

ODDEM boat.

ODDEXIM two hundred and fifty.

ODDEZ two and half.

ODDGAM-NODDGAM unfair means; sly methods.

ODDGAM-NODDGANCHO MUNIS person using unfair methods instead of being straight forward.

ODDI *f* small boat.

ODDI spasms of pain.

ODDI MARUNC to be tormented by spasmodic pains.

ODDIL *m* chief, principal.

ODDLEAN loudly, in a strong voice.

ODDLEM GHOR great house, fi: cemetery and also a jail.

ODDLI representative female exercising by right some power in domestic affairs.

ODDLLEAN ULOUNC to speak loudly.

ODDLO, -I, -EM big, great, elder; *oddlem gor*, big house; *to ticho oddlo bau*, he is her elder brother.

ODDNNEM *n* a pull.

ODDO fritter of flour either sweet or plain unsweetened.

ODDON act of bending one's head, a curve.

ODDON GALUNC to bend over something.

ODDONC to extend, to lenghten out.

ODDONC to be attracted, to feel inclined, to yield.

ODDOP *n* fence.

ODDOU to incline the head.

ODDPON duty of a representative female, especially in connection with the ceremonies of a wedding.

ODDPONN *n* superiority, dignity.

ODDUN CADDUNC to pluck, to pull violently.

ODDUNC to hedge, to wall.

ODDUNC to pull, to smoke; *dor oddunc*, to pull a rope; *chirut oddunc*, to smoke a cigar; *chimtti oddunc*, to snuff.

ODDVI *f* greatness, honour, respect.

ODIC more, much, many; *team duddvanim don annem odic asat*, in that amount there are two annas more; *odic ulounc naca*, do not speak much; *anga odic loc aslo*, there were many people here.

ODIC BORO better.

ODIC CORUN specially, in the first place.

ODIC VAITT worse.

ODIC ZAUNC to increase, to aggravate.

ODMAS *m* calculation, guess.

ODRUSTT invisible misfortune.

ODRUSTTAN unhappily, unfortunately.

OEM half part of cocoanut in shell.

OEUNC to feel tired, to be overcome by one's own patience.

OFISIN *n* office.

OGDDAINAR *m* spendrift, waster.

OGDDAUNC to spend, to waste.

OGDIM entirely, solely.

OGICH in silence, without cause, quiet.

OGLLO, -I, -EM more, much.

OGNEANIM ignorant, stupid.

OGNEANIMPON ignorance, stupidity.

OGO, -I, -EM quiet, silent.

OGO ASONC VO }
OGO RAVONC } to be quiet.

OGO RAUNNEM silence, obedience to the extreme point of tolerating injustice.

OGO VOGOT CADDUNC to pass time in idleness.

OGONNIT infinite, immense.

OGONNITAI immensity.

OGOR *m* salt-pan.

OGOT *m* necessity.

OGOT (VELL) *m* time.

OGTACHO time-serving, necessitous.

OGUNN *m* vice.

OGUNNI wicked, bad, vicious.
OI yes.
OICOND *f* orris-root.
OICUTT *n* paradise.
OIDDALLI *f* legume.
OIDUVO, -I, -EM yellow.
OIJIN *f* midwife.
OIJIN female physician, also midwife.
OIJINPONN midwifery.
OILEA-OIR exteriorly, outwardly.
OILEAN above, outwardly.
OILO, -I, -EM from above or high.
OINN *n* capital, chief town.
OINNIM insipid, not tasty, wanting in salt.
OIVATT friendly intercourse, acquaintance, dealing.
OIVATT CORUNC to manage, to direct.
OIZ *m* medical-man, doctor.
OIZAPONN medicine, physic.
OJAP *n* wonder, admiration.
OJAPAUNC to surprise, to astonish.
OJAPONC to wonder, to be surprised.
OJELCAN female carrier.
OJELCAR carrier of a load.
OJELI *m* carrier, cooly.
OJEM *n* load.
OJEM (SAGUAD) *n* gift, present.
OJIR *n* indigestion.
OJIR prime min ster.
OKEUNC to take delight in a thing, to be glad.
OKONDIT perpetual, infinite.
OKONDITAI *f* perpetuity.

OL *f* sheet, veil, mantle.
OLANDDONC to fall on one side or other.
OLCO easy, low.
OLCONONC to shake, to be unsteady.
OLI *f* small oar.
OLKEPONN facility, inferiority.
OLLCONC to know, to be acquainted with.
OLLEUNC to comb.
OLLKICHI, -O, -EM known, familiar.
OLLOC *f* knowledge, understanding.
OLLOD *f* saffron.
OLLONC to turn.
OLLONC to be twisted; *tem dor borem ollolam*, that rope is well twisted; *soglo dis cholon maje donke ollole*, by walking whole day my legs are tired.
OLLU light, slow, low.
OLLUNC to twist, to spin.
OLLUVAI *f* lightness, slowness.
OLMONC to find, to arrange.
OLO oar.
OLO, -I, -EM damp, wet.
OLO TANDUNC to ply oars.
OLOMB arrangement, agency.
OLOMB CORUNC VO } to arrange,
OLOMBUNC } to find.
OLOMB ZAUNC to complete an arrangement.
OLSAN dampness, state of being wet.
OMANIT VO OMANOT intact, untouched.
OMCO, -I, -EM a particular one.
OMOLIC precious, valuable.

Omolicai *f* preciousness.
Omorai *f* immortality.
Omoriad *f* immodesty, unmannerliness.
Omoriadi *f* immodest unmanlerness.
Omp sowing.
Ompêr sowing-time.
Ompi *m* sower.
Omponc to sow.
Ompnnim *f* sowing.
Omptea couxear udoc profitless work, useless troubles.
Ompto nidonc to sleep with face down.
Ompunc p. Omponc.
Omor immortal.
Omto,-i,-em upside down,topsy turvy.
Omto galunc to place upside down.
Omtonc to turn, to upset.
On light food, sweet conjee.
Onbaglolo, -i, -em chastened; improved by giving up past mistakes.
Onbagonc to amend,to correct.
Onbavarth incredulity, un be [lief.
Onc *f* vomit, nausea.
Oncaro *m* p. Onc.
Onconc to vomit, to throw up.
Onconn bossonc to sit reclining.
Oncunc p. Onconc.
Ondavon inclination.
Onddo *m* puddle.
Ondoc *m* obscurity, darkness.
Ondounc to incline, to bend, to bow, to be inclined, to be disposed to.
Ondounc to cherish an inclination for.
Ondounnem inclination, bending.
Ondvas troubles of exile.
Onki p. Oncaro.
Onit *f* injustice.
Onitin unjustly.
Onmonunc to hesitate, to waver.
Onn strong desire for selfindulgence, greedy, inclination.
Onn bagounc to obtain full satisfaction.
Onnbog *m* amendment, correction.
Onnbog eunc to repent, te be sorry for.
Onnbog geunc vo / Onnbogonc } to amend one's life, to correct one's self.
Onnconc to incline; *patilean onnconc*, to lie down or lean; *fuddlean onnconc*, to incline, to bow.
Onncotto, -i, -em strange, new.
Onnitio, -i, -em unjust.
Onnonim *n* rack.
Onnot *f* wall.
Onnpallo diunc to disobey.
Onnpalloc disobedient.
Onnpallon, c to disobey.
Onnunc to hold fast or tight.
Onobogot impious, wicked.
Onobogti impiety, irreligiousness.
Onod glory, spiritual splendour.
Onoprad innocence.
Onopradi innocent.
Onopradponn *n* innocence.

ONOROMBI *m* without a beginning.

ONOS *n* pine-apple.

ONOXI *f* pine apple tree.

ONS an ounce, 1/16 th (16th) part of a lb.

ONS craving passion.

ONS GALUNC to desire earnestly.

ONT sounding.

ONT ZAUNC to sound, to fathom.

ONTESTACHO,-I,-EM secret, confidencial.

ONTESTI trusty.

ONTOR *f* difference, unequality.

ONTOSCORN *n* conscience.

ONTOSCORNACHI DUC sincere repentance.

ONTROLL *n* atmosphere.

ONTRONC to lose.

ONTT *m* lip.

ONTTI *f* the lap of a woman, bosom.

ONTTI (GORVANCHI) *f* udder.

ONUPCARI ungrateful.

OP luster, gloss.

OP a long uniform garment used by members of a sodality

OPANG independence.

OPANGI independent.

OPAR *f* parable.

OPARI comparison, proverb.

OPDIUNC to polish.

OPKIRTI *f* notoriety.

OPMAN *m* injury.

OPMAN CORUNC VO DIUNC to dishonour.

OPMANACHO, -I, -EM injurious.

OPOVITR profane, unhallowed.

OPOVITRPONN profanation.

OPRAD offence, fault.

OPRADI offender.

OPRAMPOR immense.

OPROMARTH arrogant, proud.

OPROMIT *f* immense, infinite.

OPROMITAI immensity.

OPURBAECHO, -I, -EM beloved in preference to others, darling, favourite.

OPURTO, -I, -EM insufficient.

OR *m* wedding-party.

ORAÇÃO prayer, oration.

ORAMCOR wicked.

ORATOR oratory.

ORC *m* glory, satisfaction.

ORCHIL excess, remaining.

ORCONDDUNC to grind gross, not fine, to grind quickly.

ORCOTT remaing.

ORD *n* half.

ORD-MOL half-price.

ORDI (DUDDU) *f* three annas & 4 pies.

ORDO half.

ORET VO NOURO *m* bride-groom.

ORF harp, also a mouth organ.

ORG *m* family house-hold.

ORG household, family.

ORG organ, musical instrument.

ORG-VAZOINAR organist.

ORLLO big.

ORI *f* a small milet.

ORIM *m* smith's anvil, bickern.

ORISTT *m* tall man, giant.

ORJI *n* application, petition.

ORJI CORUNC to apply, to make petition.

ORKESTR orchestra.

ORN tight.

ORNOLOLO, -I, -EM tied.

ORNONC to tie, to press.

ORNUNC to make tight.
OROMB beginning.
OROMB DIUNC VO OROMBUNC } to begin.
ORONC VO ORUNC to take.
ORONDDI *f* bundle of grass.
ORONN *n* fistula.
ORONNEM *f* desert, forest.
OROONN through, by, with.
OROU *m* grain, corn.
ORPONC to work hard.
ORS year, annual period of time.
ORT *n* garden.
ORTH *m* explanation.
ORTHUNC to explain.
ORTI esteem, value.
ORTICHO, -I, -EM esteemed.
ORTO, -I, -EM superior, high in merits.
ORUCH inappetency.
ORVAI VO ORVALLI (TONN) *f* green grass.
ORVALLI (SOROP) green snake.
ORVIM through, by, with.
ORVO, -I, -EM green, not ripe.
OS VO (CHOROB) *f* fat.
OSCOT weak, feeble, insignificant.
OSCOT CORUNC to weaken.
OSCOT ZAUNC to become weak.
OSCOTAI weakness, frailty.
OSO *m* contagion, infection.
OSO this side, like this.
OSO LAGONC to get contagion.
OSO LAUNC contaminate, to pollute, to corrupt, to spread cantagion.
OSOCT weak.
OSOCTAI, *f* weakness; debility.
OSOINAR *m* cultivator.
OSOLO, -I, -EM of this kind or quality.
OSONC VO NONDONC to last, flourish.
OSOSO,-XI,-XEM voracious, greedy to eat.
OSOSO VO OSOSPONN voracity, greediness to eat.
OSOSUNC to be greedy.
OSOUNC to take care of, to look after, to mind, to treat.
OSRAI VO OXIRAI narrowness.
OSRAUNC to make narrow or narrower, to straighten, to clasp.
OSRI *f* small room.
OSRO *m* hall.
OSSONC to fare prosperously.
OST *f* valuable article, thing.
OSTAD *m* antagonist, opponent, competitor, opposer.
OSTAD master, teacher, superior.
OSTAR VO VACOR *m* razor.
OSTOMTI *f* west.
OSTOMONC DIS to sun set.
OSTUR *n* thing.
OSUC *n* small pox.
OSUC VO ASUC small pox.
OSUR the piles.
OT *n* sun.
OTCAMI founder.
OTHOIM there, near by.
OTI *m* elephant.
OTIN *f* female elephant.
OTIR *n* versatile, fickle.
OTIRPONN inconstancy, unsteadiness.
OTLOLO, -I, -EM melted.
OTMO *m* soul.
OTONC to flow away, to blah

out; *boron olonc*, to overflow.
OTORON cheat, deceit.
OTOUNC p. OTUNC.
OTREC vo OTREG aspiration, earnest desire.
OTREGONC vo OTREGUNC to aspire, to desire ardently.
OTUNC to drain, to melt; *udoc olunc*, to empty water; *gantl olunc*, to melt a bell.
OU *m* bubo.
OU CADDUNC to work unwillingly, to untwist.
OU (DORACHO) twisting.
OU GALLUNC to twist.
OUCHIT suddenly.
OUCHITAEN suddenly, unexpectedly.
OCHITAI sally, spur.
OUCONC vo OUCUNC to know, to recognize.
OUDIXEA misfortune, ill-luck.
OUDUO yellow.
OUDUO ZAUNC to become yellow, to become pale.
OULLI *f* invited guest.
OULLIC *f* invitation.
OULLIC SANGONC to invite.
OULLO *m* invited guest.
OULLOLO, -I, -EM twisted; *oullolem lugotl*, woven cloth.
OUNDUM this year, in the current year.
OUTUBR october, the month of october.
OUUNC to twist.
OUVICHAR indescretion, imprudence.
OUVICHARI indescrete, reckless, imprudent.
OUVICHARIN inconsiderately.
OVIDEA inertness, indolence.
OVIDEACHO, -I, -EM OVIDEVONT inert, sluggish.
OVOGNNI vicious.
OXACHO, -I, -EM contagious; *ti pidda voxeachi*, that sickness is contagious.
OXADDO curse.
OXADDO GALUNC to curse.
OXARIR incorporeal.
OXECHO,-I,-EM full of fat, fleshy.
OXEM in this way, in this manner like this.
OXIG nastiness, sluttisnessh, obscenity.
OXIGAUNO,-I,-EM nasty, impure, obscene.
OXIGONC to be defiled.
OXIR narrow, straight.
OXIR VATT narrow path.
OXIRCAI *f* narrowness, not lenghty.
OXIRVOZON *n* blessing.
OZ *f* habit, custom.
OZ ASLOLO habituated, accustomed.
OZ CORUNC to accustom one's self, to habituate.
OZ NANTLOLO new, raw, lacking practice.
OZ ZAUNC to be accustomed, to be habituated.
OZAR *m* one thousand (1000).
OZARCAR *m* wealthy, rich, milionaire.
OZIB *m* ambassador.
OZIBI *f* ambassade.
OZIBI DIUNC to take ambassade.
OZON weighty, importance.

Ozondar weighty man, a person of importance.

Ozri intestines.

Ozro *m* diamond.

P

P the sixteenth letter of the Roman Alphabet.

Pac *n* feather.

Paċ pure; perfect.

Pacaddi *f* hut, shed.

Pacam caddunc to remove feathers.

Pacam futtonc to fledge.

Pacam pissuddunc to deplume.

Pacan vo Pacannim fator *m* very hard stone.

Pacancho,-i,-em feathery, winged.

Pacatto *m* wing.

Pacharem *n* wedge, quoim.

Pacharnem vo Pacharonn *n* salutation, visit of condolence.

Pacharunc to salute, to wish health, to pay a condolence visit.

Pacheman injury, offence.

Pachemanacho, -i, -em injurious, offensive.

Pachur brackish (water).

Pachurai *f* brackishness.

Pachvo (rong) green colour.

Pacli *f* petal, flower leaf.

Pacli dolleanchi *f* eye-lid.

Paclin white woman, European woman.

Paclo white man, European man.

Paco *m* bat.

Pacotte naslelem finless wingless.

Pacotto *m* wing.

Pacrum *n* bird, fowl.

Pactto wing, piece of cloth, rag.

Pad act of belching wind.

Padd mountain.

Padd *n* destruction, ruin.

Padd uncultivated, vacant; *ti zomin padd assa*, that ground is uncultivated: *tim goram paddonc asat*, those houses are vacant.

Padd corunc to destroy.

Padd poddonc to remain unused, to be ruined, to lose former prosperity.

Paddan sailing vessel.

Paddavi plucker.

Paddavi (sucnem) *n* wren; *padavi munis*, one that climbs on trees.

Paddco *m* steer.

Paddculem *n* calf.

Padd-do vo Podd-do curtain.

Paddgo fault-finder, exposing defects either real or imaginary.

Paddi young cow.

Paddo *m* gathering of fruits.

Paddo *m* ox.

Paddo envious, critical, evil-minded.

Paddos shed, protection against sun and rain.

Paddsan roof, top part of a building.

Paddunc to gather fruits; *narl paddunc*, to gather cocoanuts; *fatran amble paddunc*, to throw down mangoes by stones; *angac ec ful paddunc*, to paint a flower on the body; *to laca tondar paddla*, he tells him on his face.

PADONC to fart.

PADR CUR curate, assistant priest.

PADR TIU reverend uncle, respectful greeting of children addressed to a priest.

PADR VIGAR vicar, parish priest.

PADRI *m* priest, father.

PADRINCHO ZOMO clergy.

PADRIPONN priesthood.

PADRO, -EM windy person.

PADROAD patronage of mission.

PADXA VO PADXAI *m* king.

PADXAI emperor, king, chief ruler.

PADXAIC CADDUNC to depose a king.

PADXAIC SODREILO CADDUNC to dethrone a king.

PAE NASLOLEM callow, fatherless.

PAEAM PODDONC to prostrate, to confess one's gratitude, to ask favour.

PAEM feet, legs.

PAG *n* pay, salary.

PAGA BHAIR DUDDU emoluments.

PAGACHE MUNIS hirelings, salaried men.

PAGAMENT payment, salary, wages.

PAGAR *n* parapet.

PAGAR BANDUNC to build a parapet.

PAGEM *n* a cable to tow a ship along with a carpenter's plane, a kedge.

PAGER a casting net, a sweep net.

PAGER MARUNC to fish with the casting net.

PAGUI fisherman.

PAGUNC to fish with the casting net.

PAI *m* father.

PAI creator, progenitor.

PAI-TIU uncle, elder.

PAIC p. SIPAIC.

PAICUO *m* p. PAIKILLO.

PAIEANCHI GADDI cycle.

PAIKILLO VO PAICUO *m* privy, water closet.

PAIM *m* foot.

PAIM DAVO *m* left foot.

PAIM UZVO *m* right foot.

PAIM-EANCHE TALAT soles of the feet.

PAIM-EANCHIM BOTTAM toes.

PAINDD *m* lane.

PAINEL VO PAINOL *n* frame, picture.

PAINNEM *n* cradle.

PAINNEM ALOUNC to rock the cradle.

PAINSOR purpose, motive.

PAIPUS VO MOCHO *m* shoe, boot.

PAIZ a threat.

PAIZAN civilian, civilian's dress.

PAIZDAR threatener, intimidator.

PAKHO, -I, -EM clean, neat, clear, fair.

PAL canopy, pall.

PAL (MONZAT) small lizard.

PALAS *f* palace.
PALEUNC to sprout leaves, to bud.
PALKI *f* palanquin.
PALL (ZADDACHEM) root.
PALL FUTTONC to take roots, to root.
PALL GĔUNC to take root.
PALLAMBO *m* root.
PALLAMBONC VO PALLAM FUTTONC to take roots, to root.
PALLO obedience.
PALLO DINAM ZAUNC to disobey, to disregard.
PALLO DIUNC to obey, to comply with.
PALLOC p. RAJEDAR.
PALLONN goverment.
PALLUNC to maintain, to supply food, shelter and raiment, to bring up.
PALLUNC to excente, to perform.
PALMATOR *f* ferula.
PALO foliage,quantity of leaves.
PALO top end of woman's saree.
PALO DORUNC to assist, to work together,to sing with another.
PALOU a peak or point, top, head, summit.
PALOUNC to extinguish.
PALOUNC to put out, to extinguish.
PALSANN declivity, slope.
PALSO inclined, bent, indirect.
PALSO SORONC to go indirectly, to leave the straight road.
PALTAUNC VO PALTO CORUNC to observe, to spy.
PALTO spy, listener.
PALTO CORUNC VO PALUNC to observe, to spy.
PALU *m* stone fish.
PALVI thistle.
PAMPLIT *m* pamplet.
PAMPRAI a fib, a falsehood.
PAMPRER one that tells idle tales.
PAN KAŬNCHEM betel-leaf.
PAN (KOLO) *n* leaf.
PAN LUGOT *n* broad cloth.
PAN (PUSTOCACHEM) page.
PAN (VODCHEM) *n* tobacco.
PANAUNC VO DUD CADDUNC to milk.
PANC *m* bird-lime.
PANCH (five 5).
PANCHANG almanach.
PANCHANIM infive folds.
PANCHLAUM *n* metal.
PANCHVO fifth.
PANCO VO AINNOM fan; *pankean varem galunc*, to fan.
PANCONC to stick, to adhere, to cohere.
PANCOTT glutinous, sticking.
PANCOUNC to attach.
PANDIT scholar, teacher.
PANDREM *n* a cage.
PANDRO *m* skeleton.
PANDRO SOROP cobra snake.
PANDUDDU a pie, 12 th part of one anna.
PAN-EL plant yeilding betel-leaves.
PANG *f* favour, dependence, gratitude.
PANGI dependent-on, grateful.
PANGLEPONN *n* dependence, reliance.

PANGLO, -I, -EM VO / PANGO,-I,-EM — dependent, one that subordinates to another.

PANGO crook-legged.

PANGRAUNC to cover with a blanket etc.

PANGRONN VO / PANGRUNC VO / PANGURCHEM — *n* bed-cover such as sheet, blanket etc.

PANJIREM *n* cage.

PANKITT *n* glutinous, sticky.

PAṆNIM *n* water, tide.

PANOM *m* a teat, a breast.

PANON *m* soldering, solder, sodder.

PANRO SOROP *m* cobra snake.

PANSUNC to file.

PANT line, lineament.

PANTTEM, *n* VO / PANTTLI *f* — basket.

PANTTLON pair of trousers.

PANTTULO *m* a small basket.

PANVOL foot, step.

PANVOL GALUNC to start, to commence.

PANVOLL *f* soldering, sodder.

PANVOLI DIUNC to sodder, to mix, so that one part qualifies another.

PANVOLI VO PAUNLLI gutter tile; flaps, valance.

PANZ basket like a cage or with holes about it.

PANZONNC to speak much about, to agitate.

PANZONVO agitator, person speaking much about.

PANZREM *n* cage.

PANZRO *m* skeleton.

PAO *m* fulfilment, compliance.

PÃO, UNDDO loaf of bread.

PAOM *m* foot, leg.

PAONC to reach, to help, to assist; *aum cal mapxeam paulom*, yesterday I reached Mapuça, *to ixit mojea acantac pauta*, that friend helps me in my difficulties; *mozo thuim al pavo nam*, my hand does not reach there; *tichen rinn tica paulem*, she has received her debt or money.

PAOUNC to accompany, to extend, to satisfy; *avem Pedruc techem gor pasun pavoilo*, I accompagnied Peter up to his house; *kuntton amvem mozo al pavoilo*, by standing on tiptoes I extended my hand; *hem godxem amim sogleanim paoun kelem*, we equally divided the sweets among us.

PAP *n* sin.

PAP plaster, poultice.

PAP CORUNC to commit a sin.

PAP (SAIB) *m* pope.

PAPI *m* sinner.

PAPINN *f* female sinner.

PAPUS *m* shoe.

PAR *f* mango-seed.

PAR space of 3 hours, *donpar*, mid-day.

PAR ZAUNC to disappear.

PARAMOS *f* care.

PARAMPOR *f* perpetuity.

PARATUNC to entreat, to beseech.

PARCO, -KI, -KEM hiding.

PARCONNEM *n* riddle.

PARCONNNEM solution or explanation of a problem or riddle.

PARCUṄC to guess, to solve, to find out.

PARECAR *m* sentry.

PARECAR guard, sentinel.

PARKI *m* fortune-teller, sooth sayer, guesser.

PARO *m* sentry.

PARO *m* rough wall.

PARO CADDUNC VO / PARO GALUNC } to build a rough wall

PAROI *f* crow-bar.

PARONC to produce effect, to be efficacious.

PAROZ *m* quick silver ; *thondd thondd paroz*, very cold.

PARPOLL vagabond, licentious.

PARPOLLAI *f* licentiousness, libertinage.

PARPOLLPONN *n* p. PARPOLLAI.

PARPOTI *n* crier.

PARSEANCHEM POVITR zend-avesta.

PARTICUL particle.

PARTID party, faction.

PARTIDAR bigot, factious.

PARVE doves; *parveanchem gor*, dovecot.

PAS GALLUNC to make a knot.

PAS (IGORJEN) representation of a religious scene of the saviours' life.

PAS (VATTECHO) pass issued by competent official.

PASAM *n* raisins.

PAS VO FAS *m* knot.

PASCAM *f* easter.

PASO *m* liver.

PASO *m* socket, any hollow thing or place which receives and holds something else.

PASOT therefore.

PAST worse; *Pedru Forsu passt*, Peter is worse than Francis.

PASUN therefore, on account of.

PAT CORUNC (FATT CORUNC) to turn back.

PAT (FUL) *n* chives.

PAT (OLEACHEM) *n* the blade of an oar.

PAT (SAOZ) *n* gander.

PATALL the other end downward through the earth.

PATANG kite.

PATAUNC to extend, to unfold.

PATEM (DOLLEACHEM) *n* the eye-lid.

PATEM (PITTACHEM) *n* paste.

PATI *f* lamina, a copper-plate.

PATIENAR one that relies, trusty.

PATIENNEM *n* confidence, reliance.

PATIEUNC to confide, to trust in or to.

PATKI VO PATKIN sinner.

PATMAR *f* sailing ship.

PATMARCAR owner of a sailing vessel.

PATOC *n* sin, fault ; *mapatoc*, mortal sin ; *ubem patoc*, venial sin.

PATOC CORUNC to commit a sin.

PATOLL thin, rare.

PATOLLI a kind of pastry.

PATOU p. PATOLL.

PATOU CORUNC to rarefy.

PATOUNC to extend, to spread.

PATRIARC *m* Patriarch.

PATRON protector, patron, defender.

PATSEUNC to aggravate, to become worse than previously.

PATSEUNC (JIB) to feel a pungent taste.

PATT *f* back.

PATT *m* stripe or streak (in cloth).

PATT (BANDCHO) strap, leather strap, saddle-girth.

PATT CORUNC to make strap.

PATT FODDUNC to beat on the back.

PATTA-PATTI behind.

PATTA-PATTI VOCHONC to follow, to go behind, to persecute.

PATTI *f* beam.

PATTI URONC to delay.

PATTICHO CONNOM the spine.

PATTIM behind.

PATTIM GALUNC to leave behind.

PATTIM SORONC to draw back, to fall back, to recoil; *to vaurac patti soronam,* he does not refuse work.

PATTLEAN behind, previous.

PATTLO,-I,-EM previous, behind; *pattlem voros,* last year; *aum tuje pattlo,* I am next to you.

PATTLO-PAIM hind-foot.

PATTO *m* bridge.

PATTOUNC to send, to remit; to despatch.

PAU p. PALL.

PAU (MAP) *m* quarter, fourth part.

PAU (ZADDACDEM) *m* root.

PAULO, -I silver coin worth one quarter of a rupee.

PAUM-VATT foot-path.

PAUNC to accompany, to attend, to follow: *Luisac gor pasun pai,* accompany Luis up to his house; *Pedruche duddu pai,* pay Peter's money; *tuvemlachi codel paili?* have you returned his chair ? *tem gor kitleac paulem ?* at what amount was that house auctioned ? *Pedru alpem utor sodancal paita,* Peter always keeps his word; *tuvem techem soglem rin paileim?* have you paid up all his debts ?

PAUNDDO VO SOPONN *m* stap.

PAUNLEO eaves.

PAUNLI *f* gutter-tile, flaps, valance.

PAUNNE p. PAU (MAP)

PAUNNEM arrival, accompaniment; *nourea ocleche paunne,* retinue of the bride and bride groom.

PAUNNEM VO PAINNEM *n* cradle.

PAUNNER GALLUNC to sell by auction.

PAUNNIM sale by auction.

PAUNNINDAR auctioneer.

PAUNNOM LOC people joining a procession.

PAUNNO *m* one that accompanies, attendance.

PAUS *m* rain.

PAUS BARIC VO / PAUS XIDDXIDDO } small rain.

PAUS PODDONC to rain.

PAUS XENDONC to drizzle.

PAUSACHE DIS monsoon, wet season.
PAUSAO, -I, -EM rainy season.
PAUT ruler for drawing lines.
PAUTI *f* receipt.
PAUTT time, return ; *avem don pautti keleo Joseger*, I went twice to Joseph's house ; *maca don pautti zor ailo*, twice I had fever.
PAXANNIM FATOR *m* very hard stone.
PAXTT worse.
PAZ̃ equal.
PAZ stone steps on a steepy place.
PAZI *m* unfortunate unlucky.
PAZOR VO PAROZ quicksilver.
PAZRONC to infiltrate.
PAZUNC to edge, to sharpen.
PECLOLO,- I, -EM cured, healed.
PECONC VO PECOUNC to cure, to heal.
PECTO cure, healing.
PEDD *n* pedestal.
PEDD mound, a heap of earth (to cover the roots of trees).
PEDD CURSACHEM *n* pedestal of a cross.
PEDD (DANTIACHEM) *n* a piece of the mill.
PEDD (MASOLI) shad.
PEDDI shop.
PEDO *m* servant, grave digger.
PEI *f* distaf-ful; *capsachi pei*, the distaf-ful of cotton.
PEINNIM swimming, a float.
PEL *m* ball.
PELEACHO, -I, -EM of other.
PELEAN VO POILEAN further.
PELO, -I, -EM remote, far off.
PELO neighbour; *amim amchea peleacho mog corcho*, we must love our neighbour.
PEN *n* pen.
PEN (GARACHEM) wall.
PEN PATACHEM quill pen.
PEN TIKEACHEM steel pen.
PEN TINTACHEM fountain pen.
PENCOTT *n* waist.
PENDD *f* pinnace of cocoanut.
PENDDI *f* a small bundle.
PENDDI BANDUNC to pack in bundles.
PENDO ostentation, vanity.
PENDONC to be ostentation, to be vain.
PENDRO, -I, -EM vain boaster, person betraying false pride.
PENEDI *f* pendents.
PENNCUL *n* a small bundle.
PENNEM *n* stopping place.
PENNOC faggot, bundle, sheaf; *lonnachem pennoc*, bundle of grass.
PENSAUM *n* pension.
PENSIL *n* pencil.
PENTT *n* market, bazar.
PENTTECAR bazarman, shop-keeper.
PER *n* joint, juncture, junction; *bollachem per*, joint of the finger.
PER knot, knucle, joint; *uxichem per*, joint of the sugar-cane.
PER (FOLI) *n* goava.
PER (ZADD) *f* guava-tree.
PERGAUM *m* proclamation.
PERGAUM GALTA TO *m* crier.
PERI *f* p. GABOLLI.

PERUM *n* turkey.
PERUNC to sow.
PERZUNT *m* ham.
PETT *f* box.
PETT *m* beating.
PETT CADDUNC to beat.
PETT DUDDUANCHI coffer, safe.
PETT FOLINACHI box, trunk.
PETT GAVETANCHI cabinet.
PETTARO box of bamboo cane-work.
PETTLOLO, -I, -EM burning.
PETTNEM *n* beating instrument.
PETTNEM beater, pounder.
PETTO *m* dog.
PETTO DACTO *m* poppy.
PETTON to burn, to catch fire.
PETTOP beating, knock.
PETTOUNC to burn, to set fire.
PETTUL *n* a small box.
PETTUNC to thresh, to beat severely; *dorn pettunc*, to nivel the ground by beating; *bangar pettunc*, to flatten the gold ; *tallio pettunc*, to clap.
PEUN VOCHONC to go by swimming.
PEUNAR VO PEUNEDAR swimmer.
PEUNC to swim; *to noint peita*, he is swimming in the river.
PEUNIM *f* swimming.
PEZ *f* rice gruel, canji.
PIAU VO CANDO *m* onion.
PIC *f* product, crop.
PICANDOR *n* pick-axe, mattock.
PICAR VO PIKER in harvest time.
PICLOLO, -I, -EM riped.
PICO ripe; *o ambo pico*, this mango is ripe.
PICONC p. picunc ; *xel piconc*, to ripe the field or corn ; *kens picunc*, to get the hair white; *kensoli picunc*, to suppurate the furuncle.
PIDDA *f* sickness, disease.
PIDDA PARCUNC to diagnose.
PIDDA VOXEACHI contageous disease.
PIDDA ZAUNC to get disease.
PIDDAPID *f* persecution.
PIDDENT ASONC to be sick.
PIDDEVONT sick, diseased.
PIENN *n* drink.
PIGOLLONC to drip, to meet off.
PIL *n* chicken.
PILGI *f* generation.
PILI MORGI *f* tuckey-hen.
PILICAN *n* eagle.
PILLUC *f* piclo, fife.
PILLUNC to squeeze, to press, to wring ; *olem lugot pillunc*, to wring the wet cloth; *gollo pillunc*, to press the throat ; *nac pillunc*, to wipe the nose.
PILLUNC GOLLO to extort, to recover debts by harsh means or forcibly.
PILOT *m* pilot.
PIMPLLO *m* hole ; *te caillic pimpllo poddla*, that frying pan has got a hole.
PIMPOLL *m* *fecus indica.*
PINDD *f* fern.
PINDDONNIM envy, jealousy.
PINDDONNOM,-I,-EM jealous, envious.
PINDOUN *f* obstinacy, fury.

Pindounc to be obstinate, to be stiff in a purpose; *to Pedruc pindouta*, he has aversion to Peter.

Pingle kens *m* fair hair.

Pinglo, -i, -em bright, yellow, light.

Pinh *m* pine tree.

Pinhor *m* pledge, pawn.

Pinnea generation.

Pinnea mag irly posterity, generation to come.

Pinnea pattli past generation, ancestry.

Pint *n* gall.

Pintolli, Pituu *f* nettle.

Pintur *m* painter.

Pintvel *f* elephantiasis.

Pinzari *m* carder, wool-comber.

Pinzcor old, worn-out, a rag.

Pinzonc to tear, to rend, to burst.

Pionc to drink.

Pioncho,-i,-em drinkable, potable.

Pionn *n* drink.

Pionnar *m* drinker, swimmer.

Piop beverage, potion.

Pip *n* tub.

Pip dacttem keg.

Pip ugtem cask.

Pip voddlem barrel.

Pir *f* saucer.

Piradic vo / **Piraecho,-i,-em** } venerable, old man, elder.

Pirai *f* age; *matari pirai*, old age; *torni pirai*, youth.

Pirajit *n* penance.

Pirajit cornar *m* penitent.

Pirann *m* soul, spirit.

Pirapidd *f* persecution.

Pirapidd dinar tyrant, persecutor.

Pirder corunc to spoil, to corrupt, to deprave.

Pirluc *f* fife.

Pirluc vazounc to play a fife.

Pirt love, affection, dedication.

Pirtum universe, world.

Pirtumicho, -i, -em universal.

Piscari pumping instrument.

Piscati vo Suri *f* knife.

Piscati marunc to hit with a knife.

Pisddunc to pull off the leaves; *ful pisadunc*, to pull off the leaves of a flower; *cuzneran combiechim pacam pisuddlim*, the cook pulled off the feathers of the hen.

Pissai foolishness, folly.

Pisso, -i, -em foolish person.

Pitro *m* commemoration of the dead.

Pitt *n* flour.

Pitt marunc to powder with meal.

Pitt moulelem dough.

Pitt mouunc to knead flour.

Pitto *m* powder; *miriancho pitto*, pepper powder; *Pedrun moderache sallintlo pitto addla*, Peter has brought the saw dust from the timber-yard; *locondacho pitto*, filings.

Pitto marunc to dust, to powder.

Pittolli vo Bunchundi (sucnem) bull-bull.

PITTOU (NISTEM) *n* sheat-fish.

PITTULL vo PITTUU *f* brass; *angac pittuu futtonc*, to have erytema on the body.

PIUNC vo PILLUNC to squeeze, to press; *limbo piunc*, to squeeze lime; *nac piunc*, to wipe the nose.

PIXEM mad; *tem cheddum pixem*, that girl is mad.

PIXEM madness, foly.

PIXEM LAGONC to be mad.

PIXEPONN madness, foolishness.

PIXI *f* mad.

PIXPONN p. PIXEPONN.

PIZUNC to tear, to cut asunder, to make an opening.

POC *n* an overtopped navel.

POCHCO SORO *m* weak spirit.

POCHCOUNNIM brakish water.

POCHONC to digest, to prove harmless.

POCHPOCHIT milk-shop, worthless.

POCHPOCHO, -I, -EM babbler.

POCHPOCHOUNC to babble.

POCLLAI *f* hollowness, vacuum.

POCLLO vo POCOU empty, vacant.

POCORLI vo POCORN *f* shaft, cavity.

POCRUNC to sift, to pierce all over.

POCSO, -I, -EM watery, windy, fat but not strong, puffed up.

POCXEAM vo POCXIM better than; *Pedru pocxeam Andre boro*, Andre is better than Peter; *Anna Mari pocxeam odlem*, Anne is older than Mary; *ti achea pocxeam lann*, she is younger than her; *hea bala pocxeam tem bat chodd*, that rice is more than this.

POCXIM, OSTOMTI the west; the west wind.

POD *n* song.

PODD enfilade, chain; *chear fulanche podd*, four enfilades of flowers.

PÔDD (MAP) *f* measure, seer.

PÔDD (SUTACHO) *m* thread, string, wire.

PODDI porch.

PODDIT *n* loss.

PODDONC to fall, to drop; *aum dornir poddlom*, I fell down; *soponn poddonc*, to dream; *nid poddonc*, to sleep; *paim-eam poddonc*, to prostrate, to cast at the feet; *epar angar poddonc*, to suffer loss in business; *tallo poddonc*, to grow hoarse; *paus poddonc*, to rain; *visor poddonc*, to forget; *angac kotam poddonc*, to get marks on the body; *kinna poddonc*, to harden, to grow callous; *mateac korod poddonc*, to be bald headed; *taca aplench poddlam*, he thinks only of himself; *dis poddonc*, at sunset; *distti poddonc*, to appear; *sasuc anim sunenc borem poddonam*, the mother-in-law and the daughter-in-law are not living amicably; *sovoim poddonc*, to be accustomed; *patcant poddonc*, to fall in sin; *tuca kitle norl poddlal dor paddeac?* how many cocoanuts do you get for each crop? *reddo xetant kaunc poddla*, the buffalo is occupied in eating in the field.

PODDOS neighbourhood.

PODDOVEM *n* snake-gourd.

PODDOXI neighbour.

PODDSOUN work of filling up gaps, discussion, enquiry.

PODDSOUNC to fill up gaps in the corn-fields, to discuss, to enquire.

PÔDDZIR *f* epiglottes.

PODERKHON bakery.

PODEST rich, plentiful, opulent.

PODESTAI wealth, riches.

PODVELOLO,-I,-EM proud, insolent.

PODVENNC to become proud.

PODÊR *m* baker.

PODON *m* a god-father.

PODOR *m* end, extremity.

PODVEDAR *m* powerful; *sorvpodvedar*, all powerful.

PODVI *f* power, authorithy, strength.

POGDI *f* turban.

POGLONC UDOC to drop or tricle water.

POI VO POLLI *f* cake, bole.

POI (MADDACHI) spata, spathe.

POICO *m* article, subject, matter.

POILEAN there, yonder.

POILO first; *poilo put*, eldest son.

POILO,-I,-EM the other side, yonder; *to polle toddi asa*, he is on the other side.

POIR the day before yesterday, few days ago.

POIREAN every [illegible] day.

POIRO *m* the third day.

POIRO ZOR tertian fever.

POIS far, at a distance.

POIS ASUNC to be far, to be at a distance.

POIS CORUNC to remove, to put away, to separate.

POIS GALUNC to remove, to keep at a distance.

POISAUNC to lengthen, to leave or quit, to be far off.

POISILO p. POIXILO.

POISO *m* one pice.

POIXILEAN from far.

POIXILO,-I,-EM remote, far off.

POL *n* void, vacuum.

POL chaff.

POLAS *f* palace, court.

POLENNC to heal, to diminish the pain of a sore or would.

POLEUNC to become void.

POLKE GUNN superficial qualities.

POLKEO GOZÁLI useless gossip, idle conversations.

POLKO, -I, -EM hollow.

POLLA-POLL *f* flight, escape.

POLLAUNC to drive away, to put to flight.

POLLEUNC to see, to observe, to think, consider, to examine, to visit; *aum tuca pollelam*, I see you; *poilem tujem mon palle anim magir maca sang*, first consider yourself and then tell me; *voiz vaittacarac polleunc aila*, the doctor has come to visit the sick; *voiz vaittacarachi nadd polleta*, the doctor feels the pulse of

the sick man; *hem lugot borem zolear polle*, see if this cloth is good; *tuzo fuddar polle*, take care of your future.
POLLI *f* p. POI.
POLLIT ugly, dirty.
POLLITAI *f* deformity, ugliness.
POLLITPONN p. POLLITAI.
POLLONC to fly away, to flee.
POLLOUNC p. POLLEUNC.
POLLOUNC p. POLLAUNC.
POLLPCTTO, -I, -EM fugitive.
POLLTODD *f* across the river, the other side.
POLLTONN *f* regiment.
POLO *m* cheek.
POLONC to become void.
POLONG *m* bedstead, a furnished bed.
POLONGPUX *m* bed-sheet.
POLTODDI-VOCHONC to go across the water.
POMAD *m* pomatum, pomade.
PONCHEANG calendar, almanach.
PONCŎT *f* banquet, festival, social gathering.
POND bottom.
PONDA at the bottom, below.
PONDCHEAN from below, from the bottom.
PONDEN large drain on a roof made of suitable tiles for rain-water.
PONDEN-ACHE NOLLE tiles suitable for drains of rain-water.
PONDEU *m* canoe.
PONDIAM from the bottom.
PONDLEAN from below, interiorly.
PONDRA fifteen (15).
PONDROS *f* fortnight.
PONG *n* hump.
PONGO, -I, -EM hump backed.
PONJI *f* great-grand-mother.
PONJO, PONZO *m* great-grand-father.
PONNOS (ZAD) jack fruit tree.
PONNOS (FOLL) *n* jack-fruit.
PONNSUL small jack-fruit.
PONTTI *f* small lamp.
PONTTI, PONTURUM *f* great-grand daughter.
PONTTU *m* great-grand-son.
PONVONC to drop water.
POPAI *f* papaw.
POPAI (ZADD) *f* papaw-tree.
POPIS *n* lung.
POPLI small hand-made bread.
POPSO fat, portly.
POR *n* before yesterday; *cal-por*, a few days ago.
POR *m* orphan; *Rama melo anim tache dog por asat*, Rama died and he leaves two orphans.
POR, PILO *m* brood of animals.
PORAI *f* orphanage.
PORAM-PORIM differently, diversely.
PORATUNC to beseech, to implore.
PORBEM congratulation.
PORBEM DIUNC to congratulate.
PORBU indian caste.
PORCAR vicissitudes, change of circumstances.
PORCAR manner, behaviour.
PORCAS light, splendour, brilliancy.
PORCHO,-I,-EM of before yesterday.

Porco, -ki, -kem stranger, new.
Porcond honour, respect.
Porcondunc to praise or commend.
Pordan secretary, minister of state.
Pordês exile, foreign country.
Pordexi *m* exiled, stranger.
Porganv foreign country.
Porgott propagated, diffused.
Porgott corunc to propagate, to generate, to diffuse.
Porgottai propagation.
Porgottunc to propagate, to generate, to diffuse.
Pori female of angelic form and beauty.
Poriallo *m* deluge, flood.
Poriant up to, till.
Poricxa *f* experience, knowledge, examination.
Porim mood, manner; *he porim*, in this manner or way.
Porim-porinni in various ways.
Poripurn abundant, plenty.
Poripurnai *f* abundance, opulence.
Poripurnaien abundantly.
Porjecho, -i, -em public, popular.
Porl *n* hearth.
Porma venereal disease.
Pormesvor *m* God.
Pormoll *m* scented smell, perfume, fragrance.
Pormoll diunc to give scented smell to perfume, to embalm.
Pormoll eunc to smell, to scent, to discover.
Pormoll geunc to inhale, to smell.
Pormollonc to smell, exhale.
Pormonn oath, curse, blasphemy.
Pormonn corunc vo / **Pormonn diunc** } to swear to take one's oath.
Pornello, -i, -em vo / **Porno, -i, -em** } old, used.
Pornipat adoration.
Pornipat corunc to adore.
Porno call old times, antiquity.
Porno zaunc to become old.
Poro far, separate, beyond; *poro rau*, stand separate, *tuguçlea gora poro*, beyond your house; *aro poro*, soon, in a short time.
Poro soronc to be separate, to get away.
Porob *f* feast, festival.
Porob corunc to celebrate a feast, to solemnize.
Poromukim by means of another.
Poros more than.
Porosporim alternately.
Poroston foreign country.
Porostonni stranger.
Porot vochonc to turn back.
Porounnim moan, wail.
Porsonn zaunc to succeed, to attain an end.
Porsum orchard, garden.
Portador *m* bearer.
Porteri passport.
Porti zab *f* reply, answer.

PORTI ZAB DIUNC to reply, to answer.

PORTIPAU reply, answer.

PORTO, -I, -EM up side down.

PORTONC to turn, to change, to return.

PORTOPAU reply, answer.

PORTOPAU CORUNC to reply, to answer.

PORTUN DIUNC to restore, to return, to give back.

PORTUN EUNC to return, to come back.

PORTUN GALUNC to replace, to reestablish.

PORTUNC to turn, to turn about, to turn round.

PORUM last year.

PORUMCHO, -I, -EM of last year.

PORVA care, obedience.

PORVA CORUNC to obey.

PORVAM after to morrow.

PORVANCHO of the other day.

PORVONIM *f* groan, mourn, complaint.

PORVOT *m* mountain.

PORVUNC to groan, to wail, to mourn, to sigh.

PORXELI fisher, fishing with hands.

PORXENNEM touching, feeling, groping.

PORXEUNC to hand, to touch, to feel, *porxeun masolli dorunc*, to fish by feeling.

PORZA *f* people, population.

PORZOL splendour, brillianey.

PORZOLIT brilliant, shining.

PORZOLUNC VO PORZOUNC to shine, to glitter, to sparkle, to be bright.

POSCO, -KI, -KEM adopted; *posco pai*, foster father; *posco put*, adopted son.

POSCOTTO *m* bladder.

POSLOLO, -I, -EM fed, domesticated; *to ducor poslolo, ranantlo noi*, that pig is domesticated and not of the jungle.

POSONC to live, to feed upon, to eat.

POSONN *n* food, nutrition.

POSORCAR shop keeper.

POSRO *m* shop, stall.

POSUNC to feed, to support, to domesticate.

POT *n* diet.

POT *f* richess, property.

POT CORUNC to be on diet.

POTEAN GALUNC to put in a sack, to sack.

POTEM *n* sack, bag.

POTI *f* small bag, satchel; *poti dudduanchi*, money bag.

POTI, OOU *m* husband.

POTONG VO PISOLEM *n* a small butter-fly.

POTOTONC VO PORTONC to return, to come back.

POTREM zinc.

POTRI VO KHOLI *f* a dried leaf.

POTRIC VO ROC *f* letter.

POTT *n* belly.

POTT BORUNC to eat, to earn one's means of livelihood.

POTT ZAUNC to be pregnant in consequence of illicit amours.

POTTACHO, -I, -EM of belly (fig) ilegitimate child.

Pottaro *m* a great eater.
Pottarth *n* gluttony.
Pottarth p. pottaro.
Pottarthponn gluttony.
Potti *f* book; *burge apli potti vachiat,* boys' are reading their book.
Pôtti *f* a patch of cloth, satches.
Pôtti *f* lamina, a copper plate.
Pottic *m* prawn.
Pottio glutton, excessive eater.
Pottli *f* a truss, a pack.
Pottli bandunc to pack.
Pottnno,-i,-em glutton, a great eater.
Potto *m* belt.
Pounllem coral.
Povecho public, popular.
Povitr sacred, holy.
Povitr corunc to consecrate.
Povitrponn consecration, holiness.
Poxeunc to caress, to sooth, to fondle, axeunc poxeunc, to caress, to smooth, to fondle.
Pozddeponn nastiness, impurity.
Pozddo, -i, -em nasty, slovenly, obscene, impure.
Pracas light, brightness.
Prachit diunc to give penance.
Prachit vo **Pirajit** *n* penance.
Pramos care.
Prann vo **jiv** vo **otmo** soul, spirit.
Prann vochonc, vo **prann soddunc** to die, to expire.
Prapti worthy, deserving, meritorious.
Prartonn prayer, supplication.
Prasanga for instance.
Prat propitious, useful.
Pratonnem entreaty, prayer.
Preg *f* bodice.
Pregador *m* preacher.
Prelad prelate.
Prem *m* prize, reward.
Prem vortato prize winner.
Prestau *m* cause, reason.
Pret vo **Moddem** *n* corpse, dead-body.
Prieo vo **Priev** esteem, estimation.
Priti vo **Mog** *m* love, affection, tenderness.
Pritivont affectionate.
Pritum *f* universe.
Procar feature, mode, manner.
Procoll arrogant.
Procurador *m* solicitor.
Produar *m* adultery.
Produari *m* adulterer.
Produari *f* adulteress.
Profet *m* prophet.
Progott public.
Progott corunc to public, to propagate, to diffuse.
Promannim vo / **Promonnim** vo / **Ea porim** } in this manner or way.
Promonn swearing, oath.
Promonn corunc to swear, to take an oath.
Promott supernatural cause.
Pros p. **Poros.**
Prosad *m* oracle.
Prosadaunc to consult an oracle.
Prosong accidently, by chance.
Prosonn p. **Porsonn.**

Prosud deliverance, child birth.
Prosud zaunc to bring forth young.
Proti vo Mog *m* love, affection.
Protigaz echo.
Protipall reply, answer.
Protivadi defendant before a court of justice.
Protivont dear, kind.
Protom in the beginning, at first.
Protomlem fol first production.
Protomolo, -i, -em first, principal, chief.
Proton *n* prayer, supplication, entreaty.
Protum *f* universe.
Protuvi land.
Prus *m* male.
Prusotann mankind, humanity.
Pu *m* matter, pus.
Pu mandonc to form pus.
Pudd (nacacho) nostril.
Pudd powder; *tea addamchi pudd cor*, reduce those bones to powder.
Puddem *n* p. **Bidd-ddem.**
Puddo *m* a mallet, a small parcel a packet; *chaucho puddo*, a packet of tea.
Pudin *n* pudding.
Pulaunnem suppuration.
Pulaunnem zunc, to suppurate.
Puleunc to suppurate
Pulpit *n* pulpit.
Pun p. **Punem.**
Pundd *m* a highway man.
Punem *n* merit.
Punevont deserving, worthy, meritorious.
Punn but; *tum boro borgu asloi punn alam vait zaloi*, you were a good boy, but now you are spoiled; *hem dinaim zaliar tempunn di*, if you don't give this, give at least that.
Punnam punnam frequently, ly, often.
Punnim p. **Punn.**
Punoum *f* full moon.
Punza, Puja worship.
Punzaunc to gather, to assemble.
Punzo *m* gathering.
Pur *f* city.
Puraton tradition.
Purau *m* satisfaction.
Purau diunc to satisfy.
Purem sufficient.
Purg *n* physic, purgative.
Purgator *f* purgatory.
Puri *f* city.
Purling masculine.
Purnim cementing work on building.
Puro enough.
Puro corunc to stop, to halt, to satisfy; *taca udoc puro corunc sang*, tell him to stop the water, *tica diun mojean puro cori nozo* I cannot satisfy her.
Puro zaunc to suffice, to be enough, to satisfy; *tuca tem udoc puro zalem*? did that water sufficed you ? *maca uloun puro zalem*, I was tired by speaking.

Purot p. **Puro.**

Purounc to like; *tuca puroita zaliar victem ge*, buy if you like; *ti cornim corunc maca puroi nam*, I cannot afford to do that action.

Purounc to fill up.

Purounc to fill with rubbish, *ti baim mati poddon purouli*, that well was filled up by mud.

Purounc to groan, to wail, to moan, to sigh, (of certain birds) to coo.

Purounc vo **Puro corunc** to provide, to purvey, to supply.

Purounnin groan, moan, complaint.

Purto,-i,-em equal, sufficient, like; *aple purto tannem soiro adla*, he has brought a guest like himself; *tachea purtem mojean cori nozo*; I cannot do as he likes.

Purunc to cover with earth, to burry, to close.

Purvilo,-i,-em former, ancient.

Purvim formerly, before, in ancient time.

Purvincho, -i, -em former, ancient, of old.

Purvo oriental.

Purvoz ancestor.

Puscoll very much.

Pusovam flower, blossom, bloom.

Pusovonc to flourish, to bloom, to flower.

Pusti *f* favour.

Pustivont protector.

Pusnnc to wipe, to clean; *fatravelim acxeram pusunc*, to wipe the letters from the slate; *naloch ang pusunc*, to wipe the body after bathing.

Put *m* son.

Putli, venetian coin.

Putnnem *f* niece (brother's daughter).

Putnnio, vo **Putno** *m* nephew (brother's son).

Putr *m* son.

Puttounc to agree, to be of the same opinion, to please; *tuca cosem puttoulem vaitl corunc*, how did it please you to do evil.

Puz point, full stop.

Puza *f* sacrifice.

Puza corunc to sacrifice.

Puzad *n* inn.

Puzad diunc to keep boarders.

Puzadcar inn-keeper.

Puzunc to sacrifice.

Q

Q the seventeenth letter of the Roman Alphabet.

Quadrad square, four sides being equal.

Quadril square dance.

Quaresm lent.

Quart room, fourth part.

Quartel quarter.

Queij *m* cheese.

Quellem plantain.

Queimbo plantain-tree.

Queisco, -ki, -kem intriguing, capable of carrying tales.

Queix complaint, accusation.

QUELLUNC to entertain.
QUESTANV dispute, discord.
QUIZIL intrigue.
QUIZILI MUNIS intriguer.

R

R the eighteenth letter of the Roman Alphabet.
RABNAR dweller, inhabitant ; one stopping for some purpose.
RABNNEM *n* waiting.
RABONC to wait.
RAC ashes.
RACNNOM *m* guardian, protector, shepherd; *anj guard*, guardian angel; *gorvam racnnom*, shepherd.
RACONC to keep, to preserve, to watch, to guard, to defend; *gorvam raconc*, to put the catle into pasture; *upordes raconc*, to observe the commandments.
RACONN watch, vigilance, care.
RACOS *m* monster.
RACXIN she-monster, fierce woman.
RAG anger.
RAGABORIT furious, raging.
RAGAR furious, raging.
RAGAR ZAUNC to get angry, to be angry.
RAGIST ill-tempered,(fig) choleric.
RAI nobleman, aristrocrat.
RAIA *m* a petty king.
RAIBAR *n* mediation.
RAIBARI *m* mediator.
RAJ *n* kingdom.
RAJ-CARBAR the administration of a state.
RAJ-CARBARI minister, high official of a state.
RAJEDAR *m* governor.
RAJVODD *n* empire.
RAJI consented.
RAJI willing, agreeable.
RAJI ZAUNC to consent, to agree.
RAJI ZAVOP *n* resignation.
RAJINAMA resignation.
RAJINAMA DIUNC to resign a post.
RAJVODDKI *f* government.
RAM *m* palm.
RAM salutation, greeting.
RAMACHO AITAR *m* Palm-Sunday.
RAMOSI private policeman.
RAMP *m* colour.
RAMPONC to redden, to grow red.
RAMPONC to get coloured.
RAMPONN *f* fishing net.
RAMPONN MARUNC to throw fishing net, to catch fish, (fig) to gather together, to collect.
RAMPOUNC to colour.
RAN *n* bush-wood, bush, wood.
RANANTULO, -I, -EM wild, woodish.
RAN-COMBI *f* wood-cock.
RANCOTTI wild, uncivilised.
RAND *m* widower.
RANDD concubine, mistress.
RANDD BAIL VO RANDDAU *f* widow.
RANDD ZAUNC to become widow or widower.
RANDDGUEPONN state of a widower.

RANDDPON *n* widowhood.
RANDO *m* dough, paste.
RANDON *f* fire place.
RANDOP *n* cooking.
RANDPI *m* cook.
RANDPIN *f* female cook.
RAN-DUCOR *m* wild-boar.
RANDUNC to cook.
RANIAM through a forest.
RANIO, -I, -EM wild, woodish.
RANNIM *f* queen.
RAONĀ farewell, dismissing, takeing leave.
RAONĀ CORUNC to dismiss, to discharge, to send away.
RAONC to wait, to stop, to dwell in, to reside in ; *to tuca vatler raota*, he waits you on the road ; *hea garan conn raota?* who resides in this house ?
RAS *f* heap.
RAS CORUNC to heap up, to accumulate.
RAT (zoc) *m* pound.
RAT *f* night.
RAT ZAUNC to grow night.
RATCHEM JEVON *n* supper.
RATER *m* trap.
RATRICHO, -I, -EM nightly, happening at night.
RATT *n* wheel.
RATT(SUTACHEM) *n* reel,spindle.
RATT VO / RATAOL (vaur) *f* work, labour.
RAUNC to wait, to stop.
RAUNNAR *m* resident, dweller.
RAUNNEM waiting.
RAUNS *m* sturgeon.
RAVANC to hatch.
RAVOILELEM *f* maid-servant.
RAVOILOLO *m* man-servant.
RAVULO *m* palace.
RAXI heap.
RAXI country liquor of weak strength.
RAXIC in a heap, mixed up; *te tanduu raxic gol*, make a heap of that rice; *tem batt te raxic boglat*, they enjoy the property in common.
RAXICHEM BENS joint family property.
RAZA king, governor.
RAZ-ANGON a yard.
RAZÃO reason, logic.
RAZÃO reason.
RAZDONI *f* capital.
RAZEDAR *m* governor.
RAZU *m* rope.
RAZVODD *f* kingdom.
REB *n* mud, mire..
REBEC *n* violin, fiddle.
REBECAUM *m* double-bass.
REBECAUM DACTO violencello.
RECAD compliments.
RECET prescription.
RECIT receipt,acknowledgment.
RED *f* veil.
REDDCO young buffalo.
REDDI *f* she buffalo.
REDDO *m* he buffalo.
REDDUC *f* young she buffalo.
REDOND MEZ round table.
REDRANCHI ZAT class of toddy-drawer.
REFETOR *f* refectory.
REFORM pension on retirement from the public service.
REFORMAD pensioner, retired from the public service.

REITOR prefector, or rector.
REITOR jackof the playing cards.
REJIDOR chief village official.
REJIMENT *m* regiment.
REJIMENT armancho infantry.
REJIMENT GODDEANCHO cavalry.
REJIMENT NALLINCHO artillery.
REKINT *n* clarionet in E b.
RELIC token, something reminding of anbasent person.
RELOJ *f* watch, clock.
RELOJER *m* watch-maker.
REMATIZM *n* rheumatism.
REND *n* lace.
REND (USUL) *m* income.
RENDCAR *m* renter.
RENDEIR toddy-drawer.
RENG *f* file.
RENJI *f* matter, pus.
RENTTO germ in a sore.
RENVALL sands, sandy ground.
RENVOTT sandy, abounding with sand.
RENZONC to suffer chronic disease enzonnim, chronic disease.
REODD sandy.
REODD anything round and spiral winding of a serpent.
REODD GALUNC to roll round or about, to curl up.
REODD GAUM sandy village.
REODDONC to roll, to wind.
REODDUNC to roll, to tie round.
REONT CORUNC to chew, to ruminate.
REPIC *f* chime.
REPOST reply, answer.
RETRAT likeness, picture, photo.
REUM *f* sand.
REVEZ *n* screech-owl, owl.
REVODD coil, twist.
REVODD-CANTTI rod of an axle.
REVONT ZAUNC tosuffer from illness due, as supposed to eating in the presence of a greedy person.
REZM *n* ream.
RICAMBO, -I, -EM VO } idle, not
RICAMI VO } occupied,
RICAMO, -I, -EM } empty.
Aum ricambo asam, I am idle; *tem aidon ricambem asa*, that vessel is empty.
RIG *m* admittance, entrance.
RIGAU p. RIG.
RIGO,-I,-EM VO } just now.
RIGOCH }
RIGONC to enter, to go inside.
RIGOUNC to make one enter, to put inside.
RIGUNC to enter, to introduce.
RINN *n* debt.
RINN CADDUNC to borrow money.
RINNCARI *m* debtor.
RINNDARI, RINNDINNAR *m* creditor.
RINNTO *m* vegetable soap.
RINTTEACHEM ZAD *n* vegetable soap-tree.
RISC *f* line.
RISC peril, danger.
RISC MARUNC to rule (a paper).
RISCAR CORUNC to strike off.
RISCO MARUNC to rule or draw lines.
RIT *f* custom, usage, form, order.
RIT DACOUNC to explain a method, to teach a custom.

RIT XICOUNC to train, to educate.

RITI BHAILO unfettered by custom, unorthodox.

RITICHO, -I, -EM customary, habitual.

RITIN formally, properly.

RITIN CHOLONC to behave properly, to follow popular customs.

RITIN DOURUNC to arrange, to put in order.

RITO, -I, -EM empty.

RITO CORUNC to empty.

ROANN *f* brooding, hatching.

ROANNENC BOSSONC to hatch, to brood.

ROANNINCHI COMBI brooding hen.

ROBOR, ROBON rubber, rubber goods.

ROC of course, a term of self-justification.

ROCHNAM *f* creature.

ROCHNAR *m* creator.

ROCHUNC to create; *Devan Sorg anim sounsar rochlo,* God created the heaven and earth.

ROCO *m* letter.

ROCODDE DUDDU cash down, payment on demand.

ROCODDO, -I, -EM quick, immediate.

ROCSALO cavalry, mounted troops.

RODD lamentation, wail of complaints.

RODDCUO,-I,-EM somewhat sad.

RODDIO,-I,-EM weeping, in tears.

RODDONC, RODDUNC to cry, to weep; *combo roddla,* cock crows; *ducor roddonc,* to grunt; *manki roddonc,* to croak; *undir roddonc,* to chirp; *natuc roddonc,* to pule; *colo roddonc,* to howl, to yelp; *goddo roddonc,* to neigh; *xelli roddonc,* to bleat; *uu-duiam roddonc,* to weep bitterly.

RODDNEM *n* cry, weeping.

RODDUNC p. RODDONC.

ROG *m* sickness, illness.

ROGDDO *m* millstone.

ROGDDOP *n* unction, ointment.

ROGDDUNC to rub, to apply.

ROGIO,-I,-EM sickly, unhealthy.

ROGOT *n* blood.

ROGOT NAM TOSLI PIDDA anaemia.

ROGOT TONDDAR EUNC to blush.

ROGOT VOSNEM hemorrhage.

ROGOTPINTI *f* elephantiasis.

ROGSUNC to eat voraciously.

ROGTABORIT sanguinary, bloody.

ROGTAILO,-I, -EM sanguine, sanguineous.

ROGUEUNC to suffer from a chronic disease.

ROI *f* a small bit.

ROINN *f* nest of ants.

ROIS *f* custom, style.

ROIT subject people, people of a state.

ROJA *f* permission, leave.

ROJA DIUNC to grant leave, to dismiss.

ROJEN ASSONC to be on leave.

ROLUO *m* precious stone.

ROM rum, a kind of liquor.

ROMARI pilgrimage.
ROMBONC to strike, to penetrate.
ROMPI VO ROMPO a small plant.
ROMOTT drum.
RONG *m* colour.
RONGARI painter, dyer.
RONGI *m* dyer.
RONGONC to redden, to growred.
RONGOUNC to paint, to colour, to imbue.
RONGTTO painted.
ROS *m* juice, sap.
ROS CADDUNC to extract juice, to overwork.
ROS NARLANCHO milk of cocoanuts.
ROS TAD abandoned, useless, dispised.
ROSMACHO, -I, -EM silken made of silk.
ROSMIM *f* satin.
ROSNI light, sunshine, brightness.
ROSROSSIT brilliant, beautiful, charming.
ROSROSSONC to shine brightly, to produce impression of beauty and splendour.
ROSSACHO, -I, -EM juicy, full of sap.
ROST face, likeness of face.
ROSTAD PODDONC to be unfit and helpless.
ROSTEAR PODDONC to be homeless.
ROSTO *m* road.
ROT cane, walking stick.
ROTANCHO,-I,-EM made of canework.
ROU *m* sprout seeds.
ROUNC to sow.
ROUNTO *m* hand-worm.
ROUNTUNC to ruminate.
ROUP clothes, clothing, wardrobe.
ROUPEIR clothier, dealer in piece goods.
ROVI *f* small piece.
ROVIS *f* style, custom.
ROVO *m* small bit.
ROVONT *f* rumination.
ROVONTUNC to ruminate, to brood upon a subject.
ROXIM *n* silk.
ROZ *n* rose.
RŌZ *f* rose-tree.
ROZAD rosy, rose coloured.
ROZAI mattress, cushion.
ROZAR prayers, act of devotion.
ROZAR CORUNC to pray, to meditate on spiritual matters affecting one's self.
ROZ-MORO daily wages.
RUBIM *f* ruby.
RUC *m* tree.
RUCH taste.
RUCH LAGONC VO RUCHONC to taste, to savour, to like, to be fond of.
RUCHIC relishing, savoury, pleasing.
RUCHIC LAGONC to be pleased with, to taste.
RUCHICHO, -I, -EM appetising, fond of satisfying one's tastes.
RUCHONC to like, to be tasteful or suitable.
RUDAN weeping, lamentation.

RUDAN CORUNC to mourn, to lament, to weep.
RUMBDDI *f* the plough-tail.
RUMBODD wild fig-tree.
RUMBRAM *n* wild figs.
RUND broad.
RUNDAI breadth.
RUNDAUNC to widen, to extend, to expend, to stretch.
RUNDI breadth.
RUNDOUNC to grow wide.
RUNV *n* ulcer.
RUP feature, face.
RUP NANTLO, -I, -EM ugly, deformed.
RUPCAR photo, likeness.
RUPEA BHAXEN argent.
RUPEM *n* silver.
RUPEST beautiful.
RUPIA *m* rupee.
RUPNEM *n* photograph.
RUPNEM *n* features.
RUPNEMCAR *m* photographer.
RUZAI rosary, roll of beads.
RUZONC to roots, to take roots.
RUZU certain.
RUZU CORUNC to certify; *rinn ruzu corunc*, to verify the debt.
RUZU ZAUNC to enlist.

S

S the nineteenth letter of the Roman Alphabet.
SA CORUNC to close a bargain.
SABAGI fortunate, happy.
SABAGINI fortunate, happy.
SABAR many; *sabar loc thuim aslo*, many people were there, *sabar manus coxl cortatt*, many people are working.
SABARANCHO, -I, -EM public, general.
SABRI MAN *f* a hollow bamboo.
SABSUBO in vain.
SABU *m* soap.
SAC *m* sack, bag.
SACADAM jutties.
SACADOR *m* collector.
SACALL early, soon; *zaito sacal asa*, it is very early; *call sacallim*, yesterday morning; *sacallim, ie, sanj coru naca*, come early and do not be late.
SACALLINCHO,-I,-EM of morning.
SACAROLH *f* cork-screw.
SACOR *f* sugar.
SACOR, CODDI *f* loaf-sugar.
SACOR LIMBO *m* orange.
SACOR VICTA TO *m* grocer.
SACRICHO,-I-EM sweetened with sugar, sweet.
SACTTO drunkaid.
SACXI testimony, evidence.
SACXI DIUNC to give evidence.
SACXI VO SACXIDAR *m* witness.
SACXIDAR *m* witness.
SAD *m* sound, echo.
SAD COMBEACHO cock's crow.
SAD GALUNC to cry, to proclaim.
SADAUNC to sing, to cry; *combo sadaita*, the cock crows.
SADAUNC to cry, to proclaim, to divulge.
SADD the act of making blunt, the act of taking off the edge or point.
SADD GALLUNC to blunt, to dull, (fig) to enervate, to dull.
SADD PODDONC to be blunted,

dulled: *he suriec sadd poddlea*, this knife is blunt.

SADDI woman's dress.

SADDO bride's dress.

SADE TIN three and half; *sade chear rupia*, four and half rupees.

SADEPONN sincerity.

SADEPONNIM, sincerely.

SADO,-I,-EM simple, pure, innocent, plain, sincere, common, ordinary, smooth; *em cagol xikeachem temsadem*, this paper is sealed that is plain; *em follem nocxechem dusrem sadem*, this plank is carved the other is smooth; *to manus sado*, that man is simple or sincere.

SADO SORO *m* weak liquor.

SADONO, -I, -EM capable, dexteroux.

SADU brother or sittes-in-law, a term confined to persons who are married to two brothers or sisters.

SADU ascetic person, religious beggar.

SAEL *m* teakwood tree.

SAF clean, chaste, pure.

SAFAI cleanliness, purity.

SAFIR saphire.

SAFLO teakwood tree.

SAGÔR *m* ocean, sea.

SAGRAD sacred, holy.

SAGRAD *f* tabernacle.

SAGUAD *f* present, gift.

SAI *f* cream; *dudachi sai*, *cream* of milk.

SAI ink.

SAI (NESCHI) petticoat.

SAIA VO SOIA physionomy.

SAIB lord, master, owner of a thing, sir; God, the sacrament of the Holy Eucharist.

SAIBACHEM FUL passion flower.

SAIBIKI dominion, command.

SAIBIN *f* lady.

SAIBINIM lady, a mistress, Dame.

SAIDI *f* witness.

SAIPAKI *m* cook.

SAIPAKIN *f* a woman cook.

SAIT cold.

SAL *f* the outer cover of a fruit; *keleachi sai*, the outer cover of a banana.

SAL *n* hall.

SAL VO VOROS year.

SAL ZADDACHI bark.

SALAMI exchange of greetings and courtesies.

SALAMOTIN without any mishap, safely; *salamotin pavonc*, to reach safely.

SALL school, shop.

SALL establiment, factory, workhouse; *camarachi sall*, a smith's shop, smithy; *burge sallint vetat leunc anim vachunc siconc*, boys are going to school to learn to read and write.

SALL forge.

SALLANDOR VO SALLERI VO SALLI VO SAL } porcupine; *amim ranant don sallandranchim poram dorlint*, we caught two young ones of the porcupine in the forest; *te dollint eoc sall asa*, there is a porcupine in that den.

SALLO VO SAVOC (ZADD) *n* lotus tree.

SALLOC (FULL) lotus.

SALS purgative salts. [fire.

SALUTT, SULUTT salute of gun-

SALV salver.

SAMBALL care, protection.

SAMBALLI protector, guide.

SAMBALLNAR protector, preserver.

SAMBALLONC to keep, to preserve one's self; *mojea atan samballonam*, it cannot be hold in my hand; *tem malear samballonam*, it cannot be carried on the head.

SAMBALLUNC to keep, to save; *Josen aple lagim sogle duddu sambaule*, Joseph kept all the money with himself; *connsamballita team burgeanc?* who is taking care of those children? *zo conn Devachem xastr samballita ta bagevont*, those who keep the law of God are blessed; *tachean apli jib sambullu-nozo*, he cannot hold his tongue; *apnnem aple caide samballunc zai*, one must do his duty.

SAMBAR spice, seasoning.

SAMBARI dealer in spices.

SAMBCAILO, -I, -EM facing, being in front of.

SAMBCAR opposite to.

SAMBOI *n* pocket.

SAMBOLKAR arsenic.

SAMBOLLI *f* pouch.

SAMCO, -KI, -KEM straight, right, *hi vatt samki*, this way is straight; *samki nit cor*, do the justice correctly.

SAMCO VOCHONC to go straight.

SAMKILO, -I, -EM frontier, that which is on the front.

SAMOGORI *n* household-goods.

SAMON *n* furniture, goods.

SAMP snake.

SAMPADDNEM conclusion, finishing touch.

SAMPADUNC to terminate, to put an end, to finish.

SAMPDDAUNC to catch, to arrest, to pounce, to detain.

SAMPDONC to be caught.

SAN *f* a broom.

SAN MARUNC to sweep with a broom.

SAN VACXANI economy.

SANCHRISTÃO sacristan.

SANCLAUNC to chain.

SANCNOLLI VO (SANCNOI) VO SOCNOLLI *f* } the throst, gullet.

SANCOW *m* a pool, bridge.

SANCRIST vestry, sacristy.

SANDDLELEM deserted, lost.

SANDDNAR deserter, forsaker.

SANDDONC to lose.

SANDDOUNC to lose.

SANDDUNC to let go, to lose; to forsake, to leave; *moje chear rupia sanddle*, I lost four rupees; *to aplo gaum sonddun Goeam ailo*, he came to Goa leaving his native land; *Joaunchean soro sandu nozo*, John cannot stay without drinking liquor; tum tin annem vor anim maca eoc anno sodd, you take three annas and leave me one anna.

SANDO *m* limb.

SANDONC to join, to juncture.

SANDOUNC to join, to juncture.

SANDOP *n* union, junction.

SANDUNC to join, to unite, to conjoin, to miss, to incorporate, to bind, to tie.

SANDUS file.

SANG shell of beans.

SANGALLO *m* bagre fish.

SANGAT company.

SANGATA in company.

SANGATI *m* companion.

SANGDDAUNC to join, to unite, gather.

SANGNAR informer, reporter.

SANGNNAM declaration, expression.

SANGNNAR narrator.

SANGNNEM GOODCHEA ADIM act of foretelling, prophecy.

SANGO *f* shells of beans.

SANGODD *m* raft.

SANGODD *m* even, pair.

SANGONC to tell, to inform.

SANGONC FOTTI to tell lies, to fabricate.

SANGONC GUTT to divulge, to disclose.

SANGONC SOTEN to dictate, to enjoin.

SANGONC SOTH to tell the truth, to admit facts, to confess.

SANGONC SOTHA VOIR to exaggerate.

SANGONC THODDEAN to summarise, to shorten, to abbreviate.

SANGONC UTRAN UTOR to detail, to specify.

SANGONC VODDLEAN to exclaim, to shout.

SANGOTT (MASOLLI) *n* a bagre fish.

SANGRAM fight, combat.

SANGRIXEC medicated foot-bath.

SANGTER *n* a small bagre fish.

SANGUNC to tell, to inform, to converse with.

SANJE in the evening; *sanje ie*, come in the evening.

SANJECHEA VELLA at evening time.

SANJECHO ADÊS *m* afternoon.

SANJERI in the evening.

SANKOLL *f* chain, fetters.

SANN a grind stone; *vacor sannicher galunc*, to grind the razzor.

SANNI frenzied.

SANNONG VO SONNONG cloth.

SANNOS *f* moth; *sannos cagotkata*, moth eats paper.

SANNOS pincers, nippers; *camar vinglio carta sannoxim*, the black smith takes the coal with the pincer.

SANSOUM *n* mustard.

SANSPONC to feel, to touch, to affect.

SANSPONNO, -I, -EM feeler.

SANSVEL mustard-plant.

SANT a fair, market.

SANT VO BOGT a saint.

SANTAB affliction, trouble.

SANTAP chagrin, vexation.

Santiponn holiness, spiritual purity.

Santtonc to stagnate.

Santvol *f* holy oil.

Sanvori *f* megpie.

Sanvorzonnar economical.

Sanvorzonni economy.

Sanz evening time, evening, late hour.

Sao, -i, -em, vo Savo, -i, -em sweet: *saem udoc*, sweet water; *saem anim karem udoc eellaim zala*, sweet and salt waters are joining together.

Saoc, (ful) *n* lotus.

Saott *n* shade.

Sap vo Sorop *m* snake; *pandro sorop*, cobra snake, agio sorop, carpet snake.

Sapuso vo Sapuxi snake root.

Sar tke heart or the hardest part of a tree.

Sarangi cithern.

Sarbot syrup, sweet drink.

Sarco,-ki,-kem, right, straight, lawful, reasonnable, just; *ho ixeop sareo asa*, this account is right; *hi zomin sarki cor*, make this ground proper.

Sarco corunc to concert, to settle, to dispose, to put in order, to repair, to mend, to make agree, to conciliate, *dar sarkem corunc*, to repair the door.

Sarcos Circus.

Sardar *m* captain.

Sardin *n* sardin.

Sarem *n* manure.

Sarem galunc zaddac to put manure to the tree.

Sari ashes.

Sari corunc to reduce to ashes.

Sarj serge, a kind of woolen cloth.

Sarkem *n* face, feature, likeness; *lichems arkem borem*, her likeness is beautiful.

Sarkench exactly, definitely.

Sarkench socla downright.

Sarkench zaunc to fit, to adjust.

Saronn *f* broom; *garac saronn marunc*, to sweep the house.

Sarunc to poke, to light; *uzo sarunc*, to light the fire.

Sarunc to snuff; *dio sarunc*, to snuff the lamp.

Sarunc to spend; *duddu sarunc*, to spend money; *avem vaitlac zaite duddu sarle*, I spent lot of money for sickness.

Sarunc to earth up, to prop, to buttress; *eca zaddac mati sarunc*, to earth up a tree.

Sarvolli p. **Sanvori.**

Sasnnachea sasnanc everlasting.

Sasnnancho, -i, -em perpetual.

Sasonn *n* perpetuity.

Sasro vo Maum *m* father-in-law.

Sasu *f* mother-in-law.

Sat seven (7).

Satrazi a carpet.

Satt sixty (60).

Sattonc to stagnate.

Sattvonnem *n* stagnation.

Satvo seventh (7th).

Satxim seven hundred (700).
Sau *f* anvil.
Saucar *m* banker, merchant, money-lender.
Saucarponn *n* act of a merchant.
Saucas vo **Soucas** slowly, quietly.
Saud toast, health.
Saulli *f* shade.
Saullo (sucnem) sparrow, hawk.
Saumllo, -i, -em grey.
Savo, -i, -em innocent.
Sec hot fomentation.
Seclolo, -i, -em chastened.
Seconc to be chastened by trials.
Secretar *m* secretary.
Secretari *f* secretariat.
Secunc to foment with hot bath.
Secuni an eft or newt, a small lizard.
Sed *n* silk.
Sed victato *m* silk merchant.
Sedachem lugott *n* silk cloth.
Segun *m* virtue.
Segunni honest, virtuous.
Segur, Sugur safe, free from fear.
Sekim finally, atlast.
Sel seal, stamp duty.
Selêr sadler.
Semetery cemetery, graveyard.
Seminar *f* seminary.
Seminarint sictato *m* seminarist.
Semitt cement.
Semitt caddunc to cement.
Sencuddo *m* hairy-worm.
Sendri *f* mat.
Ser seer, measure for grains, also a measure for liquids.
Sercam (sucnim) *n* sparrows.
Sercar government.
Sercar goddcho caido constitution.
Sermão sangonc to preach.
Sermaum *m* sermon, preaching.
Sermon cerimony.
Serpent *f* serpent, snake.
Serpent pacottanchi dragon.
Sertidão certificate.
Seruc sparrow.
Servej beer.
Servej calli porter.
Set *n* field.
Set camotponn agriculture.
Setcamti *m* farmer.
Setembr *m* september.
Setim *f* setin.
Setuc (masolli) *n* a handsome fis.
Siadd p. **Aac.**
Siassonn throne, royal seat.
Siassonnar bossonc to enthrone.
Sicar *f* hunting.
Sicari *m* hunter.
Siclolo, -i, -em educated, well-informed.
Sicnar studious.
Siconc to study.
Sicop learning, education, training.
Sicounc to educate, to instruct.
Sicxa *f* punishment.
Sicxa launc to punish.
Sidd sail.

SIDDCAUNC to be aware of sudden doubts or fears, to awaken mentally.
SIDDUC cunning, artful, astute.
SIDDUCAI cunning, alertness.
SIFR cypher, zero.
SIGI spit, a long sprong.
SIGI LAUNC to spit.
SIGNIFICAD *m* meaning.
SIGRI stove for cooking.
SIGRUR gridiron.
SILONC p. XILONC.
SIM boundary, limit, frontier.
SIMANLI gallery.
SIMLI ferrule.
SIMPDDAUNC to disperse, to spread.
SINAL-POTR a written document.
SINALL prostitute, woman of loose character.
SINALLPONN prostitution.
SINDUR p. XINDUR.
SINET seal.
SING horn.
SINGANCHO,-I,-EM having horns.
SINKELELEM congealed, frozen.
SINKEM arrangement to keep food and food-stuff hanging on high.
SINKEUNC to congeal, to freeze.
SINN complain of injustice.
SINNONC to complaint of grievance.
SINOD synod, religious council.
SINS disciple, follower.
SINSLI dicanter, a small bottle.
SINSO flask.
SINSO (LANCUDD) blackwood.
SINTARI bamboopole.
SINTARPAR sarcasm, taunt.
SINTARPARI sarcastic, ironical.
SINTID sense, attention, alertness.
SINTID DIUNC to attend, to head.
SINTIDACHO, -I, -EM attentive, watchful.
SINTIDAN watchfully, attentively.
SINTOR black guard.
SINTORPONN blackguardism.
SINTUR girdle, waist-band.
SINXEM *n* lead.
SIPAI *m* soldier.
SIPAI NOVO recruit.
SIR MARUNC to open a vein.
SIR piece, slice, plot.
SIR vein, blood-vesel.
SIRAP *m* curse.
SIRAP DIUNC to abuse, to curse.
SIRBO, -I, -EM spotted.
SIRCO vinegar.
SIRSIRI PIDDA *f* cholera.
SIRSIRONC to quiver, to shiver.
SIRVISTTO ceremony, observance, of a customary practice.
SIRVISTTO CORUNC to observe a custom with no good-will.
SITOU refreshing, cool.
SITOUCAI freshness, coolness.
SITSÃO citation, intimation, summons.
SITSÃO LAUNC to serve summons.
SIVAI without.
SIZLELEM cooked.
SIZOUNC to cook.
SIZOUNCHEM CAM cookery.
So six (6).

Soad taste, flavour.
Soai vo Sovai cheap.
Soai corunc vo Sovai corunc to make cheap.
Soaiki cheapness.
Soar orderly.
Sob *f* beauty, handsomeness.
Sob diunc to beautify, to adorn.
Sobai fairness, neatness.
Sobagi fortunate, happy.
Sobar many p. **Sabar.**
Sobd expression, phrase.
Sobdh a word, expression.
Sobe mazar in a public manner.
Sobechem, Sobaichem comely, appropriate, beautiful.
Sobit beautifull, handsome.
Sobitai beauty, handsomeness.
Sobonc to grow pleasant, to be come agreeable; *hem gor alam borem sobla,* now this house looks pleasant; *tuca cosem soblem ti corni corunc,* how did it afford you to do that action.
Sobcunc to make pleasant or agreeable.
Sobrecazac *m* frock coat.
Sobrepeliz *f* surplice.
Sobri patience, time of waiting.
Sobri khaunc to be patient, to wait.
Socall early morning time.
Socallcho adês *m* morning.
Socallim morning.
Socar essence.
Socla vo Kala down, below, under; *tem socla asa,* it is down; *tachea socla fator asa,* there is a stone under it; *socla voch anim hie,* go down and come.
Socla caddunc to lower, to take down; *vat socla caddunc,* to turn down the light; *unchai unni corunc,* to lower; *voddun caddunc,* to pull down.
Socla sorønc to stoop down.
Socla-voir uneven, unbalanced.
Socnoi vo Socnolli *f* throat.
Socoilean from below.
Socoilo at the bottom.
Socoilo, -i, -em of the bottom.
Socol below, at the bottom.
Socol caddunc to lower, to take down.
Socol soronc to stoop down.
Soconc to dry, to parch; *tallo soconc,* to feel thirsty.
Socot *f* strength.
Socott all leverything.
Socti *f* strenghth, vigour.
Soctivont strong, vigorous.
Sod *n* soda water.
Sod *f* search, quest.
Sod vo Sud corunc to search, to procure.
Sodam always, every day.
Sodam sorvotam for ever, perpetual, everlasting.
Sodamanki cuttle fish.
Sodancal daily.
Sodanch always.
Sodancho, -i, -em usual.
Soddi *f* holi-day.
Soddounar gulamponnantlo emancipator.
Soddounc to free, to deliver from.

Soddounni *f* salvation, deliverance.

Soddun diunc to deliver, to release.

Soddun marunc to fling, to pelt.

Soddunc to leave, to abandon, to untie, to extend, to stretch; *amvem to epar soddlo,* I left that trade; *sorpan cat soddli,* the snake left a skin; to *aplo gaum soddun Bomboi gelo,* leaving his country he went to Bombay; *tanduu soddunc,* to clean the rice by pounding; *moje duddu amvem gelle anim taca jur soddlo,* I received my money and left him the interest; *khastintlo soddunc,* to deliver from punishment; *tica gor soddlem anim set anvem gellem,* I ceded her the house and took the field; *suscar soddunc,* to breathe, to inhale; *vatt soddunc,* to give way; *hat anim paim soddunc,* to stretch one's hands and legs; *bonnconnintlo soddunc,* to set free.

Soddunc nitintlo to acquit, to discharge.

Soddvonn *f* remission.

Soddvonddar *m* deliverer, liberator, saviour.

Soden *f* search.

Sodim always.

Sodol bodol exchange.

Sodonicai *f* intelligence, understanding.

Sodri *f* throne.

Sodunc to search, to find out, to procure.

Sofa *m* sofa.

Soglem all, everything.

Soglo, -i, -em whole, entire.

Sogott all, everybody.

Soi, Chun *f* scraped cocoanut.

Soia *f* physionomy.

Soimb *n* nature.

Soimbacho, -i, -em natural.

Soimba-orto, -i, -em extraordinary, supernatural.

Soimbim naturally.

Soinn *n* lineage, race.

Soiran *n* sense, use of reason.

Soirboir stupid, silly, foolish.

Soirboir zaunc to become dull, or senseless.

Soirboirponn *n* nonsense, foolery.

Soiri *f* female relation.

Soiric relationship, kindredship.

Soiro *m* male relation.

Soiro atvo *m* host.

Soit *n* lash.

Soit together with.

Soitan *m* devil, satan.

Soldad *m* soldier.

Solmitt *n* saltpetre.

Solod *m* basket.

Solog *m* castrated pig.

Solep vo Soupó billet or log.

Solpaunc to smooth, to plane.

Solpi *m* planer, moulding-worker.

Solpotti *f* small billet.

Solunc to peel, to unhusk.

Somar *m* Monday.

SOMBALCAR arcenic.
SOMBRAN *f* ostentation, pomp.
SOMBRUT rich, fertile.
SOMBRUTCAI *f* richness, fertility.
SOMDIR *m* sea, ocean.
SOMEST all, many ; *somestam boglancho ecott,* communion of all saints.
SOMANDAN *n* ease, tranquility, quietness.
SOMJIC intelligent, prudent.
SOMJICAI *f* prudence, intelligence.
SOMOIA-PORMONNEM according to time ; *somoia pormonnem cholonc zai,* it is necessary to accomodate with the circumstances.
SOMOIO time, period, of time.
SOMONZ VO SOMOZ understanding, comprehention.
SOMORPIUNC to dedicate, to offer, to sacrifice.
SOMORPONNI *f* dedication, offering.
SOMPADDNEM consummation.
SOMPADONC to finish, to terminate.
SOMPEPONN *n* facility, ease.
SOMPEPONNIM easily.
SOMPO, -I, -EM easy, not difficult.
SOMPONC to finish, to terminate, to die.
SOMPOUNC to finish, to accomplish.
SOMPTIC rich.
SOMPTICAI *f* riches.
SOMPURN full, perfect.
SOMPURNAEN fully, completely.
SOMPURNAI *f* plenitude abundance.
SOMUDUR *m* ocean, sea.
SOMURT *f* law.
SOMZAUNC to explain, to persuade, to reconciliate.
SOMZONC VO SOMZUNC to understand, to comprehend.
SOMZONIM *f* meaning, understanding.
SOMZUT understanding.
SONAR *m* gold-smith.
SONBIAM linseeds.
SONDDI *f* muzzle.
SONDEU doubt.
SONEM *n* gold.
SONG VO SONGOT company, society.
SONGIN quiet, peaceable.
SONIM BEGOT *f* tin, leaf-brass, tinsel.
SONIMAN *n* reception, refuge, shelter.
SONIMAN CORUNC to receive, to entertain, to shelter.
SONKEM wind-pipe, mouth.
SONKESTT difficult, hard.
SONKESTTAI *f* difficulty.
SONKIRN melancholic.
SONN, SAL bark.
SÔNN *f* flax.
SONPITOLL *f* tinsel.
SONSNICAI patience, endurance.
SONSO *m* rabbit.
SONSONNUNC to throb, to beat, to palpitate.
SONSOT *f* lineage, race, generation, descendents.
SONSUNC to bear, to forbear, to endure.

Sont loliday.
Sontab *m* affliction.
Sontaban indignantly.
Sontos *m* joy, happiness.
Sontosaunc to satisfy, to please.
Sontosonc to be contented or satisfied with, to content one's self with.
Sontosponn *n* joy, happiness.
Sonvem with, about, for.
Sonvôd *f* conversation.
Sonvodunc to converse, to talk.
Sonvoim habit, custom, usage.
Sonvoim assonc to be used, be habituated.
Sonvoim corunc to practice, to to accustom, to train.
Sonvoim permonnem according to custom or usual habit.
Sonvoim zaunc to get accustomed.
Sonvoincho,-i,-em usual, habitual.
Soo vo Solla sixteen (16).
So-ong farce, part of dramatic play.
Soongui actor of dramatic scenes.
Sôp *n* remains of grapes, caju or other fruits. soup.
Sopecar *m* a sealer.
Soper *m* soup-plate.
Sopnneunc to dream, to think idly.
Sopo *m* seal, mark.
Sopo marunc to seal.
Sopó, Soponn seat, a bench of stones.
Soponn *m* dream.
Soponn *n* seat, steps.
Soponn puddonc to dream.
Sopter *m* shoe-maker.
Sopur small, light, swift.
Sopurai *f* smallness, subtilty, thinness.
Soput *m* oath.
Soput diunc to swear.
Sôr threaded garland; *fulancho sôr*, garland of flowers.
Sôr comparison.
Sor corunc to compare, to equalize.
Sorad around.
Sorap dealer in money, banker.
Sorasori fully, completely.
Sorbountim around, all around.
Sordar *m* officer.
Soreachi batti distillery of liquor.
Sorg *m* heaven.
Sorguincho, -i, -em heavenly, celestial.
Sori *f* string, wire; *tambeachi sori*, copper wire.
Sori *f* repair, renewal.
Sori corunc to repair; *gor sori corunc*, to repair the house.
Sori guntunc to string, to thread.
Sori pounlleanchi string of corals.
Sorm *n* sense, understanding.
Sorngo *m* kite.
Sorngo (masoli) *m* pomfret black.
Soro *m* wine, spirit.
Soronc to finish, to end, spend; *tin dis sorlet anim choutea disa*

to amger ailo, three days were over and on the fourth day he came to our house; *moje lagim 2 rupia sorlet*, I spent 2 rupees; *bitor sorunc*, to enter; *bhair soronc*, to go out; *aro soronc*, to approach near; *poro soronc*, to move; *tinnem ti corni corunc soro nasli*, she should not have done that action.

SORONC to end, *aucsoronc*, to die.

SOROUNC to finish, to spend; *sogle duddu tannem soroile*, he spent all the money.

SOROP *m* snake.

SORPOLLI *f* chain.

SORPOTTO, -I, -EM prostated, lying flat on the ground.

SORPOTTONC VO / SORPOTTUNC } to prostrate, to fall at one's feet.

SORTO, -I, -EM nearly exhausted.

SORV all.

SORVOI everything, all.

SORVOI LOC all the people.

SORVOI THAIM every where.

SORVOTAM always, for ever.

SORVZANNAR omnicient.

SORXILO, -I, -EM of near.

SOSNAI *f* patience, endurance.

SOSNAR patient, endurer.

SOSNICAI *f* patience, endurance

SOSONC to agree, to accomodate; *maca soro sonsonam*, wine does not suit me.

SOSTA cheap.

SOSTAUNC to appease, to pacify.

SOSUNC to bear patiently, to to endure.

SOT *n* truth.

SOTEA *f* right, power.

SOTEVONT true, real, honest, sincere.

SOTMANDCHEO VOSTU a creed.

SOTMANDUNC to believe, to accept.

SOTOR seventy.

SOTRI *f* umbrella.

SOTRI BAILANCHI parasol.

SOTT CON VO / SOTT CORUN } at once, instantly.

SOTTO *m* thick-short stick.

SOUCAS slow.

SOUCASAIEN slowly, leisurely.

SOUCOLOLO, -I, -EM inured, habituated to.

SOUCOSAI *f* leisure, peace.

SOUEM *n* a large mat.

SOULI a small billet or log.

SOUNCOUNC to accustom, to inure.

SOUNG ANCAR comedian, actor.

SOUNGANCHO, -I, -EM frivolous, not serious.

SOUNGODDO *m* companion.

SOUNNEM *n* bird.

SOUP a billet or log.

SOUPAUNC VO SOLLPAUNC to be [plane.

SOUPOTTI p. SOULI.

SOURATAI avidity, greediness, eagerness.

SOUTI-DHU step-daughter.

SOUTI-MĀI step-mother.

SOUTO-PAI step-father.

SOUTO-PUTR step-son.

SOUVOT co-wife.

SOVAI cheap; *hem nislem tuvem sovai addlaim*, you have brought this fish cheap.

Sovai a quarter, a fourth part; *sovai rupia*, one rupee and 4 annas.

Sovai zaunc to become cheap.

Sovaiki cheapness.

Sovaixinn *f* virgin, maid, maiden.

Sovem with; *lache sovem tachi maim asli*, his mother was with him.

Sovo, -i, -em sixth.

Sovoim *f* habit, custom.

Sovost *f* quiet, peaceable.

Sovost corunc to still, to appease, to calm.

Sovostai *f* peace, happiness.

Sovostcai quietness, calmness, tranquility.

Sovostonn *n* pacification.

Sovostonnim quietly, peaceably.

Sovostponn p. **Sovostoai.**

Sovrat insatiable.

Sovratai insatiableness, greediness.

Sozonc to agree, to fit, to suit.

Srap curse, imprecation.

Srapunc to curse.

Srungar dress, deck, ornament.

Srungar corunc to adorn, to deck.

Suad *m* taste.

Suad-diunc to flavour.

Suadacho, -i, -em tasteful, appetising.

Suadic tasteful.

Suam sir or master, lord.

Suanim prelate, the superior of a convent or religious house.

Suart ambition, [illegible]

Suarti avaricious, ambitious.

Suat *f* place, ground.

Subdican subdeacon.

Suc happiness, joy, pleasure.

Sucannem *n* helm.

Sucavont happy, fortunate.

Sucmaiecho happily brought up.

Sucnnem *n* bird.

Suco, -ki, -kem dried.

Sucoll vo **Sucou** abundance, plentifulness.

Suconc to dry, to desicate; *ti masolli sucli*, that fish is dried up; *Joaum heam disanim sucla*, John has become lean in these days, *to vagac decon suclo*, he was surprised by looking at the tiger; *doriachem pannim suconc*, to reflux the water of the sea or ocean.

Sucop dryage.

Sucou abundance of corn.

Sucounc to dry.

Sucti doriachi reflux of the tide, low water.

Sucti eunc to be refluxed.

Sucum clean, neat, pure.

Sucumai cleanliness, neatness, purity.

Sud *f* search.

Sud corunc to search.

Sudarnar reformer.

Sudaroup reform, amendment.

Sudarunc to reform, to improve.

Supd candid, sincere.

Sudd free, independent, innocent, bold.

SUDD ZAUNC to be free.
SUDDCA freedom, liberty.
SUDDOLPONN *n* simplicity.
SUDDSUDDAI agility, diligence.
SUDDSUDDIT active.
SUDEU VO SUDEVO hallowed, blessed.
SUEL awl.
SUEL a big needle.
SUFFOL hallowed, blessed.
SUGRAT *m* ambition.
SUGRATI ambitious.
SUGROM glossy (fig.) polite, refined, polished.
SUGUR ' JIU CORUNC to insure life.
SUI *f* needle.
SUI the heaping of a measure, overfilling.
SUKEM dry.
SUL VO DOKIN south.
SULLSULIT VO TUUTUIT lubrious slippery, loose.
SULLSULLITAI lubricity.
SUMAN *n* weak.
SUMAN SANT holy weak.
SUMANCAR one attending to a weekly turn of duty.
SUMAR mediocrity, about.
SUMARACHO, -I, -EM, VO SUMARSUMAR middling, ordinary.
SUMB *n* rope.
SUMBRONN reason, understanding.
SUMORONN adoration.
SUMORUNC to adore.
SUMURT *f* law, rule.
SUMURTICHO, -I, -EM religious, canonical.
SUN *f* daughter-in-law.
SUNC *n* sharp point.
SUNCR UDEUNC to dawn.
SUNCR VO ARUUN dawn, dawn of day, morning.
SUNCRAR *m* friday.
SUNDOR fine, curious, beautiful pretty.
SANDORAI fineness, beauty, elegance.
SUNGOTT *n* shrimp.
SUNNEM *n* dog.
SUNTT *f* dry ginger.
SUNTTO *m* a small piece.
SUP *n* winnowing fan.
SUPARI VO FOFOLL betel-nut.
SUPARUNC VO ASDUNC to winnow.
SUR *f* tody juice of the palmtree.
SUR VO PISCATI *f* knife.
SURI VODLI poniard.
SURIO *m* sun.
SURIO COMOLL turnsol, girasol.
SURMAI *f* surmullet.
SURNGAR CORUNC to adorn, to deck, to trim.
SUROI not boiled.
SUROP fine, curious, beautiful.
SUROPAI beauty.
SURUNGAR adorn, deck, trim.
SURUNGAR CORUNC to adorn, to trim.
SUSCAR sigh, breath, earnest, desire.
SUSCAR SODDUNC VO SUSCARONC VO SUSCARUNC to sigh, to desire earnestly.
SUSMUDDIT puffed up, flabby, apparent.

Sustaunc to accomodate, to provide for, to reconciliate.

Sustaunnim accomodation, reconciliation (fig) adoption.

Sut *n* thread.

Sutachi gaddi reel of thread.

Sutachi gulli *f* clew of thread.

Sutar *m* carpenter.

Sutli *f* cord, twine.

Suttavem truth, veracity, reality.

Sattavo, -i, -em truly, infact, indeed.

Sut *n* thread.

Sutor funich, fuse, connecting wire or string.

Sutt discount, allowance.

Suttca freedom, act of setting at liberty or letting loose.

Sutti leave, holiday.

Sutti corunc to make pieces; *nistem sutti corunc*, to clean the fish.

Suttlolo, i, em loose, light, swift, able, free, easy.

Suttonc to get loose, to disengage one's self, suttonc (ballont), to bring forth young.

Suunc to put, to set; *cacnam suunc*, to put bangles.

Suvsuit level.

Suvsuit corunc to level.

Suz swelling.

Suzonc to swell.

T

T the twentieth letter of the Roman Alphabet.

Ta llu brain-pan, cranium.

Taat *m* the palm of the hand.

Tabean under responsibility.

Tabelião *m* notary.

Taboad tables of addition, substraction and multiplication.

Tac *n* butter milk.

Tacot *f* strength, vigour.

Tacticho, -i, -em urgent.

Tactin quickly, hurriedly.

Tadd palm-tree (not cocoanut tree).

Taddgullo or targullo fruit of palm tree.

Taddi juice of palm tree.

Taddimidi *f* caper, skip.

Tae twigs of tree.

Taful dandy, coxcomb.

Tagaït from, then.

Tagddi *f* balance, scale.

Tai *f* branch, a shoot; *zaddachi tai*, branch of a tree.

Tainnen poddonc to be tempted, to be seduced.

Tainnim *f* temptation.

Taix fee, charge for service.

Taji fresh.

Takit *f* haste, hurry, urgency.

Tal mode, fashion, smart appearance.

Talam lies, appearances.

Talem *n* padlock.

Talic *f* copy.

Talic caddunc to copy.

Tall symbols.

Talla below, under.

Talli, Kandi *f* bough, twig.

Talli, talu *f* Sinciput.

Tallio pettunc to applaud, to extol with shouts.

TALLNIM temptation.

TALLO *m* voice; *mozo tallo poddla*, my voice is hoarse.

TALLO *m* the throat; *mozo tallo ducta*, my throat pains me; *mozea talleac cantto laglo*, a thorn was stuck in my throat.

TALLO *m* tone, tune; *dogui gatateca tallean*, both are singing in the same tone; *donuïm podancho ecuch tallo*, both the songs have the same tune.

TALLO *m* branch; *ambeacho tallo*, branch of a mango-tree.

TALLO PODDONC to grow hoarse.

TALOB pay.

TAMATAM apples of love.

TAMB *f* rust.

TAMBACU *m* tobacco.

TAMBDDO (RONG) red.

TAMBDDO CORUNC to make red.

TAMBDDO ZAUNC to grow red.

TAMBEM *n* copper.

TAMBETT sledge hammer.

TAMBETT CADDUNC to thresh, to hammer.

TAMBEUNC to rust.

TAMBIO *m* copper-pot.

TAMBIO PITTULCHO brass water pot.

TAMBONN copper goods.

TAMBOR large drum.

TAMBOURINE small drum, toy drum.

TAMBRET *f* stool.

TAMBSO, -I, -EM reddish.

TAN *f* thirst.

TAN LAGONC to be thirsty.

TANC power, means, possibility.

TANCH pace, step.

TANCH attachment of property in lieu of debt.

TANCH MARUNC to secure payment of debt by attaching property.

TANCH MARUNC to step forward, to walk.

TANCHAUNC to pick holes.

TANCHEAN by them.

TANCHOUNNO, -I, -EM fault-finder.

TANCONC to be possible, be able.

TANCOT means, resource.

TANCSALL *f* mint.

TANCUNC to gain, to finish; *sorg tancunc*, to gain heaven; *vatt tancunc*, to finish a journey.

TANDD tight.

TANDD CORUNC to make tight.

TANDD RABONC to be stiff.

TANDDEL *m* helmsman.

TANDDELI *m* a rower.

TANDDI *f* crowd, throng; *tinttear locachi tanddi zalea*, there is a crowd of people in the bazar.

TANDDUNC to row.

TANDDUNC (TOMBU) to raise, to lift.

TANDU VO TANDULL *m* rice.

TANELELO, -I, -EM thirsty.

TANENCHO SORANTO *m* acute thirst.

TANEST thirsty.

TANEUNC to be thirsty.

TANG one anna or 16th part of a rupee ?

TANKI *f* picking.

TANKI *f* cistern.

TANKI picking of small holes

on mill stones and grinding stones.
TANKICAR *m* one that picks grinding stones.
TANKIO *m* the herb mercury.
TANNOM *m* weaver's loom.
TANTI nerve, sinew.
TANTIACHEM COL shell of an egg.
TANTIACHI MUNDDON yolk of an egg.
TANTIACHO BOU white of an egg.
TANTIAILO likely to give eggs. fertile, promissing.
TANTIALLO nervous, snewy.
TANTIM *n* egg.
TANTUM inside of that.
TAO *m* voice, throat p. TALLO.
TAO *m* branch.
TAOT *m* palm of the hand.
TAP *m* fever, heat.
TAP EUNC to get fever.
TAPIOC tapioca.
TAPKIR *f* small bottle.
TAPLOLO,-I,-EM warm, hot, excited.
TAPONC to be warmed, to warm, to heat, (fig.) to get angry.
TAPONNC to get excited by drink.
TAPOUNC to warm, to make hot, to heat.
TAR *m* wire.
TAR *m* telegram, wire.
TAR, VODDEM, FIN ferry.
TAR CADDUNC to go by a ferry-boat, to go across a rive.
TAR CORUNC to wire, to telegraph.
TARANN *m* strength, vigour.
TARANTTUNC to stretch, to stiffen.
TARCAR *m* ferryman.
TARIC *f* date.
TARICHEM VODDEM *n* ferry-boat.
TARLO *m* sardine.
TAROCK *m* saviour, mediator.
TARUM *n* ship.
TARUM FUDDTATEM shipwreck.
TARUM PORTONC to capsize.
TARUM ZUZACHEM man-of-war.
TARVACHEM SUCANNEM rudder.
TARVACHEM VOZON ship's ballast.
TARVACHI BOR *f* cargo.
TARVACHO CUNVO ship's mast.
TARVACHO MAL CHODDOUNC to ship goods or merchandise.
TARVACHO NANGOR anchor.
TARVAR CHODDONC to embark.
TARVOTTI *m* sailor, mariner.
TAS *n* furrow.
TAS *n* hour.
TAS GALUNC to plough.
TASNNIM pin, also act of scraping.
TASNNIM *f* adz.
TASSOP THICACHEM facet.
TASSUNC to shave, to polish.
TASUNC to scrape.
TATT *n* tray.
TATT, THAGDDECHEM scale.
TATTO *m* girdle, sling.
TAU p. TALLU.
TAUCULLO herb-mercury.
TAUG talisman, charm.
TAUNC to bear, to suffer.
TAUNNIM *f* temptation.
TAZ *m* pole.
TAZO, -I, -EM fresh, new.

TAZUN ASSONC to be eager, to be alert,

TĒ *m* she, that.

TEA on that; *tea disa*, on that day.

TEA BHAIR besides, over and above.

TEA PASSOT consequently.

TEA PSOOT on that account.

TEA VOLL then.

TEA VORVIM therefore.

TEATR dramatic perfomance.

TECLEM *n* vo.

TECLI *f* vo.

TECLO *m* head.

TECT *m* roof.

TECT NOLEANCHO tiled roof.

TECT POTREACHO zinc roof.

TEDIAM (TEA DISSA) the other day, a few days ago.

TEDIANCHO,-I,-EM relating to a past incident.

TEDNAM then, therefore.

TEDONAM ab out that time.

TEF *n* clod; *tefam foddunc*, to break the clods.

TEFOLL *n* wild pepper.

TEFOLL (ZADD) *f* wild pepper tree.

TEL *n* oil.

TELACHO, -I, -EM oily, used for oil.

TEL, PETROL petroleum, kerosine oil.

TELL COBREACHEM cocoanut oil.

TELCAR *m* oilman.

TELCARIN *f* oil woman.

TELI *m* oilman.

TELIO greasy, oily, fatty.

TELINI *f* oilwoman.

TELLNAR observer, listener, spy.

TELLNIM peep, sly-look.

TELLUNC to observe, to spy, to listen.

TEM stubborness, obstinacy.

TEM CORUNC to be wilful or obstinate.

TEMB stubborness.

TEMB RÊVÊNCHEM downs or sandy hills.

TEMBI *f* end, point.

TEMBIST stubborn, obstinate.

TEMBON ebony.

TEMELI stubborn, obstinate.

TEMPORACHE SUMANN ember days.

TEMPR *n* sauce, gravy.

TEMPR sauce, curry stuff.

TEMRO, -I, -EM stubborn.

TENCLOLO, -I, -EM leaning, reclining.

TENCO *m* prop, fulcrum, support.

TENCONC to lean, to rest.

TENCOUNC to prop, to lean (against a thing).

TENEXI *f* end, top.

TENDDLI vegetable plant.

TENGRO bandy-legged.

TENGU dwarf, deformed.

TENKI a prop support.

TENNCAUNC to cudgel, to hammer, to cane.

TENSÃO intention, design, resolve.

TENTUM in that.

TEONC to perspire, to moisten.

TERA thirteen.

TERAO thirteenth.

TERNAM then.

Terrin tureen.

Ters a form of prayer, rosary.

Testament last will, testament.

Testament cornar testator.

Testament pallnar executor of a last will.

Teste jest, mock, derision.

Teteg three by three.

Teugo,-i,-em playful, amusing.

Teunc to observe, to spy, to listen.

Teuxilo, -i, -em of that side.

Teuxin on that side.

Tevonc to melt, to soften, to become damp.

Texem like that.

Thaem known; *devac thaem*, God knows or known to God.

Thaim with, by; *conna thaim?* with whom?

Thainche,-i,-em of there, of thither, original.

Thali lance, pole (of a coach).

Thali metal plate, flat dish of metal.

Thambnnem vo Thamnnim cessation, suspension, discontinuance.

Thambonc to cease, to stop.

Thambounc to stop, to suspend.

Than *n* pap, breast.

Than vo Thoim than from there; *kuim than*, from where.

Thananchi chium *f* nipple.

Thanga there, thither.

Thao, -i, -em visible, manifest; *moje coistt Devac thae*, my sufferings are known to God.

Thao corunc to discover, to disclose, to reveal; *Pedrun chori thavi keli*, Peter discovered the theft.

Thao zaunc to appear, to manifest.

Thap slap.

Thap marunc to give a slap, (fig.) to deceive, to cheat.

Thapi trowel of masons.

Thapo raft; *cantiamcho thapo corun nodint gallo* we made a raft of wood and sunk it in the river.

Thapo (xennacho) cow-dung.

Thapott *n* slap.

Thapott marunc to give a slap.

Thapttaunc to slap one over the face.

Thapttunc to lull a babe to sleep, to press in.

Thar entirely, exceedingly.

Thar camponc to be overcome by fear.

Tharaunc to decide, to resolve.

Tharaunc to stop, to suspend.

Tharaunc(mol) to fix a price.

Tharaunem stopping, suspension.

Tharear nam zaunc to feel uncertain, to lose piece of mind.

Tharnnem permanency, stopping.

Tharo a dwelling place, abode, habitation.

Tharounc to stop, to prevent from falling.

Thatt *n* scale,

THAU the bottom, the ground, depth, basis.

THAU GEUNC VO / THAU POLLEUNC } to examine, to fathom, to be informed.

THAUVAR PAONC to reach the bottom or depth.

THELI small bag, hand-bag.

THELO large bag.

THEMBEUNC to fall in drops.

THEMBO *m* drop.

THEMBRI knee.

THERMOMETR thermometer.

THEUNAR depositer, trustee.

THEUNC to keep, to deposit.

THEUNNIM deposit, warehouse.

THIBO peak or a point, stop, head, summit.

THIBOUNC to make points.

THIC precious stone.

THICAN property, abode.

THICMOTI curiosity, skill, art.

THICMOTICAR curious, ingenious.

THICO sign-mark.

THICONC to stop, to be satisfied.

THIMPI *f* spit.

THIMPI UDOUNC to spit.

THINCHEAN by that side.

THINGA there.

THIR firm, certain, constant.

THIRASONN firmness, steadiness.

THIRAUNC to certify, to acertain, to make steady.

THIROUNC to make steady.

THIRSONN firmness, steadiness.

THÔC deceiver, cheater, lier, taleteller.

THOCONC to be mistaken, to mistake.

THOCONC to be tired.

THOCOR collision, impact.

THOCOR BOSSONC to collide, to strike against each other.

THOCPONN deceit, artifice, stratagem, cheat, trick.

THÔCUNC to deceive, to cheat, to seduce.

THODDARONC VO THODDARUNC to lessen, to decrease.

THODDEPONN lessness.

THODDO,-I,-EM little, less; *oundum paus thoddo*, rain is less this year; *hem tacheaki thoddem*, this is less than his; *thodde rupan bore punn callzan vaill*, some are beautiful in features but wicked in heart.

THÔI VO THÔOI *m* carpenter.

THOIM there, thither; *thoim than anga e*, come here from there.

THOIM, THUIM there, yonder.

THOINCHEAN p. TINGACHEAN.

THOINCHO, -I, -EM of there.

THOINTHAN from there.

THOIPONN carpentry.

THOND cool, calm, cold; *hem udoc chodd thond asa*, this water is very cold; *tem mas un aslem atam thond zalem*, that meat was hot but now it has become cold; *aiz doria thond asa*, to day the sea is calm; *kal Pedr chaoulolo aiz thond asa*, Peter was vexed yesterday but to-day he is quiet.

THOND CORUNC to cool, to pacify, to appease.

THONDAI coolness, calmness.

THONTTO, -I, -EM lame; *tachodonkò moddon to thontlo zala,* he has broken his leg and has become lame ; *caetanacho al modon to alam thontlo zala,* cajetan became lame by having broken his hand.

THOO p. THOVO.

THOOP graving, engraving.

THÔR a grandee, a great man.

THORTHORO trembling, fear, shivering.

THORTHORONC to get afraid.

THORTHORONC to suffer from extreme hunger.

THORUM *n* handle.

THORVAI greatness, grandeur, size, height, magnitude.

THOUNC to engrave, to impress, to implant.

THOUPI engraver.

THOVO *m* treasure, riches.

THUCUNC to spit.

THUMPI *f* spit.

THUMPI GALUNC VO } to spit.
THUMPI UDOUNC }

TI she.

TIA-MĀI, TIMAI aunt.

TIB pear or point, top, head, summit.

TIC pricking hot, acrid.

TIC LAGONC to taste acrid.

TICLEM female child born after three boys.

TICLI dot, slight stain.

TICLO male child born after the birth of three female children.

TICSAN *f* acrid, high-seasoned.

TICSANNICHO, -I, -EM acrid, biting in taste or behaviour.

TIDD restless, turbulent, noisy.

TIDDAI trick, wile, prank.

TIDDCANNE to tease, to excite.

TIDDOG aversion, detestation.

TIDDPONN trick, wile, prank.

TIDDPONNE to strain.

TIDDKICHO,-I,-EM easily vexed, excitable.

TIDDTTO triplicate.

TIKE little, few, for a little while.

TIKE-TIKE little by little.

TIKE-TIKE VOCHUNC to go slowly or little by little.

TIKEM *n* steel.

TIKET ticket, permit.

TIKET TOPALACHI postage stamp.

TIKI (ZAD) *f* cinnamon tree.

TIKI(TIKIECHI SAL) *f* cinnamon.

TILL *m* sesame.

TILL (ANGACHO) *m* mole.

TIMAUNC to wet, to moisten.

TIMPI *f* spit.

TIN three (3).

TINCDDO, -I, -EM crucked, not straigth.

TINGACHEAN p. TINCHEAN.

TINGACHO, -I, -EM from there.

TINN *n* tin.

TINSAN the time of sunset; *chondrim tinsanam distli poddlolo,* the moon was seen at the time of sunset.

TINT *n* ink.

TINT (SORO) red wine.

TINT TAMBDDEM red ink.

TINTÊR ink-stand.

TINTÊR ADDIECHO sandhorn.

TINTEIR-REVENCHO sand horn.

TINXIM three hundred (300).

Tip white, a mark to shoot at, (fig.) aim, intent, end.
Tipari spondylus.
Tipaunc to aim, to strike at the mark.
Tipêst treble, triplicate,
Tir *m* aim.
Tir rag, strip of cloth.
Tir dorunc to aim, to direct.
Tircamptti shooting bow.
Tiron ceremony commemorative of the darkness preceeding the Lord's Passion.
Tiroo, -i, -em vo Thirso, -xi, -xem, vo Thirvo, -i, -em squint eyed.
Tirponc to suffer from a strain.
Tis thirty (30).
Tisal vo Tinsal the space of three years.
Tisrai the male hawk.
Tisrai, Tisrol share of third part.
Tisri a cockle; *bazarant tisreo coseo victat,* how are the cockles sold in the bazar.
Tisro, -i, -em third.
Tissalacho,-i,-em being three years old.
Tisvaddo *m* island.
Titl title, designation.
Titlo, -i, -em so much.
Tiù (angacho) mole.
Tiu vo Mam uncle.
Tiva, Tiva-pai uncle.
Tiva-maso *m* whale.
Tivaxi a carpet.
Tixilean in all three sides.
Tixim in all three sides.

Tizal earthen pot for cooking meat.
Tizulecar *m* brick-maker.
Tizulo *m* brick.
To, -i, -em he, she, it ; *to anim aum geleaum,* he and I went; *to dadlo kitem corta?* what is that man doing ? *ansla to ansla anim roddla to roddla,* some are laughing, others are crying; *tuzean to fator ucluet ?* can you lift that stone?
Toa vo Toua down, below.
Toad tune, tone of music.
Toada bhair tunelessly; discordantly.
Toadan tunefully, combining sounds in a harmony.
Tobac vo Tobacoddi the herbage.
Tobulo stable, kennel, stall.
Tocad a piece of music.
Toch, tich tench the same, that.
Toclem *n* head.
Toclem foddunc to have headache.
Tocli head.
Tocli foddunc to have headache.
Tocolio,-i,-em having a large head.
Tocôs work, labour, toil, (fig). trouble, grief, fatigue.
Tocôs caddunc to bear hardship (fig.) head-strong.
Tocot strength, energy, ability.
Tocrar dispute, disagreement, quarrel.

TOCRARI inclined to dispute or quarrel.
TOCTTO plank of wood.
TOCXI VO TONCXI *f* end, top.
TOCXIM portion, part.
TÔDD *f* coast.
TODDCO CORUNC to inoculăte.
TODD-DDOC deceit, strategem.
TODD-DDOKI artful, dishonest.
TODDEO inoculation.
TODDI BHAIR in high seas, beyond the sight of land.
TODDICHEAN keeping land in view, along the coast.
TODDIEM VAREM land breeze.
TODDIO belonging to the land, due to land forces.
TODDIO PAUS late monsoon, attributed to land.
TÔDDOON retention, keeping back, suspension, stagnation.
TÔDDÔS *m* the highest point, a wooden peg used by shoemakers.
TODDTODDIT fast, tight.
TODDTODDIT BANDUNC to bind fast, to fasten the knot tightly.
TODDUNC to break.
TOEM VO TOLLEM *n* pond, pool.
TOEUNC to become damp.
TOG professional cloak.
TOGDIR destiny, bad luck.
TOGNNAR lasting, durable.
TOGODD waist pendant of female child.
TOGGONC to economise, to be thrifty.
TOGOUNC to last, to preserve.
TOGOUNNI economy, frugality.
TOI p. TOLLEM.
TOIAR ready,
TOIAR CORUNC to make ready, to prepare.
TOIAR ZAUNC to be ready.
TOIARI *f* preparation, readiness.
TOJVIT *f* idea, ingenuity.
TOL living strenth.
TOL night watchman for paddy fields.
TOL VOCHONC to faint.
TÔLL VO TOU *m* grasshopper, locust.
TOLLEM, *n* VO TOLLI *f* pond.
TOLLI VO TOU grasshopper, locust.
TOLLO pan.
TOLLOG *n* a grown up chicken, half fowl.
TOLLOI tank, pond.
TOLLOP VO TOOP *n* rock.
TOLONC VO TOLUNC to bear, to be able to endure, to pull on.
TOMAT tomato.
TOMBOR kettle drum.
TOMBORCAR drummer.
TOMBU *m* pavilion, tent.
TONC peak or point, top, head, summit.
TONCH *f* beak.
TONCHUNC to peck.
TONCXI end, top.
TONDD mouth, face; *londd ugddunc*, to open the mouth; *tondant bolt galunc*, to put the finger into the mouth; *tonddac moem gallunc*, to put a mask to the face; *tonddac rong caddunc*, to paint the face.
TONDD CADDUMC to salivate, to

expel disease by salivation.

TONDDAO, -I, -EM disposed to speak much.

TONDDAR MARUNC to speak in an unrestrained manner, to be outspoken.

TONDDLI small mouth.

TONKI (MASOLI) *f* needle fish.

TONN straw, grass.

TONN CADDUNC to weed.

TONNACHEM CUDDEM straw loft.

TONNCO thick stick, bludgeon.

TONNI short stick.

TONNIR state; *mornache tonnir*, at the point of death.

TONT stupid, dull.

TONTTO dispute, quarrel, fight.

TOOP VO TOLLOP *n* rock.

TÔP *m* cap.

TOPAL VORNAR postal runner.

TOPALCAR post-man.

TOPALL *n* post (office).

TOPAS examination, survey.

TOPASNAR examiner, auditor of accounts.

TOPASSUNC to examine, to verify.

TOPI *f* small cap.

TOPIO VO XIRLO *m* chameleon.

TOPLEM copper pot.

TOPNAR a borer, piercer.

TOPNNEM a borer, piercer.

TOPONC to wound, to strike.

TOPONN *n* a borer, piercer.

TOPOS ship's scavenger.

TOPUNC to bore, to pierce, to wound, to strike.

TOR green mango.

TORAS, UJEACHO the heat of fire.

TORC reasoning.

TORCA DORUNC to reprimand, to correct misbehaviour.

TOREA reprehension.

TOREA VO ZINOS quality ; *torea dorunc*, to find fault with.

TORI if, in case; *em tori tum corsi zalear, tum boro burgo zasi*, if you do this, you will become a good boy.

TORI PUNN VO TORI ZANN yet, more over, though.

TORLUC duty of night-watch in paddy fields.

TORNELO, -I, -EM p. TORNO, -i, -em.

TORNEM DACTEM a young woman, a girl.

TORNEPONN *n* youth.

TORNO, -I, -EM green, not ripe ; *tem zadd tornem*, that tree is green ; *to ambo torno*, that mango is green ; *ti bail torni*, that woman is young.

TORNO DACTO a young man.

TORO green fruit.

TORONJ *n* pomecitron.

TORÔNJ (ZADD) pomecitron tree.

TORR tower.

TORR GANTTICHI belfry.

TORR UNCH steeple, spire.

TORSAD sword.

TORVAR *f* sword.

TORVAR MOTTVI dagger.

TORVARICHI POTI scabbard.

TOST *n* basin, ewer.

TOSTAN, ZOLLI portmanteau

TOTT-TODDAUNC to frighten.

TOTTACLOLO, -I, -EM extatic.

TOTTO loss, damage.

TOTTU pony.

Tou *n* sole; *mocheanchi tou*, the sole of shoes. [cust.
Tou vo Tôll grasshopper, lo-
Touc imitation, copy, mokery.
Touchean from below.
Toucho, -i, -em of down, of below.
Touî, tiui, teui he also, she also, it also.
Touli *f* earthern vessel.
Toulo a kind of earthen cover.
Toulolo, -i, -em fried.
Toumolle tortures, extreme pain.
Toumollunc to suffer extreme pain.
Tounc vo Tollunc to fry.
Tousonc to burn, to get dried up.
Touxem *n* cucumber.
Touxinn *f* cocumber-plant.
Tovo gap, cavity, hollow.
Tovo marunc to mend, to patch; *dorji capdac tovo marta*, the tailor is patching the clothes.
Tovoi *m* carpenter.
Toxem like that.
Trall *m* world, earth.
Trombet trumpet.
Tualo *m* towel.
Tualo jeuncho napkin.
Tualo mezacho table cloth.
Tuboc carbine, rifle, carabine.
Tuc weight.
Tucaddo vo Cuddco *m* piece.
Tucunc to weigh, to ponder, to consider.
Tufan *n* tempest, storm.
Tugelo, -i, -em your, yours.
Tujean by you; *tujean tem cori nozo*, you cannot do that.
Tull balance.
Tullos wild basil.
Tulltullit lubrious, shining, loose.
Tulltullitai lubriousness, looseness.
Tulltullonc to be full, to overflow.
Tum you.
Tumb coffin, bier.
Tumban galunc to emtomb.
Tumbu *m* pavilion, tent.
Tumcho, -i, -em, vo Tumgelo, -i, -em } yours.
Tup *n* butter.
Tupikionn raising up, making higher.
Tur millet.
Turo ear of corn.
Turo fulancho bunch of flowers, plume.
Tus *n* broken rice or grain.
Tutl *m* hammer.
Tutt shortage, loss.
Tutt eunc to get shortage.
Tuttonc to break, to split.
Tuttounc to break.
Tuzo, -i, -em you, yours.

U

U the twenty-first letter of the Roman Alphabet.
U *f* a louse.
U podre bogunc to undergo severe torments.
Uar *n* flood.
Ub *f* heat, warm, ardour.
Ub diunc to warm, to make hot slightly.
Uball *m* longing, great desire

of seeing an absent person.

UBALL warm, hot.

UBALL, UBAU hot weather.

UBALLONC to long, to desire of seeing an absent person.

UBALLONC to be breathless with heat.

UBANTORI on air.

UBANTORI ULOUNC to speak at random.

UBAR high, elevated.

UBAR CORUNC to elevate, to raise up.

UBARNEM elevation, uplift.

UBARUNC to raise, to lift up.

UBAU *m* longing.

UBAXI *f* asthma.

UBAXI EUNC to suffer from asthma.

UBECHO,-I,-EM warm, not cold.

UBEM CORNAR erector, builder.

UBGO, -I, -EM unwilling, reluctant.

UBGONC to hate, to abhor, to detest.

UBGONN *f* hatred, detestation, dislike.

UBLEM (DARACHEM) *n* moulding.

UBMODDO, -I, -EM tepid, lukewarm.

UBO, -I, -EM on foot, standing, straight; *to vatter ubo raula*, he is standing on the road, *maca ubi boddi di*, give me a straight stick.

UBONC to float.

UBONC to fly on wind.

UBOUNC to throw on wind; *xidd ubounc*, to spread the sail; *bautto ubounc*, to raise a flag; *naum ubounc* to defame.

UBOUNC to float, to throw on the surface of water, to overfloat.

UBOUNCHO, -I, -EM flying, fit to be blown away.

UBOUNNOM, -I, -EM outspoken, scandalous.

UBOT GALUNC to abandon, to forsake, to deprive of assistance.

UBOT PODDONC to be forlorn, to be helpless. *Pedru melo anim tachim burgim ubot poddlim*, Peter died and his children were helpless.

UBOXI *f* asthma.

UCASSI settler, outside, or foreign.

UCDDE TANDU rice of boiled grain.

UCDDEM BAT boiled rice grain.

UCDDO OROU boiled grain.

UCDDONC to open.

UCDDONC to boil, to be boiling.

UCDDUNC to open; *pett ucddunc* to open the box.

UCHAMBOLL unquiet, agitated, troubled.

UCHAMBOLL ZAUNC to be restless.

UCHAMBOLLAI agitation, unquietness.

UCHAR sound, expression, utterance.

UCHARONN *f* commemoration.

UCHARUNC to confess, to reveal.

UCHARUNC to pronounce, to utter.

UCHEAPOTI *f* confidence.

UCHEAV *f* delight, pleasure, satisfaction.

UCHIT *m* prize, remuneration.

UCHIT, UCHUT secretly.

UCLLAMBO shaky, moveable.

UCLLAMBONC to suspend, to hung.

UCLLAMBOUNC to hung, to suspend.

UCLONC to rise, to get up.

UCLUNC to raise, to lift, to take up, to pick up.

UCMAI tender breeding, easy life.

UCMAIECHO, -I, -EM tenderly brought up, unused to discomforts.

UCO turkish pipe.

UCODDIAM BOSONC to squat.

UCODDLOLO, -I, -EM boiled.

UCOL uplift, regeneration moral, mental and material.

UCOL-LOLO, -I, -EM raised up.

UCTTEPONN opening, nakedness.

UCTTO, -I, -EM open, sincere, plain.

UCTTO CORUNC to open.

UCTTO ZAUNC to be opened.

UCUM order, command.

UCUM BODLUNC to countermand.

UCUM BOUNDDUNC to circularise, to circulate necessary information.

UCUM DEVACHO fixed law of God, fate.

UCUM DINAR commander, person competent to issue orders.

UCUM MUSSOLMAN SERCARACHO foeman.

UCUM RUSS SERCARACHO ADLEA CALLANT ukasse.

UD *n* an otter.

UDAR generous, liberal.

UDAR ou credit.

UDAR DIUNC to sell on credit.

UDAR GEUNC to buy on credit.

UDAR MONACHO disposed to be generous, liberal.

UDARACHO,-I,-EM having credit, trustworthy.

UDARI MOL price chargeable for goods bought on credit.

UDARO,-I,-EM flat on the ground with the head upward.

UDARPONN liberality, generosity.

UDCACHO, -I, -EM due to water, caused by water.

UDCACHO LOTT flow of water, running stream.

UDCAO,-I,-EM watery.

UDDAN MARUNC to jump, to leap across.

UDDI VO UDDKI leap, jump.

UDDKI MARUNC to leap, to jump.

UDDNEM VO UDDON *n* jump, leap.

UDDO (REVENCHO) *m* downs or sandy hills.

UDDON VOCHONC to fly.

UDDONC to fly.

UDDONC to jump, to leap; *rong uddonc*, to lose colour, to fade.

UDDOUNC to throw, to put, to extend.

UDDOUDDO,-I,-EM noisy, turbulent.

UDDTO,-I,-EM superficial, fanciful, purposeless.

UDEG *m* occupation, business, work.

UDEGI diligent.

UDELOLO,-I,-EM born, nascent, springing up.

UDEM work, business.

UDEMI *m* labourer.

UDENTE EISLEAN easterly, towards the east.

UDENTECHO, -I, -EM eastern, oriental.

UDENTI east, orient.

UDEUNC to rise; *dis udeunc, to* rise the sun; *angac fodd udeleal,* appeared boils on the body.

UDEV *m* birth, appearance.

UDEV ZAUNC to born, to appear.

UDIC VO UDOC *n* water; *carem udoc,* salt water; *savem udoc,* fresh water.

UDOC SODDUNC to let water flow, to cleanse, to irrigate.

UDOC ZAUNC to melt, to dissolve into water.

UDÔR *f* womb, utero.

UEL *f* shout, clamour.

UFA loss at a game for missing the right use of a play token.

UFEG profit, advantage, gain.

UFEGAC PODDONC to be useful, to become serviceable.

UFEGACHO, -I, -EM useful, serviceable.

UFELOLO,-I,-EM floating, afloat in water.

UFEUNC to float, to bouy.

UFRATPONN *n* contrariety, vexation, opposition. [ration.

UGDASSACHI POROB commemoration.

UGDASSACHO,-I,-EM memorable, having a retentive memory.

UGDASSAN carefully, thoughtfully.

UGDDAPEM CORUNC to reveal.

UGDDAS *m* memory, remembrance.

UGDDAS CORUNC to remember, to recollect.

UGDDAS CORUNC, PATCANCHO to examine the conscience.

UGDDAPO,-I,-EM revelation, explanation.

UGDDUNC to open.

UGDDUNC (MANDD, ISCOL, etc.) to start business, to establish.

UGI quiet.

UGI RAVONC to be quiet.

UGORMOLLONC to fall out with one; to launch out into abuse.

UGOUNC to comb, to bloom.

UGTTEA MONACHO, -I, -EM frank, open, hearted, candid.

UGTTEAR PODDONC to be destitute.

UGTTEM CORUNC to expose, to disclose.

UGTTI GOZAL free discussion, plain talk.

UGTTO, -I, -EM open, naked.

UGUI CORUNC to silence, to supress.

UJEACHI COTTI Firebrand.

UJEACHO, -I, -EM due to fire.

UJETI disputing, quarrelsome.

UJIR presence, in front.

UL *f* wool.

ULANDI balance, against the weight.

ULANDDONC to turn, to revolve.

ULANDDONEM *n* vacillation.

ULAS *m* contentment, satisfaction, joy.

ULASUNC to rejoice, to make merry.

ULASVONT merry, joyful, content.

ULLOLO, -I, -EM restless, active, energetic.

ULLULONC to be restless, to be active.

ULO shout, call.

ULO CORUNC VO } to call.
ULO MARUNC }

ULOC *f* flea.

ULOP *m* heat, burning.

ULOP PODDONC to burn, to be impatient, to be eager.

ULOUNAR speaker, debater.

ULOUNC to speak, to express, to talk.

ULOUNC umanneanim to speak in riddles, to allude, to avoid plain facts.

ULOUNC ADD to oppose, to contradict.

ULOUNC DUSREA EISLEAN to defend another person.

ULOUNNEM conversation, talk, chat.

ULOUNNEM (CAZARACHEM) bethrotal, marriage agreement.

ULOUP speech, discourse, verbal report.

ULOUP DOGAM BHITOR dialogue, colloquy.

ULPAUNC to destroy with fire.

ULPO, -I, -EM burning, glowing, enthusiastic.

ULPONC to burn, to be consumed by fire.

UM *m* sweat, perspiration.

UMALLO *m* seething, bubbling, effervescense.

UMALLONC to boil.

UMANNEM *n* enigma, riddle.

UMARI *f* puberty.

UMAUM *m* kiss.

UMAUM DIUNC to give a kiss.

UMAUM GEUNC to kiss.

UMBOLL percolation of water, monsoon spring of water.

UMBOLL ZAUNC to cause seasonal springs of water to break-forth in monsoon.

UMBOLLNNEM *n* washing.

UMBOLLUNC to wash.

UMBOR VO } threshold, side or
UMBRO *m* } fold of a door.

UMBRI smelling salts.

UMCALLONC VO } to hang, to sus-
UMCALLAUNC } pend.

UMCOLLONC to hang, to be suspended.

UMED *f* care, solicitude.

UMED DENVONC to cool down energy, to feel tired. [rage.

UMED JIRONC to lose one's cou-

UMEDI cheerful, courageous.

UMEDICHO,-I,-EM energetic, active.

UMEDIN energetically, enthusiastically.

UMER p. UMED.

UMEUNC to sweat.

UMLO *m* red-ant.

UMOLLO *m* bubbling.

UMONC to smell, to ascertain by smelling.

UMOR *m* threshold.
UMOR bad blood.
UMPTHENCHO, -I, -EM fit to be rooted out, necessary to be destroyed.
UMTO, -I, -EM upside down.
UMTTONC to strive (to part from a place, thing or person).
UMTTUNC to pull violently, to pluck, to pluck away or off.
UMTUNC to pour into, to put.
UN warm, hot.
UN CORUNC to warm, to make hot.
UNAU heat.
UNCH high.
UNCHAI *f* height.
UNCHAMOLACHO, -I, -EM of high price or valuable.
UNCHAUNC to raise up, to elevate.
UNCHI p. UNCHAI.
UNCHLEAN from above.
UNCHLO, -I, -EM of above, superior.
UNCHOUNC to exalt, to elevate.
UNCTTI vo / UNCTTIO } sob, hiccup.
UNCTTONC to sob often, to hiccup.
UNDD *m* heart.
UNDDACHI PIDDA heart disease, liver-complaint.
UNDDEACHO GUIROB crumbs.
UNDDECAR *m* baker.
UNDDI *f* cheque.
UNDDI *f* handful of cooked rice.
UNDDO *m* bread.
UNDDO GODD bun, sweet cake.
UNDDO TORRAD toast.
UNDIR vo UNDUR *m* rat.
UNET *n* heat of the sun.
UNGATTI *f* finger.
UNGI *m* smeller.
UNGLOLO, -I, -EM smelt.
UNGONC to smell.
UNIM *f* sister-in-law (wife of brother).
UNNAUM loss, discount, damage.
UNNAUM SONSUNC to allow discount, to allow for depreciation.
UNNEMPONN wanting, dishonour, lowliness.
UNNO, -I, -EM less, inferior.
UNNOM CORUNC to lessen.
UNNOM ZAUNC to be less.
UNNONIM hot water, boiling vapour.
UNNONIM KHOBOR fresh news, latest report.
UNNONNIM hot.
UNS sugar-cane.
UNTT *n* camel.
UNTTI *f* bosom; *gorvachi untti*, an udder.
UNXEL *n* sugar canes plantation.
UNXEM *n* pillow.
UNXIR late.
UNXIR EUNC to be late.
UPAI *m* means, remedy.
UPAS *m* hunger, fasting.
UPAS CADDUNC to famish, to suffer from privations.
UPAS DORUNC to keep fast, to remain fasting, abstain from food.
UPAS MAR *m* extreme hunger.

Upas soddunc to stop fast.

Upaxi starved.

Upaxim hungry.

Upaxim raonc to go on hunger strike.

Upcar *m* favour, influence, power.

Upcar corunc to favour, to oblige.

Upcar mandunc to [illegible]. to acknowledge a favour.

Upcarancho, -i, -em due to [illegible]vour, mercy or patronage.

Upcari grateful to, for.

Upcari mon sense of gratitude, grateful disposition.

Upcaronc to serve, to be useful.

Upodro punishment, suffering.

Upordes *m* commandment, precept.

Upott full, brimful.

Upott borunc to fill up to the brim.

Upoz offspring, progeny.

Upoz *n* brood of animals.

Uprant vo **Uprantem** afterwards.

Uprasnnim *f* appearance, invention.

Uprasonc vo / **Uprasunc** } to appear, to find.

Uprassonc to rise up in revolt, to rebel.

Uprassonc to rise with new ideas, to invent new methods, to make one self conspicuous.

Uprassonn rise, eminence, fame.

Upvas *m* breath, exhalation.

Upxam *n* instruction.

Upxamunc to instruct.

Upzaunc to cause, to originate, to occasion.

Urba courage, boldness.

Urba diunc to animate, to encourage.

Urba moddunc to cool down.

Urbe-boronn animated, lively.

Urbeche, -i, -em energetic, active.

Urbelolo, -i, -em full of anima[illegible] enthusias[illegible]

Urbo[illegible]im arrangement.

Urbod[illegible] to arrange

Urca nolli *f* [illegible].

Urcunc, Dolle [illegible] stare, frighten by staring.

Urist[illegible] ferocious.

Uristtai *f* ferocity.

Urlolo, -i, -e[illegible] excessive, sur[plus.

Urmott haughty, proud.

Urmottai *f* haughtiness, pr[illegible]

Uronc to last, to continu[illegible]

Urponz *f* crowd, multitude.

Urvur eruption (on the skin).

Urvur futtonc to have eruption on the skin.

Urvurem *n* measles.

Us *f* sugar cane.

Uscar p. **Suscar**.

Uscaunc to hallow, to set dog.

Usco anxiety.

Usir late.

Usir corunc vo / **Usir launc** } to delay.

Uskeunc to be anxious, to be eager to see.

Uslonc to crack, to split.

Usmott *f* cough.

Usn heat, disease caused by heat.
Usnem, loan, lending.
Usnem diunc to lend, to give a loan.
Usnem ulounc to speak unkindly.
Usnnem gueunc to receive a loan.
Usounc to unstich, to unroll, to unfold.
Usponc to make empty, to rid one's self of.
Usponnem the act of voiding a place, emptying.
Ussul income, recovery, revenue.
Ussul zaunc to fetch an income.
Ustilolo, -i, -em dug.
Ustonc suffer again, to cause a relapse.
Ustto, -i, -em dirty, unclean.
Ustunc to dig; *fond ustunc*, rake up the bones of the dead; *osturiam ochunc*, to be chocked, to be strangled.
Usvas breath, respiration.
Usvas soddunc to breathe, to inhale.
Uta-o, -i, -em simple, silly.
Utar *m* passenger.
Utar advanced; *utar pirai*, old age.
Utar poddonc to be convalescent.
Utirn satisfaction, discharge.
Utirn corunc to satisfy, to discharge.
Utnnem *n* raising up.
Utom pure, excellent.
Utomponn *n* purity, excellence.
Utor *n* word, promise.
Utor diunc to promise.
Utor paunc to fulfil a promise.
Utou shallow, not deep.
Utponn production.
Utponn zaunc to produce.
Utponni productive, fertile.
Utronc to change, to depreciate.
Utronc to land, to alight, to disembark.
Utrunc to transfer.
Utrunc jadu to dehypnotise.
Utrunc mal to discharge cargo, to unload goods.
Uttaunc to raise, to take up.
Uttonc to get up, to rise from.
Uttounc to make one get up.
Uvar flood, inundation.
Uxar clever, careful, intelligent.
Uxarki intelligence, cleverness.
Uxel *n* plantation of the sugar canes.
Uzllunc to clean, to polish.
Uzo *m* fire.
Uzoll clear, bright
in presence of.
Uzot *f* quarrel, dispute.
Uzot corunc to quarrel, to dispute.
Uzounc to clean, to polish.
Uzounu starting success in a game.
Uzraunc(masolli) to clean fish.
Uzvadd *m* light.
Uzvaddaunc to illuminate.
Uzvaddi *f* flambeau.
Uzvaddic brilliant, shining.
Uzvaddonc to grow day.
Uzvo, -i, -em right.

V

V the twenty-second letter of the Roman Alphabet.
VA exclamation of surprise, or contempt.
VACANDDAR eulogist, panegyrist.
VACANDDUNC vo VACANNUNC, to praise, to commend.
VACANNEM praise, commendation.
VACHEA speech, talk, utterance, voice.
VACHEA DORONC to lose speech.
VACHIN vaccination.
VACHNAR reader.
VACHOP *n* reading.
VACHPI *m* reader.
VACHUNC to read.
VACHUNCHO, -I, -EM suitable for reading.
VACOR *m* razor.
VACRI cook-room, backroom, usually a kitchen.
VADD *f* height, loftiness, growing up.
VADDAI growth, advancement.
VADDCULO, -I, -EM round.
VADDECAR *m* neighbour, one that lives in the same ward.
VADDI vo.
VADDI oart, plot of land.
VADDLOLO, -I, -EM grown up.
VADDO hamlet, village.
VADDONC to grow, to increase.
VADDOUNC to increase, to make it grow.
VADDUNC to serve meal, to give; *bic vaddunc* to give alms.
VADDVON female watching an oart.
VADDVON resident watch of an oart.
VADI *m* plaintiff.
VADI *f* a strap.
VADIN an idler, a scamp.
VADO opinion; *to aplea vadeacho*, he is obstinate.
VADOU *n* tempest, storm.
VADOUJO, -I, -EM tempestuous, stormy.
VAG *m* tiger.
VAGARNEM gesture, aspect, appearance.
VAGARUNC to gesticulate.
VAGI *f* lobster.
VAGINN *f* a female tiger.
VAGOLEM (MASOLLI) *n* skate fish.
VAGOLLO *m* a small bat.
VAGONNIM *f* centipede.
VAGOTT cub of a tiger.
VAGOUNC to take care.
VAGOUNNIM *f* care, attention.
VAI vo VALLI a rivulet, track, train.
VAI *m* windiness.
VAICOR vo VAIKHOR windy, flatulent puffy.
VAIDI indian doctor, medical practitioner, of ayurvedic.
VAIDIC cure, healing, sanation.
VAIDICAI *f* medicinal.
VAIDOMON *n* inflamation.
VAINCHO a little.
VAINGEM *n* brinjal, mad-apple.
VAINGIN *f* brinjal plant.
VAINGON *n* after crop.
VAITOO, -I, -EM bad, wicked; *odic vaitt*, worse.

VAITT VO KHOTTO wicked.
VAITT *n* sickness.
VAITTACAR VO PIDDEVONT patient.
VAITTAN PODDONC to fall sick.
VAITTAPONN wickedness, cruelty.
VAIXICAI medicinal.
VAJEUNC to fẹel tired, to lose patience.
VAKHANNIM praise, commend.
VAKIL pleader, lawyer.
VAL VO VEL arbour, bind weed, creeper, climber.
VALL *m* river, stream.
VALL(BAJI) *f* a wine that grows up against a wall or over a arbour.
VALLES lunatic, scamp.
VALLESPONN lunacy, madness.
VALLI *f* rill.
VALLO ring, foot ornament.
VALLOI *f* white ant.
VALLUNC to drain, to pour out, to drop; *xit vallunc*, to drain the water from the rice.
VAN *n* hand-mill; *tandu canddchem van*, a mill to clean the corn or rice.
VANCDDEPONN tortuosity, curve.
VANCDDO,-I,-EM crooked, tortuous, wrong.
VANCDDO TINCDDO ULOUNC to speak unreasonably.
VANCHONC to live; *to mornantlo vanchlo*, he escaped from death; *tum chodam orsam vanch*, you live for many years.
VANCONC to halt, to limp.
VANDÔR *m* ape.
VANDONN *n* praise, commendation.
VANDUNC to offer.
VANGDDA in company with.
VANGÔDD *m* company.
VANGOUNC to dry up in the open air.
VANKI juice of manioc.
VANN *f* hempen sandal.
VANN (TARVACHEM) *n* the curve of a ship.
VANNIM *m* spider.
VANNIM VO RÔPÊR *m* hawker.
VANNPONN *n* haggling.
VANNPONN CORUNC to grudge, to haggle, to dispute.
VANNPONNIM haggler.
VANOR *m* ape.
VANSEL *n* bear.
VANSO *m* a cross piece of timber to hold fast large beams, brace.
VANTLOLO,-I,-EM ground; *vantloleo mirsango*, ground chilies.
VANTTLOLO, -I, -EM divided.
VANTTO *m* part, portion, share.
VANTTO VO VANTTE GEUNC to share, to divide.
VANTTOP distribution, division; *tannim hea gorachem vanttop borem kelam*, they have well divided this house.
VANTTOP grinding.
VANTTPI *m* distributor, divider; *vanttpean tem xet chear codden vanttlem*, the distributor divided the field into four parts.
VANTTPI *m* miller, pounder,

grinder; *gantlnear vantlpi tandu vantla*, the miller is grinding the corn on the hand mill.

VANTTPINN *f* a female distributor.

VANTTUNC to grind, to mill, to distribute, to divide.

VANVONC to flow, to transport, to remove, to purge, to expiate; *udoc vaunta*, the water is flowing; *tea dadleacho gai chodd vaunta*, that man's wound is bleeding very much.

VANVUNC to flow, to purge, to expiate, to atone, to purify; *tunnem soglem tel vanvoilem*, he poured out all the oil; *tea burgeachem nac vaunta*, that boy's nose is flowing.

VANZ void, vacuum, empty.

VANZPONN VO } sterility, bar-
VANZTTEPON *n* } reness.

VANZTTO, -I, -EM sterile, barren; *vanztti bail* sterile woman; *vanzttem zadd* unfruitful-tree.

VAO circle of metal or ore.

VAOI *f* white ant, p. VALLOI.

VAR *f* placenta.

VAR (ZOC) *m* yard.

VARAND varandah, balcony, outer gallery of a house.

VARDDIC marriage, matrimony, wedding.

VAREA DIUNC to ventilate, to winnow.

VAREM *n* wind, air.

VAREM GEUNC to breathe, to respire.

VAREM SUTTONC to blow wind.

VAROUNC to drop, to scatter.

VAS smell, bad odour.

VASPUXI request, inquiry, search, investigation.

VASPUXI CORUNC to search, to inquire, to investigate.

VASRI *f* a balcony, terrace.

VASRUM *n* calf.

VAT *f* candle; *mennachi vat*, wax candle; *chorbechi vat*, candle of fat; *capsachi vat*, wick.

VAT VO VAI *m* cramp; *mojea paiean vai aila*, I got a cramp in my leg.

VATO (DARACHO) *m* the hinge of a door.

VATT *f* way, road; *hi vatt bori noi*, this way is not good; *hi vatt oxir*, this way is narrow.

VATT DACOINAR guide.

VATT DACOUNC to show the way, to conduct, to direct; *Jose vatt noclo taka tike vatt dacoi*, Joseph does not know the way please show him.

VATT GEUNC to take an expedient, to form a new plan.

VATTAU change, exchange, banker's commission.

VATTAUNC to change, to exchange: *duddu vattaunc*, to exchange money.

VATTAUNC to save, to deliver from danger; *Franciscan Pedruc vattailo*, Francis saved Peter.

VATTCULLEPONN roundness.

VATTCULLO, -I, -EM round.

VATTEN salver.

VATTI *f* p. VATTLI.

Vattli *f* copper plate.
Vattod tough.
Vattonim *n* urine of a sick person for medical inspection.
Vattounc to be saved, to escape.
Vattsur wayfarer, traveller.
Vau *m* river.
Vau *m* wind.
Vau *f* corner or angle of the mouth.
Vau-zodd *m* tempestuous wind.
Vaum (zoc) *n* about 2 yards.
Vaulolo, -i, -em emptied, cast.
Vaunc to place, to put.
Vaunc p. **Vallunc.**
Vaunnim a flowing of humours, (fig) shame, blushing.
Vaur *m* work, labour, toil.
Vauraddi *m* labourer.
Vauti white ants.
Vaxad *n* medicine, remedy.
Vaxi inhabitant, resident.
Vaxil discount, deduction, compensation.
Vaxil diunc vo / **Vaxil corunc** / **Vaxil** } to deduct, to count, to diminish, to abate, to lessen.
Vaxtt bad; *to burgo vaxtt*, that boy is bad.
Vaxtt sickness; *aum noclom coslem techem vaxtt tem*, I do not know what kind of sickness he has got.
Vaxtt wickedness, malice; *tuca anim taca cainch vaxtt nam*, there is no malice between you and him.
Vaxtt caddunc to attend on a sick person.
Vaxttponn wickedness, malice.
Vaz vase.
Vaz hatred, detestation, dislike, tediousness.
Vazonc to play (a musical instrument).
Vazontor a musical instrument.
Vazontri *m* musician.
Vazop *n* soneta, a musical composition.
Vazounc to play (on a musical instrument).
Vazpi *m* player on an instrument.
Vazunc to read. p. **Vachunc.**
Vea *m* joint father-in-law.
Veadi vo Vechic prodigal.
Vechicai prodigality.
Vechit prodigal.
Vechitai prodigality.
Vedd ear-pendant.
Veddo *m* a screw; *vaddeacho khillo*, a screwed nail.
Veddo siege, circle, frame; *xarac veddo gallunc*, to besiege, to lay siege to a city.
Veddo strap, leather stramp, saddle-girth, belly-band.
Veddo bandunc to put a strap.
Veddunc to seige, to frame.
Veg tenesmus.
Vegim soon, at once.
Veglazar separation, difference; *Pedrucho anim Paulucho veglazar zala*, Peter and Paul have been separated; *eam don ostunim zailo veglazar asa*, there is a great difference

between these two articles.

VEGLEPONNAN disagreeably.

VEGLICAI *f* difference.

VEGLO,-I, -EM different, separate, except.

VEGLO SORONC VO VEGLO ZAUNC to separate.

VELEAN over.

VELL *m* time; *tum ea vellar ailai?* have you come at this time? *aum char vell gelom tachea gara lagim*, I went four times near his house.

VELL chance, hazard.

VELL *f* sea-shore.

VELL PODDONC to sunset; *aum vell poddonc thoim paulom*, I reached there at sunset.

VELL VO VEU VO EU pallet; *manichem vell* the pallet of a bamboo.

VELLO p. VEDDO.

VELLU VO VEU bamboo cock.

VELLUM cardamon.

VELUD velvet cloth.

VENG VO ENG embrace.

VENGM ARUNC VO / VENGOTTUNC VO / VENGOUNC } to embrace.

VÊNN joint mother-in-law.

VENTOZ fomentation with cups.

VENTT ill wind, unforeseen trouble.

VENTT a welt, braid (of hair).

VEPAR *m* business, merchandise.

VEPAR CORUNC to trade, to barter.

VEPARI tradesman, merchant.

VER till; *temcori ver to ogo raulo*, he kept quiet till he did that.

VER VO ER splinter, crack, chip, another, other; *maca ho naca ver di*, I do not want this, give me another.

VER EUNC to crack, to slit, to chop.

VERAUNC to cleave, to crack, to chop.

VERELOLO, -I, -EM cracked, choped.

VEREM VO VIREM poop, stern.

VEREM DORUNC to direct a rudder or helm.

VEREUNC to crack, to slit, to chop.

VERIAN till, until; *aum Mapuxea verian paulom*, I reached till Mapuça.

VESTID gown, skirts, female dress.

VET *f* span.

VETA THUIM everywhere.

VETT violence.

VEU screw, anything round and spiral.

VEU VO EU p. VELL.

VEU VO EU p. VELLU.

VEUC GALUNC VO / VEUC GEUNC } to roll round or about, to curl up.

VEUL VO EUL lobe.

VIA-SACRA the Way of the Cross.

VIAJ voyage; travel by sea.

VIBADD p. IBADD.

VIBADDO, -I, -EM Prodigal; waster.

VIBADDUNC *p.* IBADDUNC.

VIC, *n* poison

VIC GALUNC to poison; *Pe-*

drun vic galun marle sogleam undranc, Peter put to death all the mice by poisoning them.

VIC GEUNC to take poisoh; *Luis vic geun melo*, Luis died by taking poison.

VICAO, -I, -EM, venemous, poisonous.

VICAR, *m* poisoning.

VICARONC to poison (Fig.) to taint, to envenom.

VICAUNC p. VICARONC.

VICHAR inquiry, questioning.

VICHAR CORUNC to ask, to inquire, to question.

VICHARNEM *n* asking, questioning.

VICHARRUNC asking, inquiring, interrogating,

VICHARUNC to ask, to inquire, to question.

VICLAB suffering

VICONC to sell, to be sold.

VICOP *n* sale.

VICRAUNC to scatter, to spread, to shed, to disperse.

VICRAUNNEM scattering, effusion.

VICRECAR *m* a peddler.

VICRECARIN *f*. a female peddler.

VICRI VO VICRIT sale, act of selling.

VICTO, -I, -EM sold.

VICTO DIUNC, to sell, to vend, to betray.

VICTO GEUNC, to buy, to purchase.

VICTOLO -I, -EM, seller, trader.

VICUNC to sell, to vend, to betray.

VICXA *n* poison.

VID destruction, ruin.

VID LAUNC to ruin; *tannem gora darachi vidd laili*, he ruined all the property.

VIDI smoke, cigarette, biddi,

VIDEA art, trick, wit skill.

VIDEAVONT ingenious.

VIDES banishment (Fig.) a desert.

VIDEXI banished, exiled.

VIDIEPONN destruction; wastefulness.

VIDIEPONNAN prodigally.

VIDOU prodigality; waste.

VIDR Glass.

VIDRACHO -I, -EM, made of glass.

VIDUAS destruction.

VIDUASUNC to destruct, to ruin.

VIDUAXI spendthrift, waster, destroyer.

VIEUNC to bring forth young.

VIGAR, vicar.

VIGARPONN office of the chief parish priest.

VIGN *n* evil.

VIGNANTLO, -I, -EM unfortunate, unlucky.

VILL, a scythe, a pruning-knife.

VILLAT region, ground.

VINAX currupted, mutilated.

VINCHUN CADDUNC, to choose, to make choice of.

VINCHUNC to pick up.

VINCOP sale, auction.

VINCTO, -I, -EM, sold.

Vincunc to sold, to vend.
Vinddnnem *p.* Vinnem.
Vinddonc p. Vinnunc.
Vinddop weaving, texture.
Vinddpi *m* weaver.
Vinddpinn *f* a female weaver.
Vingans *n* revenge.
Vingans geunc, to take revenge.
Vingleponn, nakedness, want, poverty.
Vinglleponn, nakedness; destitution.
Vinglo -i, -em, naked, mere, bare; *burge vingle bountat*, boys are walking naked.
Vinglo (ujeacho), *m* coal; *dump vinglear gal*, put the incense upon the coal.
Vingllo (ujeacho) Burning coal; piece of firebrand.
Vinn without.
Vinnannim *m* carpenter.
Vinnannponn, p. Innannponn.
Vinnem, without, except p. Vinn.
Vinnem, a welt, braid (of hair).
Vinnim gallunc to braid; to interlace; to interweave.
Vinnonc vo Vinnunc to weave.
Vinnpi *m* a weaver.
Vinnpin, *f* a female weaver.
Vinnunchi sui knitting needle.
Vinot oration, request, prayer.
Vinot corunc, to intercede, to pray, to request, to ask.
Vir broomstick.
Virar zaunc to be demented.
Virgong to melt (Fig.) to move.
Viril peas.
Virlem (Caoteachem), *n* a cage.
Virnem vo Irnem-n a chisel.
Viroit vo Vinnem without; *to mocheam viroit gelo*, he went without boots.
Vironc to melt, to dissolve.
Virop dissolution, melting.
Virounc to melt, to dissolve.
Virsponn, insipidity, tastelessness.
Vis twenty.
Viscoll removing.
Viscollonc to go far, to go far away, to differ from.
Viscottunc, to unsew, (Fig.) to disunite.
Vismit miracle.
Vismitcar, miraculous.
Visoo sense.
Visoo -i, -em, twentieth.
Visor, *f.* forgetfulness.
Visor galunc, to make one forget.
Visor poddonc, to forget.
Visou rest, repose, tranquility.
Visou diunc to give time.
Visovo sense.
Visovonc to get rest, to repose, to lie by.
Visraunc to make one forget.
Visronc vo Visrunc to forget.
Vistar extension, stretching.
Vistaraunc to spread, to extent, to expand, to stretch.
Vistarlolo, -i, -em extended; *vistarlolem zadd*, extended tree.
Vistarunc to spread, to extend.
Vistt *m* friend.
Visttin *f* a female friend.

VISTTÔGOT friendship.
VISVAS *m* hope.
VISVAS DIUNC VO / VISVASONC } to hope, to expect, to confide.
VISVAS DOURUNC to trust, to have faith.
VISVAS SODDUNC to destrust, to give up hopes.
VISVASSACHO, -I, -EM confident, trustworthy.
VISVASSAN faithfully, truly.
VISVASSI faithful, confident.
VISVO world, universe, mankind.
VISVÔNN (MASOLLI) *m* a saw-fish.
VIT *n* part.
VIT estate, riches, property; *Pedru odlem vit bôgta*, Peter is enjoying a large estate.
VITT a qualm, anything that provokes omitting, nauseousness.
VITT DISONC p. VITTEUNC.
VITTELOLO afflicted with nausea, (fig.) disgusted, tired.
VITTEUNC to excite nausea, to give qualms, (fig.) to disgust.
VITTONC to discolour, to tarnish.
VIVADI contentions.
VIVAR abyss, gulf, that which is immense.
VIVEK reflection.
VIVEKHUNC to reflect, to see.
VIXARGOT signal, nod, sign.
VIXARGOT CORUNC to nod, to beckon.
VIZ thunderbolt.
VIZACHI SORI thunder-rod.
VIZMITANCHO, -I, -EM miraculous wonderful, performing wonders.
VIZMITT miracle, surprising event.
VO or, either.
VOCH go.
VOCHNNI departure, walk.
VOCHONC VO VOCHUNC to go, to pass.
VOCHONC DUSREA DHESSANT to emigrate.
VOCHONC DUSREACHE RACONNENC to ascort.
VOCHONC RONG to discolour, to fade.
VOCLECHO, -I, -EM bridal.
VOCOT *n* medecine, remedy.
VOCOT DOR PAUTTICHEM dose.
VOCTANCHEM BUTIC dispensary.
VOCTANCHO BUTQUEIR compounder.
VOCTI medicinal, having curative properties.
VODD big, large, great.
VODD DADOSPONN ecstasy, full satisfaction.
VODD DUC distress, agony.
VODD (PIDDA) convulsion, fit.
VODD RUCH eagerness, passion.
VODD (ZADD) banyan tree.
VODDANLO, -I, -EM belonging to a respectable family.
VODDE AXECHO, -I, -EM ambitious.
VODDE KHOXEN CORUNC to work enthusiastically, to do with zeal.
VODDECAR boatman.
VODDEM *n* boat, canoe.
VODDEM TARUACHEM yawl.

VODDI canoe, barge.
VODDI MARUNC to convulse.
VODDIKECHO, I,-EM eminent, distinguished, respectable.
VODDIL chief, head, ruler.
VODDIL director, principal.
VODDIL CONVENTACHI abbess.
VODDIL CONVENTACHO abbot.
VODDLEAN loudly.
VODDLO CULLIEN fidalgo, lord.
VODDÔLL VO VODDOU some time ago.
VODDOP enclosure, fence.
VODDOU GALUNC to bend.
VODDPON ZUTTIECHEM high rank, eminent.
VODDTA TOSLEM elastic.
VODDUNC to draw, to pull on.
VODDUNC (ADDO) to fence, to enclose.
VODDUNC (VIDDI) to smoke.
VODDVICAI honour, distiction.
VOGO quiet, calm.
VOGO RABONC to remain silent.
VOGOT time, period of time.
VOGOT ACANTACHO crisis.
VOGOT PAUNC to pass time.
VOGTA BHAIR irregularly, at improper time.
VOGTACHO,-I,-EM time-serving, opportunist.
VOICONDD *f* aromatic weed.
VOILEA OIR from top only, exteriorly.
VOILEAN VO VELEAN from above.
VOILO,-I,-EM of above p. OILO.
VOIR... up, on the top p. OIR.
VOIZ *m* doctor, medical practitioner.
VOIZACHEM RECEIT prescription.
VOIZACHEM AUTAM surgical instruments.
VOIZAPONNACHO,-I,-EM medical, concerning medical profession.
VOJELCAR carrier of a load.
VOJELEM female carrier of a load.
VOJEM load, burden.
VOL bed-sheet.
VOL pair of dress sheets worn by Indian women.
VOLECAR oarer, mariner.
VOLCAN woman dressed in sheets of the Indian style.
VOLL vale, valley.
VOLL twisting; *dorache vôll*, the twisting of a rope.
VOLL VO OU file, row, rank.
VOLL VO VOU bubo.
VOLLCONC to know.
VOLLEUNC to get wet.
VOLLEUNC to get tired by monotony.
VOLLKHICHO,-I,-EM known, familiar.
VOLLO *m* oar; *voddeacho volo*, the oar of a boat.
VOLLO,-I,-EM not dry.
VOLLO MARUNC VO TANDUNC, to move a boat with oars.
VOLLOC acquaintance, familliarity.
VOLLONC to turn.
VOLLONT wall.
VOLLOUNC p. VOLLEUNC.
VOLLSO p. OSO.

VOLLU vo LOU meekly, slowly, quietly.
VOLLUNC vo OVUNC to twist; *dor vollunc*, to twist a rope.
VOLLUNC to turn.
VOLLVOLLE sufferance, toleration, pain.
VOLLVOLLUNC to suffer, to tolerate, to experience.
VOLSANN *f* humidity.
VOLT return, side turn.
VOLTER easy-chair.
VOM ECHE DUS sowing time.
VOMP act of sowing.
VOMPECAR sower.
VONCARO *m* vomitting, qualms.
VONCARO ADDUNC to give qualms.
VONDD craving desire, variety.
VONDDO pit, excavation, well of low depth.
VONDOULOLO, -I, -EM inclined, bowed.
VONDOUNC to be inclined, to bow down.
VONDOUNC to incline, to bow, to tend.
VONTT lip.
VOONC vo VOLLUNC to turn.
VOP lustre, brilliance.
VOP DIUNC to give lustre.
VOPAR parable, example.
VOPARIN SANGONC to exemplify, to explain by means of proverbs.
VOR bridal party.
VORA riches, abundance.
VORATUC a piece of octave.
VORCOTT vo VORCHIT excessive, rest, remainder.
VORG *m* concert, partner.
VORN p. PROS.
VORNAR carrier, bearer.
VORNUNC to praise, to commend; *aum luca vornilam, mojea Deva*, I praise Thee, O my God !
VORNUNC to bind; *to fas vornunc zai*, that knot must be tightened.
VÕRODD *m* marriage, matrimony.
VORONC to carry, to bear.
VORONC CHORIAM to steal.
VORONC SERCARAN to confiscate.
VORONC VODDEM to take by boat.
VOROU grain, corn.
VOROUN by cause.
VORS year, the period of one year.
VORS OGLLEA DISSACHEM leap year.
VORSACHE ORSA annually.
VORSACHO, -I, -EM annual, yearling.
VORSACHO DIS anniversary.
VORSAN VOROS yearly.
VORTO, -I, -EM superior. p. ORTO.
VORTOMON event, issue, incident.
VORTOONC to happen, to occur, to come about.
VORUNC VODDUN to drag, to draw.
VORVIM p. ORVIM.
VOS tallow, fat.
VOSO *m* p. OSO.
VOSOUNC to inhabit, to prosper.
VOSSOUNNIM use, enjoyment.
VOST vo.

Vosti wealth.
Vostur an estate, a farm, a land.
Vosvosponnan greedily.
Vosvosso, -i, -em greedy, gluttonous.
Vot sunlight, daylight.
Vot right of voting.
Votac sucounc to dry in sunlight.
Votonc to be spilt.
Votounc to pour out, to empty.
Votunc to pour, to spill.
Voulolo, -i, -em bent, twisted.
Vounc p. **Vollunc.**
Voz *f* habit, custom, use.
Voz corunc to practice, to acquire a new habit.
Voz zaunc to get accustomed.
Vozon weight, sense of responsibility.
Vozṙ *n* diamond.
Vozri intestines, of an animal.

X

X the twenty-fourth letter of the Roman Alphabet.
Xa king, emperor.
Xabudin peacefully, quietly, transquilly.
Xac cooked vegetables, cooked meat.
Xai *f* ink.
Xal shawl.
Xamaim *f* grand-mother.
Xamarog ostrich.
Xami *f* visit.
Xamp stamp, sign-mark.
Xanneponn *n* intelligence, prudence, knowledge.
Xanneponnacho, -i, -em prudent, wise, intelligent.
Xannim wiseacre.
Xannom, -i, -em prudent, learned.
Xannuleponn innocence, simplicity.
Xannulo, -i, -em innocent, guileless.
Xant quiet, mild, meek.
Xantiponn *n* meekness, mildness.
Xantounc to appease, to pacify.
Xapai *m* grand-father.
Xap-cannem *n* printing-press.
Xapi printed.
Xapnar printer.
Xapunc to print.
Xapuncho, -i, -em concerning a printing or publishing work.
Xar *n* city, capital.
Xarachi bondobost civic arrangement.
Xaracho, -i, -em belonging to a city.
Xarati *m* intercessor.
Xarti paunc to fulfil, to perform.
Xarti-pavop fulfilment.
Xaratin *f* intercessor, intercessoress.
Xarantlo, -i, -em dwelling in a city.
Xarop syrup.
Xastr *n* law.
Xastri *m* learned.
Xastridar *m* legislator.
Xastrovont doctor, learned man.

XATI courage, boldness.
XATIDAR courageous person.
XATIVONT daring, audacious.
XAT-TI end, conclusion.
XAT-TI PAUNC to comply with, to fulfil, to terminate.
XAULO teakwood.
XEAN rarely, seldom.
XEBAS! well-done!
XEBASKI *f* honour, respect.
XEBASKI DIUNC to applaud, to cheer up.
XEBOI shout of triumph.
XEC hot fomentation.
XEC DIUNC to foment.
XECAC *f* intercessor.
XECDDEANCHE XECDDE in course of centuries, from century to century.
XECDDO century, one hundred.
XECONC to warm.
XECONC to be chastened, to improve under trials.
XECOUNC to heat, to make hot or warm, to foment.
XECTI *f* strenght, vigour.
XECUNC to apply hot fomentations.
XECUNNI *f* an eft or newt, a small lizard.
XEDDEM *n* alburnum.
XEGUNN virtue, good quality of human being.
XEGUNNACHO,-I,-EM possessing a good character.
XEGUNNI virtuous, well-behaving.
XEKIM finally, at last.
XELEM *n* a bunch of cocoanuts.
XELI *f* a twig, a rush etc., tying up sheaves of corn etc.
XELL *f* humidity.
XELL EUNC to become humid, to moisten.
XELLEUNC to get cold, or stale.
XELLI *f* sheep.
XELL-MODDO,-I,-EM tepid, luke warm.
XELLO,-I,-EM cold, stale; *ho unddo xello*, this bread is stale, *hem mas xellem*, this meat is not fresh ; *hem xellem udoc*, this is cold water.
XELLO MANDONC to grow seaweed.
XEM VO XEMBOR, one hundred (100).
XEMBOR ORSAM century, centenary.
XEMP VO / XEMPADDO VO / XEMPDDI VO / XEMPDDO — tail.
XENCARO *m* gravel.
XENCREM *n* the comb of a cock, crest.
XENDDI *f* small bunch of hair on the top of the head.
XENDDO *m* a lock of hairs.
XENDDONC to lose, to miss.
XENDLOLO,-I,-EM lost, missing.
XENDRI *f* mat.
XENDUR red, vermilion, paint (for the face).
XENET *n* dry leaf of plantain-tree.
XENIVAR p. SONVAR.
XENN *n* cow-dung.

XENN CADDUNC to put cow-dung.

XENN PAUSACHI *f* drizzling of rain.

XENNOIM school-master.

XENNOIPONN teacher's duty.

XENTTO *m* grandson's grandson.

XENUR *n* short tail.

XEO *m* sea-weed.

XEOTT *n* cloudy, mild sun.

XEOTT *m* end, conclusion.

XEOTTIM finally, at last.

XER *m* seer, pound.

XERAT *f* intercession.

XERATIN *f* intercessor.

XERNOGOT *m* plaintiff.

XERONVARTH *n* veneration.

XET *n* field.

XET-CAMOT agriculture.

XETCAMTI *m* agriculturer, cultivator.

XETCAN *f* owner of the field.

XETCAR *m* owner of the field.

XETT *m* gold-smith.

XETTIN *f* wife of gold smith.

XETTIO *f* mockeries, jests.

XEU *n* humidity.

XEUCUNN dry dung cake used for fuel.

XEUGO press for making vermicelli.

XEUNC to get cold.

XEUNC to receive; *saib xeunc*, to receive Holy Communion.

XEUMODDO, -I, -EM luke-warm, tepid.

XEUMODDO CORUNC to make lukewarm.

XEUMODDO ZAUNC to become cool.

XEUTTAI *f* mullet (fish)

XEUTTIM at last, finally.

XEUTTO *m* large mullet.

XEUTTONC to fall down with a great force.

XEUTTUNC to beat violently.

XEVA *f* service.

XEVA CORUNC to serve.

XEVOC *m* servant, attendance.

XEZAN *f* (female) neighbour.

XEZAR *m* neighbourhood.

XEZARI *m* neighbour.

XIB *n* a sort of small mackerel.

XICAR *f* game.

XICAR MARUNC to hunt.

XICARI *m* hunter.

XICNAR *m* student.

XICO *m* seal.

XICO MARUNC to seal.

XICOINAR *m* instructor, teacher.

XICONC to study.

XICONN *f* instruction, teaching, doctrine.

XICOP *n* study, learning.

XICOP ATMEACHEM psychology.

XICOP BASSECHEM grammar.

XICOP DEVACHI VOLLOC GUEUNCHEM theology.

XICOP ENGINANCHEM mechanics.

XICOP LETRADPONNACHEM jurisprudence.

XICOP PORZANCHI VOLLOC GUEUNCHEM history.

XICOP SOUNSARACHI VOLLOC GUEUN geography.

XICOP VOIZANCHEM medical studies.

XICOP XASTRANCHEM religious studies.

XICOP ZADDANCHEM botany.

XICOP ZANVARANCHEM zoology.

XICOUNC to teach, to instruct.

XICUNC to learn, to study.

XICXA *f* punishment.

XIDAU *m* quit. rent.

XIDD *n* sail.

XIDD SODDUNC to set sail.

XIDDCAUNC to caution to advise against.

XIDDCOLOLO, -I, -EM guarded, cautioned.

XIDDCONC to be on guard.

XIDDI staircase, ladder.

XIDDOLL VO } large, loose.
XIDDOU }

XIDDOU CORUNC to enlarge, to make loose.

XIDDUC careful, cautions, perennial.

XIDDUCAI *f* caution, vivacity, carefulness.

XIDDXIDDO PAUS *m* drizzling rain.

XIDDXIDDONC to be drizzling.

XIDDXIDDONCPAUS *m* to drizzle.

XIDOU *m* the dew or moisture of the night.

XILI *f* cholera.

XIL-LO chamelion.

XILOC *n* remainder, rest.

XIM *n* cold.

XIM limit, boundary.

XIM KHAUNC to feel cold; *aiz zobor xim khata*, to-day is very cold.

XIM NANTLELEM limitless, vast.

XIMBRO, -I, -EM snuffling.

XIMBUR *m* the mucus voided by the nose.

XIMBUR CADDUNC to wipe the nose.

XIMECHO,-I,-EM connected with boundary line, relating to boundaries.

XIMEILO,- I,- EM occupying or belonging to the boundary line.

XIMPDDAUNC to scatter, to spread.

XIMPDDONC to be scattered.

XIMPDDUNC to scatter, to spread, to pour out.

XIMPI *f* shell; *tisrechi ximpi*, shell of cockle.

XIMPI (ODDEACHI) mouth of the stomach.

XIMPNNEM *n* watering.

XIMPNNENCAR *m* one that waters.

XIMPO *m* big shell.

XIMPONC to water.

XIMPTTEM *n* bunch of cocoanuts.

XIMPUNC to water.

XINC *f* sneeze.

XINC EUNC to sneeze.

XINCOLL *f* empilade.

XINCONC to sneeze.

XINCONC to study, to learn.

XINDDOLL *f* adulteress.

XINDDOLL *m* adulterer.

XINDDOLLPONN *n* adultery.

XINDONC to cut.

XINDUNC to cut into small pieces.

XINDUR red, vermilion.

XING *n* horn.

XING *n*. cornet.

XING VAZOUNC to play a cornet.

XINGADI stag.
XINGAO, -I, -EM cornuto, horned.
XINKELOLO, -I, -EM congealed, frozen.
XINKEUNC to freeze.
XINN *m* complaint.
XINN CORUNC to complain of.
XINNANEO mussles.
XINNCAR *m* complainant.
XINNCAN *f* complainant.
XINNONC to complain.
XINS CAPUNC to behead.
XINS *n* head.
XINS *m* disciple.
XINSO *m* flask, bottle.
XINSLI *f* phial, small bottle.
XINSOR *f* crocodile.
XINTARI, GÓROUNCHI *f* angling cane.
XINTODDO *m* aspersion, sprinkling.
XINTODDO MARUNC to sprinkle.
XINVIN lioness.
XIODD *m* lobster.
XIONC to stitch, to sew, to cover, to retile.
XIONN *f* whistle, sewing.
XIONN CADDUNC to sew.
XIONN GALUNC to whistle.
XIOR *f* aspersion, sprinkling.
XIOR MARUNC sprinkle.
XIR *f* vein, slice, piece, the internal divisions of oranges, lemons.
XIR MARUNC to open a vein, to take out blood.
XIRANTOL artery, blood-vessel.
XIRAP *m* curse, imprecation.
XIRAP GALUNC VO } to curse.
XIRAPUNC } to curse.
XIRBO, -I, -EM threshed.
XIRCO *m* vinegar.
XIRCAUNC to entangle.
XIRCONC to be entangled; *xirconc tarum*, to run aground, to strand.
XIRISTTO *m* custom, practice.
XIRLI *f* lizard.
XIRLI (PIDDA) *f* cholera.
XIRLO *m* chamelion.
XIROI *f* vermiceli.
XIRONTT *f* punishment.
XIRONTT MARUNC to punish.
XIRVOLLI *f* vermicelli.
XIRXIRI (PIDDA) *f* cholera.
XIRXIRO *m* shivering cold.
XIRXIRO EUNC VO } to feel shivering cold.
XIRXIRONC } to feel shivering cold.
XIT *n* boiled rice.
XITOU cool, mild.
XITOUCAI *f* coolness, mildness.
XIUM *m* lion.
XIUNC to sew.
XIUNNICAN *f* female tailor.
XIURAUNC to sprinkle.
XIUXIONC to boil.
XIVAI without.
XIVAUNC to lay a ship aground.
XIVI abuse, abusive words.
XIVI DIUNC to abuse, to insult.
XIVONC GHOR to repair the roof of a house.
XIZONC to cook.
XIZOP *n* cookling.
XIZOUNC to cook.
XIZUNC p. XIZONC.
XOR, XER pint measure.
XYRING syringe.

Z

Z the twenty-sixth letter of the Roman Alphabet.

ZAB VO.

ZABAB *m* reply, answer.

ZABAB DIUNC to reply, to answer.

ZABABDAR responsible man, chief.

ZABABDAR responsible, accountable.

ZABAN word, utterance.

ZABTO inventary, catalogue.

ZABTO UTRANCHO vocabulary, dictionary.

ZACAT *f* custom duty.

ZACHO, -I, -EM whose.

ZADD *n* tree, plant.

ZADD-PALO botany, herbage.

ZADD PORMOLLACHEM balm.

ZADD-PALO VOLLCONAR botanist.

ZADD VICACHEM aconite.

ZADD VICARACHEM aconite.

ZADDAM LAUNC to plant trees.

ZADDNI hypnotic strokes or passes.

ZADDO *m* search, review.

ZADDO GEUNC to search.

ZADDOP *n* the act of sweeping, sweepings.

ZADDPI *m* sweeper.

ZADDPIN *f* a female sweeper.

ZADDU broom.

ZADDU MARUNC to sweep, to dismiss.

ZADDUNC to sweep with a broom.

ZAG *f* murmur, buzzing.

ZAG noise, uproar.

ZAGO *m* place, ground.

ZAGO, -I, -EM awake, wakefull ; *aum sogli rat zago aslom*, I was awke whole night.

ZAGO CORUNC to awake.

ZAGO ZAUNC to awake.

ZAGOR *m* theatre.

ZAGOUNC to awaken.

ZAGRACHEM GHOR play-house, theatre.

ZAGRACHO, -I, -EM theatrical, dramatic, entertaining.

ZAGRIST comedian, actor.

ZAGRONN night-duty, night entertainment, loss of sleep.

ZAGRONN *n* act of being awake.

ZAGRUT awaked, watchful.

ZAGRUTAI *f* watchfulness, vigilance.

ZAGUICHO,-I,-EM suitable for vigilance.

ZAI *f* net.

ZAI ZAUNC to want, to require, to be in need.

ZAIFOLL *n* walnut, nutmeg.

ZAITE PAUTTIM frequently.

ZAITE PAUTTIM HAJIR ZAUNC to frequent.

ZAITE PAUTTINCHO frequent.

ZAITEAM. JINSA, CHEM diverse, various.

ZAITEAM RONGANCHEM dapple, of mixed colours, variegated.

ZAITEM copious, abundant, much, considerably, abundantly.

ZAITEM abundance, plenty.

ZAITIM SERCARI TARUVAM navy.

ZAITIM ZUZARI TARUVAM squadron.
ZAITO, -I, -EM many, much, lot.
ZAITO LOC crowd, throng, mob.
ZALL p. ZAI.
ZALL detestation, abhorrence.
ZALL *n* burning sensation.
ZALLI p. ZAI.
ZALLI KENSANCHI cawl.
ZALLONNENCAR *m* administrator.
ZALLONNIM *f* administration.
ZALLONNIM CORUNC to administrate, to govern.
ZALLUNC to burn, to blaze.
ZAMAN p. zamin.
ZAMB *m* jamb.
ZAMB (ZADD) jamb tree.
ZAMB VO / ZAMBAI } *f* gaping, yawning.
ZAMBAI CADDUNC VO / ZAMBAI EUNC } to yawn.
ZAMBKHAN *f* carpet.
ZAMBLAM *n* jambulans.
ZAMBOLL *f* jambulan tree.
ZAMIN surety, bail.
ZAMIN RAVONC to stand bail, to guarantee, to assert.
ZAMINDAR surety, bail.
ZAMINPONN *n* security.
ZAMPI *f* lethargy, dawn, approach of day.
ZANC *f* delirium, frenzy.
ZANCNNEM *n* dilirium, frenzy.
ZANCONC to talk wildly, to rave.
ZANCRO, -I, -EM one that talks wildly; frenzied.
ZANG VO ZANGOT thigh.
ZANA ZAUNC to know, to acknowledge.
ZANNAR wise person, well-informed personage.
ZANNAR VODDLO sage, philosopher, scientist.
ZANNARPONN *n* wisdom, knowledge.
ZANNARPONNIM according to knowledge or experience.
ZANNAUNC to make known, to publish, to warn.
ZANNOUNC to warn, to tell before hand.
ZANTTI elderly female.
ZANTTICAI *f* wisdom, knowledge, experience.
ZANTTO, -I, -EM wise, chief.
ZANTTO elder, principal.
ZANVAI prudence, science.
ZANVAI *f* ring-worm.
ZANVAR animal, brute, beast.
ZANVAR CHIAR PAIEANCHEM quadruped.
ZANVARACHEM POR cub, puppy.
ZANVUIM *m* son-in-law.
ZANZU *f* lay, ditty.
ZAO-ZAUNC to be in want.
ZAP DIUNC to answer, to reply.
ZAP VO ZAB *f* answer, reply.
ZAZUR *n* necessity, want, need.
ZAZURAI *f* necessity.
ZAT *f* caste, class.
ZATOC *n* birth, nativity.
ZATOCACHO, -I, -EM native.
ZAU burning sensation.
ZAU *f* (GOVACHEA BHAVACHI BAIL) sister-in-law.
ZAU (MASOLLI MARCHEM) net.
ZAUNC to become, to happen; *Caeten dorji zaunc gela,* Caetano has gone to become a

tailor; *cal ec cazar zalam*, there was a wedding yesterday; *aiz ec novol zalem*, to-day happened one miracle; *borem zaunc*, to succeed well; *ho caoto zalo*, this cocoanut tree has taken roots; *him angaulim tuca zatat?* these clothes fit you? *tica coc burgo zala*, she gave birth to a son or she has brought fourth a son; *calloc zaunc*, to become dark; *uzvadd zaunc*, to dawn; *sovai zaunc*, to become cheap; *marog zaunc*, to become dear; *mollo zaunc*, to fatten, to grow fat; *baric zaunc*, to grow thin; *ragar zaunc*, to be angry; *favo zaunc*, to merit, to deserve; *tuje lagim to vepar zata?* can you do that business? *ballont zaunc*, to bring forth a young; *utpon zaunc*, to profit; *chori lhai zali*, the theft was found out; *toclean zaunc*, to have headache; *mutonc zaunc*, to have necessity to make water; *bair zaunc*, to have motions; *cosoloi zata*, anything will do; *dinam zaunc*, to refuse, to decline to give; *melolo jivo zaunc*, to rise from the dead; *pidda zodd zaunc*, to aggravate the sickness; *potant zaunc*, to have stomach-ache; *zun zaunc*, to ripen; *noco vo neno zaunc*, to ignore, not to know; *sonvoim zaunc*, to be accustomed; *piddentlo boro zaunc*, to be cured from the sickness; *hea battac kille narl zatat?* how many cocoanuts do this property produce?

Zauuim *m* son-in-law.

Zenzronc to rub against a thing.

Zenzronnem weeding; *baki utram borcileant "Je"*.

Ziconc to win, to prove victorious.

Ziczic brilliante, lustre, glitter.

Ziczicong to shine, to glitter.

Zilla district.

Zin *n* saddle; *goddeac zin gallu-no*, to saddle a horse.

Zinôs kind, sort.

Zinzdunc to get loose out one's hands.

Zioni *f* puberty.

Zirn digestion.

Zit dispute, opposition.

Zo who; *zo conn boreo corneo corta to boro*, one who practices good works is good.

Zoar *f* mosquitoes.

Zoari *m* jeweller.

Zobab answer, reply.

Zobor obstinate, much; *to zobor*, he is obstinate; *tannem zobor coist gelle*, he took much troubles.

Zobor-dost *f* violence, impetuosity.

Zobor dosti *n* violently, forcibly.

Zobor dosti violent, impetuous.

Zoc measure, weight; *tachea angachem zoc cadd*, take the measurement of his body.

Zoc caddnar one that takes measurement.

Zoc caddunc vo Zoc geunc to take measure, to weigh.

Zocat toll-house.

Zocmi wounded, hurt.

Zocmi corunc to injure, to hurt.

Zocmi zaunc to be injured.

Zocot tuft, lock.

Zocteponn *n* equality, conformity.

Zocto equal, similar, alike.

Zocum responsibility.

Zocunc to measure to weigh.

Zôdd heavy, weighty, difficult; *zodd zaunc*, to be heavy, to be difficult.

Zodd gain, income.

Zodd acxer double letter.

Zodd (addos) protection, shelter.

Zodd (toclen) dull, stupid.

Zodd zaunc to gain; *ea orsa bori zodd zali*, this year there was a good gain; *jib zodd zaunc*, to lose the speech, to have the tongue paralised; *zor zodd zaunc*, to aggravate the fever.

Zoddavonc to aggravate, to increase.

Zoddcan earning female.

Zoddcar *m* winner, one that earns.

Zoddem *n* pair, couple.

Zoddi-couli dropsy.

Zoddiem pair of earings.

Zoddnar bread-winner, earning member of a family.

Zoddo hinge.

Zoddo pair, couple.

Zoddonc to fall.

Zoddounc to throw down.

Zoddponc to be shaken.

Zoddpunc to shake, to toss, to bit, to chastise with blows.

Zoddtti *f* examination, judgement.

Zoddtti corunc to examine, to judge.

Zoddtti nimanni last judgement.

Zoddunc to gain, to obtain.

Zoddunc to join, to unite; *kille anim follim zoddunc*, to join planks with nails.

Zoddunc to solder, to mend.

Zogddem quarrel, dispute, fight.

Zogddecar *m* one that quarrels.

Zogddonc to quarrel, to fight.

Zogllaunc to lighten, to glitter.

Zogllaunnem Zogllaunnem.

Zogllo p. **zogllaunnem.**

Zogllo marunc to lighten, to glitter.

Zogllonnem lightning.

Zogoinar saving man.

Zogol that part of the plough that enters in the earth.

Zogoonn *f* economy, sparing, saving.

Zogounc to spare, to save.

Zogzog splendour.

Zogzogunc to shine, to glitter.

Zogzokit brilliant, shining.

Zogzokitai brightness, splendour.

Zoi *f* gut, intestine.

Zoimoim here and tehre, in different places.

Zoit voronc to win.

ZOITT *n* victory, gain.
ZOITVONT victorious.
ZOLLI *f* gut, intestine.
ZOLLIM-MOLLIM here and there, in different places.
ZOLLONC to burn, to heat.
ZOLLOU firewood.
ZOLLPONC to roam, to wander about.
ZOLLÚ *f* leech.
ZOLLZOLLAUNC to rinse.
ZOLM *m* birth.
ZOLMANCHI SUAT birth place.
ZOLMANCHO, -I, -EM native, original.
ZOLMANCHO DIS birth day.
ZOLMANCHO DHES natice land.
ZOLMANCHO GUNN inherited quality.
ZOLMONC to born.
ZOMAN sum, total.
ZOMAN bail.
ZOMA ZAUNC to flock, to gather.
ZOMAT community, meeting.
ZOMBAZOMBI vo } combat, fight,
ZOMBI } contest.
ZOMBI MARUNC to fight, to combat.
ZOMBO *n* assembly.
ZOMBONC to penetrate.
ZOMIN *f* earth, ground.
ZOMIN PETTLELI floor, pavement.
ZOMIN VOSSOINAR farmer, cultivator.
ZOMIN VOSSOUNC to farm, to cultivate.
ZOMIN VOSSOUNCHI farm, field.
ZOMINDAR landlord.
ZOMO assembly.
ZOMO sum ; *somestam christavancho eoc zomo*, union of all the christians.
ZOMO CHRISTANVANCHO congregation.
ZOMO DACTTEAM TARVANCHO flotilla.
ZOMO TARVANCHO fleet, squadron.
ZOMONC to join, to congeal.
ZOMONG jagma (tree).
ZOMONG jagma (fruit).
ZOMOUNC to sum up, to total.
ZOMPOI sea-saw, assault, attack.
ZOMPOI MARUNC to attack, to assault.
ZOMPOI MARUNC to swing.
ZONDVO *m* maize.
ZONEL *n* window.
ZONGLI ANS fenduck.
ZONGLLI wild, woodish.
ZONGOLL, *n* forest.
ZONN *m* *jono.*
ZONN *m* person, individual.
ZONN dividend of a village community ; right of each member to such dividend.
ZONN EOC, each one, every one.
ZONSORI teasing habit.
ZONTTA *f* hair clotted.
ZONTTA ZAUNC, (kensanchi), to plait the hair.
ZONTR *n* dhoty.
ZONTIR *n* wire drawing iron.
ZONVAR *n* animal.
ZOPTI confiscation.
ZOPTI CORUNC to confiscate.
ZOR *f* fountain.
ZOR CULCULEACHO ague fever.
ZOR (pidda), *m* fever.
ZOR SUCTA TOSLI spring.

Zorcottung, to rub one's self against a thing.
Zorcottunc to cut down, to fell.
Zori if.
Zori tori if, although.
Zorlo *m* cockroach.
Zoronc to wear out.
Zorounc to rub a thing against another thing.
Zorpati *f* galon.
Zorst *n* zinc.
Zor-tor if, although.
Zot, *n* yoke of oxen.
Zot-coxi *m* cultivator of the land.
Zotexi *m* prophet.
Zotixi *m* astronomer.
Zotnaen carefully.
Zoton *f* care.
Zoton corunc to take care.
Zott-tti *f* judgement.
Zou *f* leach.
Zouconc to discern confusedly.
Zounle twins.
Zoupounc to roam about.
Zovai foolishness.
Zug *n* danger, peril.
Zui *f* jasmim.
Zulum *m* offence, harm, grievance.
Zulumunc to oppress.
Zulo hammock.
Zum *n* yoke for oxen.
Zumor *m* chandelier.
Zun seasoned, old.
Zun zaunc to season, to get riped.
Zuno, -i, -em old.
Zunvo *m* island.
Zuri *f* flight.
Zuronc to run away, to flee.
Zutti duty, office, post.
Zuz *n* war.
Zuzari *m* warrior, soldier.
Zuzonc to fight, to combat.